turn d on or bef

HEINEMANN
SCHOOL
MANAGEMENT

Financial Management for Schools

The Thinking Manager's Guide

BRIAN KNIGHT

Series Editor Michael Marland

About the author

Brian Knight is an Honorary Research Fellow of the University of Exeter. His earlier book *Managing School Finance* (1983) advocated financial delegation to schools long before it was fashionable. He has lectured and provided training on school financial management extensively in the UK and overseas since 1977. He has also written books on the management of school time and public relations for schools (co-author).

Heinemann Educational Publishers
Halley Court, Jordan Hill, Oxford OX2 8EJ
a division of Reed Educational & Professional Publishing Ltd

MELBOURNE AUCKLAND
FLORENCE PRAGUE MADRID ATHENS
SINGAPORE TOKYO SAO PAULO
CHICAGO PORTSMOUTH (NH) MEXICO
IBADAN GABORONE JOHANNESBURG
KAMPALA NAIROBI

A catalogue record for this book is available from the British Library

ISBN 0 – 435 – 80481 – 2

97 98 99   10 9 8 7 6 5

Typeset by Taurus Graphics, Kidlington, Oxon
Printed in Great Britain by Athenæum Press Ltd, Gateshead, Tyne & Wear

Contents

Introduction

This book is written for all those who manage school finance – head-teachers and principals, senior staff, members of governing bodies and local administrators. It is primarily intended for those who wish to reflect about that task. It will appeal less to those who just depend on common-sense, or see management as administration. It is not mainly a 'how to do it' book – though I hope there are plenty of practical examples – but rather a 'how to think about it' book.

When I first wrote and lectured about school finance in the mid-1970s and suggested that those responsible for schools should manage their own budgets, the idea was considered mildly crazy, if not indecent. Audiences were distinctly cold. Worldwide, with a few exceptions, state maintained schools in developed countries lived in a wonderland where they did not know what their costs were, and were responsible for not more than 5 per cent of their funds. (Many schools in developing countries were responsible for much more, but only because they had to raise their own finance.) Independent schools were the exception. But from the early 1980s financial delegation has spread rapidly in Canada and the USA, Australia, New Zealand, South Africa, Holland and Belgium, and in the UK where over 20 000 schools will be responsible for their own budget by 1994.

When I wrote *Managing School Finance* (Heinemann, 1983), one sentence in particular drew some attention:

> **A school is a cost-accountant's nightmare: a labour intensive, non-profit-making service organisation, with ill-defined objectives, with uncosted and unquantifiable outputs and ill-costed inputs, in a straitjacket of constraints and with an arthritic lack of flexibility in buildings and staff.**

Today, less than ten years later, the sentence should begin 'A school is a cost-accountant's paradise . . .', so extensive is the financial data on schools which is now emerging and so varied is the practice.

Whatever their initial reactions, the vast majority of headteachers, principals and governing bodies have responded positively to their new responsibilities. Often under great pressure they have reacted pragmatically, working out practical solutions to practical problems as they clamber up the learning curve. Inevitably theory has been largely absent. Yet 'there is nothing so practical as good theory'. We need a firm theoretical framework to underpin our actions. So I have tried to draw out the principles and key issues beneath good financial management in schools, drawing upon my own experience as headteacher for many years and as educational consultant in financial management to many different clients in the UK and worldwide. I have also drawn extensively upon that growing body of books and articles on educational economics and finance. Although I come from a secondary background I have tried to bear primary schools particularly in mind – in many ways they need the most help in responding to current pressures.

I do not believe the book is too technical. It certainly is not about accountancy – I share the Monty Python view of that dark art – 'so utterly, incredibly, boring . . .'. So the philosophy of management adopted is not a technocratic one. I might define management as the application of inspiration, imagination and empathy to the improvement of a school, so I have assumed that intelligent management of a school's finances and resources needs above all:

a clear vision of where the school should be going, based upon a coherent philosophy and set of values;

a sharp focus on results, matching achievement against outlay;

a thoughtful, analytical approach to issues and problems;

a capacity for lateral thinking.

Of course it does also need some concepts and skills – and the back of an envelope . . . .

The material in the book follows a logical sequence. The early chapters examine some key concepts and terms and then consider general financial planning and responsibilities. The next three chapters deal with the acquisition, accumulation and maintenance of funds, while the next three deal with their expenditure through the budget process, and the management of the resources that they buy. The next chapter examines the difficult areas of costing and cost-effectiveness and opens up perhaps the most important deep issue underlying school financial management – productivity. The final chapter carries the productivity theme into that fascinating arena of possible future developments and alternative strategies. At that point I run for cover.

Each reader will see the book differently. It is relatively context-free, so it should be of use to anyone managing a school of any size or type, anywhere in the world. But because of this broad approach you will need to bridge from the principles discussed to your own everyday situation. Ideally it would help if you could pause after each section and ask 'How could I apply that in our school?' Readers from small primary schools will need to be a little forbearing; I do realise your situation is very different, but I certainly believe the principles and the issues I have set out are still relevant for you, though they need scaling down and simplifying.

I am most grateful to those who have answered my pesky queries or who have helped in other ways. In the UK I am indebted to: John Davies, Director of the Educational Publishers Association; Noble Hanlon of MacIntyre & Co; George Kelly of Acorn Fundraising; Jackie Hardie, Senior Adviser to Enfield LEA; Janet Ouston, Head of the Management Development Centre, University of London Institute of Education; Alan Quilter, South West Regional Director of the Independent Schools Information Service; George Reekie, Headmaster of Tatworth County Primary School, Somerset; Les Walton, Headmaster of Norham Community School, North Shields. I have also received valuable information from the Department of Information, HM Treasury, and the Central Statistical Office. I have received great help from the University of Exeter School of Education Library, and particularly Anne Dinan. I am also most grateful to Rosalind Levačić of the Open University and Richard Canning, Manager of Holyrood School Chard, for their invaluable help in wrestling with the difficulties of Chapter 6, and greatly improving it.

Outside the UK I have received equally valuable help from: Dave Bonner, Senior Teacher of Willeton Senior High School, Perth; James P. Boyle, President of Ombudsman Educational Services Ltd, Libertyville, Illinois; Professor Daniel Brown of the University of British Columbia; Ross Harrold of the University of New England, NSW; Professor G. Alan Hickrod of the Centre for the Study of Educational Finance, Illinois State University; John King of the Australian Council for Educational Research Ltd; Gary Marx, Senior Executive Director, American Association of School Administrators; Ken Rae, Senior Policy Analyst, New Zealand Ministry of Education.

I am also extremely grateful to five busy and highly respected people who so kindly read the draft text and made helpful suggestions to improve it: Brian Caldwell, Reader and Associate Dean, University of

Melbourne Institute of Education; Peter Downes, Headmaster of Hinchingbrooke School, Huntington; Tim Simkins, Head of the Centre for Educational Management and Administration, Sheffield Hallam University; Bob Smilanich, Associate Superintendent, Edmonton Public Schools, Alberta; Joe Winston, Department of Arts Education, University of Warwick.

Finally, I owe as always an enormous debt of gratitude to my wife and partner Joan, who has done most of the detailed processing of this book and has contributed to it in so many other ways. To her support and help I owe more than I can possibly say.

Acknowledgements

The author and publisher would like to thank all those who gave permission to reproduce the following copyright material.

Almqvist & Wiksell Publishing Ltd, Figure 31 (p. 175) from *Managing School Time* (1989) by B Knight adapted from *International Encyclopedia of Education* (1985) eds. Husén & Postlethwaite.

The Australian Council for Educational Research Limited, Figure 16 (p. 83), Figure 17 (p. 84) from 'Curriculum and Financial Performance in Non-Government Schools' (1988) by R. Harrold.

The Chartered Institute of Public Finance and Accountancy, Figure 3 (p. 27) from 'Local Management in Schools Training Package, Level 1' published by CIPFA – sponsored LMS Initiative (1988).

Controller of Her Majesty's Stationery Office, extract (p. 134) from 'Management within Primary Schools' (1991) by the Audit Commission.

The Educational Publishers Council, the Publishers Association, 19 Bedford Square, London, WC1B 3HJ, Figure 12 (p. 68) from *Book Check Action file* (1989).

Enfield LEA, Figure 21 (p. 116) from 'Annual Replacement Costs for Science Equipment' (1991) by the London Borough of Enfield.

Falmer Press Limited, Figure 24 – original model (p. 137), Figure 25 – refined model (p. 138), Figure 2 (p. 139) from The *Self-Managing School* (1988) by B Caldwell and J Spinks.

Longman Group UK Limited, Figure 36 (p. 207) from *Designing The School Day* (1992) by B Knight; Figure 23 (p. 133) from *Local Management of Schools – Training Materials* (1989) by B Knight; Figure 30 (p. 173), Figure 34 (p. 196), Table 9 (p. 179), all from *Managing School Time* (1989) by B Knight.

McREL Institute, Figure 32 (p. 176) from *Achieving Excellence – A Site-Based Management System for Efficiency Effectiveness* (1988) by McREL. Also quoted in *Managing School Time* (Longman 1989).

Routledge Publishers, Figure 29 (p. 164) from *Performance Related Pay in Education* (1992) by G Sapsed.

Royal County of Berkshire, Figure 4 (p. 28) from 'Berkshire LEA' (1989, revised 1993).

Transaction Publishing, Table 10 (p. 188) from *Public Schools Issues in Budgeting* by J Augenblick. Adapted from H Levin (1985).

Every effort has been made to trace all copyright holders, but if any have been inadvertently overlooked the publishers will be pleased to make the necessary arrangements at the first opportunity.

List of tables

List of diagrams

1 A theoretical framework

This is the most difficult chapter in the book, because it explores some of the central concepts and principles of school financial management. But it is the foundation for the chapters that follow. If you are a good manager, thinking about what you are doing, you need a secure theoretical framework. And the theory is not really that difficult . . . .

■■■ A model for school financial management

If you are managing something, it helps to have a mental model of the operation you are managing. Think of the school as a volatile 'system' within which finance is an interactive element.

In figure 1, within the bold broken line defining the boundaries of the school four components are suggested. The first is the input of financial resources, derived from outside the system from central or local government funds raised by taxation, or by fund raising and income generation and including where appropriate school fees. This element also includes capital assets, funded from similar sources but built up over previous years.

The revenue element of these resources is allocated among and converted into the next component, human and physical resources, by the budget mechanism. This will include all human resources, goods and services, and the maintenance of capital assets. There may be some additional resources donated from outside the system, e.g. given by the PTA or sponsored by a firm.

At first sight it appears that these human and physical resources are then used in the educational process. This is a misconception, because they can only be used after conversion into the third component, units of time use ('resource hours'). For example, a teacher can only be used if he or she is on the school timetable; a room can only be used if it is allocated for a specific time. Skilful management can often expand the resource hours available considerably and sometimes dramatically.

r-------- THE ECONOMIC, SOCIAL AND POLITICAL ENVIRONMENT ◄

Delegated funds

Central and local government,
trust or church funds, etc.

Monitoring and evaluation

FINANCIAL RESOURCES	HUMAN AND PHYSICAL RESOURCES	TIME UTILISATION

Capital assets   B
      ↑   U
           D
           G
Total   →   E
income   T
(revenue)
	Teachers
	Ancillary staff
	Premises
	Learning resources
	Other goods and ser-
	vices
		School day/year
		Timetable and time
		  for groups
		Time for individuals
		Use of time

Donated funds

Fees
Fund-raising
Income generation

Donated
resources

Donated time

Staff
Students
Parents
Community

L------------ THE ECONOMIC, SOCIAL AND POLITICAL ENVIRONMENT ◄

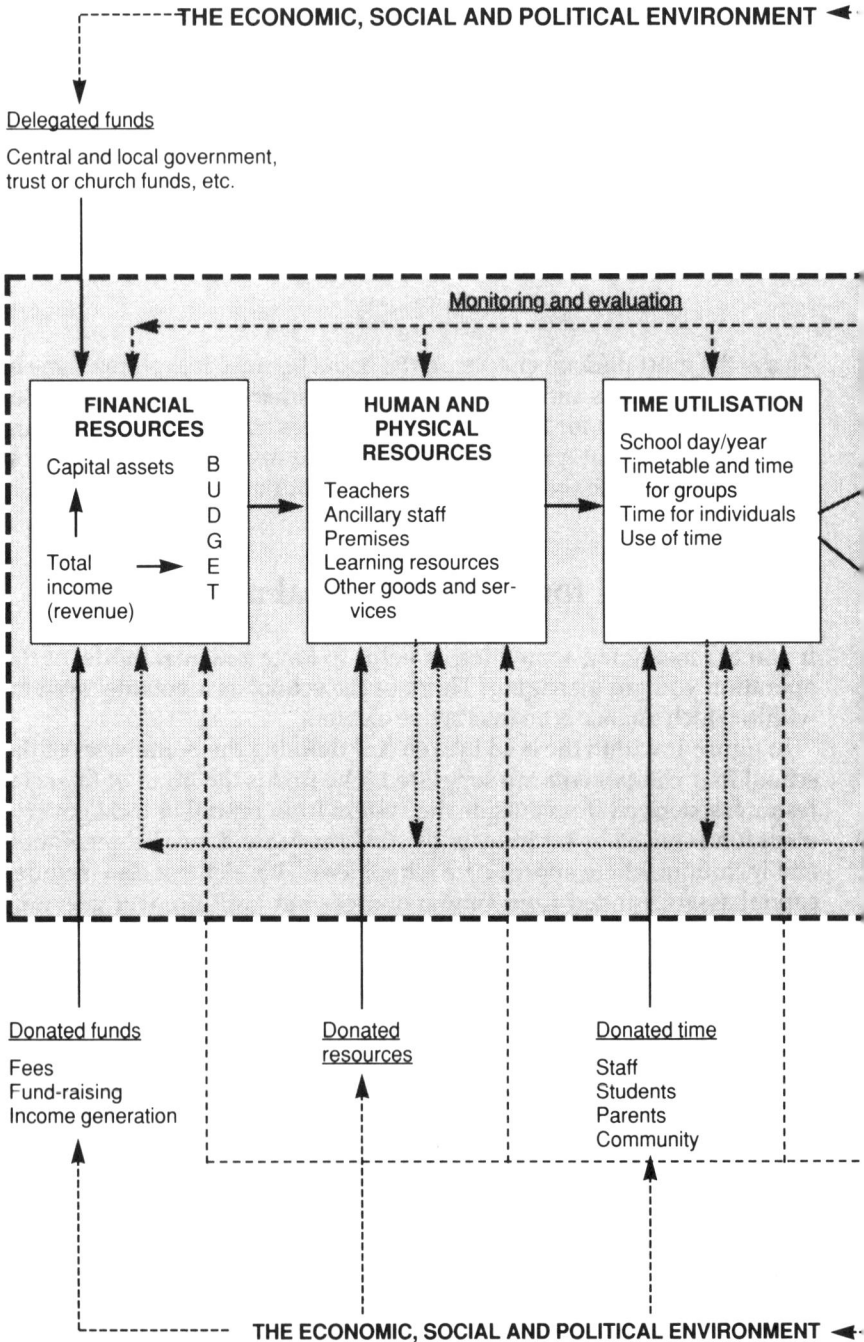

Figure 1 A systems model for school financial management

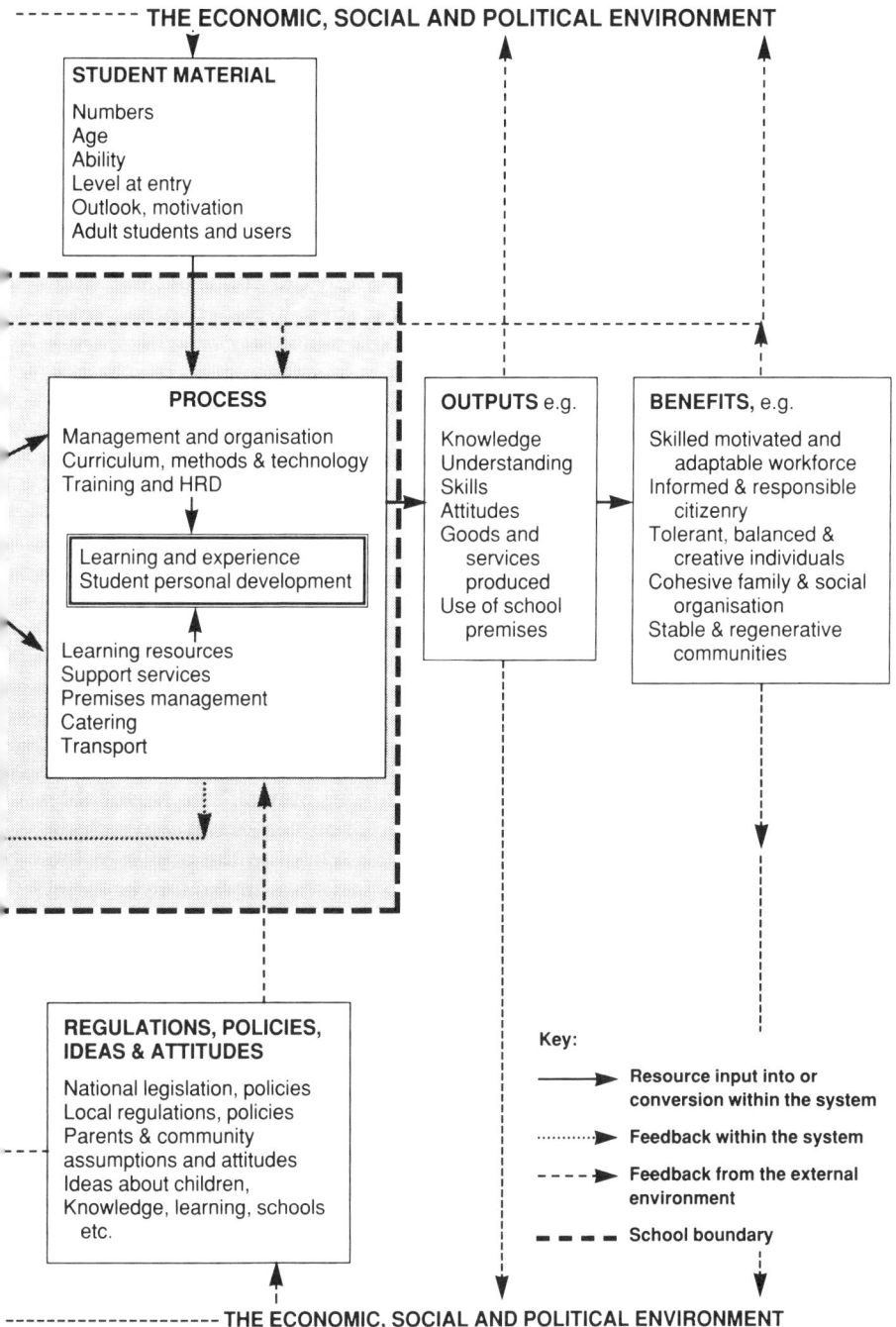

THE ECONOMIC, SOCIAL AND POLITICAL ENVIRONMENT

STUDENT MATERIAL

Numbers
Age
Ability
Level at entry
Outlook, motivation
Adult students and users

PROCESS

Management and organisation
Curriculum, methods & technology
Training and HRD

Learning and experience
Student personal development

Learning resources
Support services
Premises management
Catering
Transport

OUTPUTS e.g.

Knowledge
Understanding
Skills
Attitudes
Goods and
  services
  produced
Use of school
  premises

BENEFITS, e.g.

Skilled motivated and
  adaptable workforce
Informed & responsible
  citizenry
Tolerant, balanced &
  creative individuals
Cohesive family & social
  organisation
Stable & regenerative
  communities

REGULATIONS, POLICIES, IDEAS & ATTITUDES

National legislation, policies
Local regulations, policies
Parents & community
  assumptions and attitudes
Ideas about children,
Knowledge, learning, schools
  etc.

Key:

⟶ Resource input into or
   conversion within the system

⋯⋯▸ Feedback within the system

- - -▸ Feedback from the external
   environment

▬ ▬ School boundary

THE ECONOMIC, SOCIAL AND POLITICAL ENVIRONMENT

Example The same sum of money is set aside in two schools to purchase a computer. In school A the computer is locked in a cupboard by an over-zealous caretaker; in school B it is in use throughout school hours, at lunch-time, after school and often in the evening. Result – for the same expenditure school B gets perhaps 1000 'computer-hours' in a year and school A none!

Total resource-hours can be supplemented by donations of time: from teachers, giving time voluntarily beyond their 'directed time'; from students, doing homework or helping with voluntary activities; from parents or members of the community, volunteering their services. These additions may be very considerable, and again can be influenced by effective management.

The final component of the system is the educational process itself – that combination of managed arrangements for learning, with support arrangements, which is the core of a school. At its heart is 'the black box' of the classroom (or any other location) in which actual learning takes place. The process is affected by three major variables – the resources provided by the three earlier components, the student material on which it works, and regulations, policies, ideas and attitudes formed by society outside the system.

Emerging from the system are the outcomes of the process – both measurable and non-measurable but assumed by reason of students' experiences. So, for example, a residential experience may not leave measurable changes in student behaviour but may still be reasonably assumed to leave beneficial outcomes. School outcomes can also include any goods or services sold or given by the school to the public or the local community, including the use of its facilities. In the longer term, and much less measurable still, outcomes lead to benefits to society and to individuals – the final justification for the whole system.

The static page does scant justice to this model. We really need to imagine one of those moving computer simulations, where coloured blobs wobble and jerk from one point to another, setting up forces which judder through the system. For fundamental to this model is the idea of *feedback*. This may be entirely within the system – perhaps a new curriculum development that needs a reallocation of financial, human and physical or time resources, indicated by the dotted lines in figure 1. Or it may come from outside the system, as perceived outputs and benefits from the school affect the external environment and so alter the framework within which the school operates (broken lines in figure 1).

Example Introduction of a new curriculum, such as the National Curriculum in England and Wales, may require additional financial resources, converted into specific human and physical resources and possibly new time allocation arrangements. Experience of this new curriculum in operation will then feed back within the school the need for some changes to those resource allocations. But later, if outcomes and benefits of the new curriculum become apparent, other feedback operates. This may influence student material, perhaps by increasing the staying-on rate; or may make society more willing to grant funds or make donations to the school; or affect other attitudes towards the school, or policies; or affect the system through monitoring and evaluation mechanisms.

Several features of this model stand out:

1 Finance triggers and controls the system. Any change in the scale of financial resources or conditions on their use have an immediate effect on the rest of the system. Therefore schools that acquire greater responsibility for their own funds will want to augment them and gain more freedom over their use.

2 On the other hand, financial resources, and even the human and physical resources which they buy, are only a part of the system. The further away from the initial financial input, the more its direct impact is reduced. So, for example, a 10 per cent increase in funding may lead to a 10 per cent increase in tangible resources – but not necessarily to a 10 per cent increase in learning within the 'black box' – and it will be less likely still that a 10 per cent improvement in outputs can be identified (and even less, clearly attributed to the financial change); while any effect on benefits is likely to be incapable of separation from other factors – or even imperceptible.

3 The whole system is susceptible to good management. And effective management of the third or fourth components may be equally as important for good financial management as effectiveness with the first two. Also, management possibilities are clearly not confined to the system: as responsibility for finance increases, schools will increasingly wish to influence their external environment, to improve public funding, increase donation of funds and resources, and influence policies, regulations etc. So marketing and public relations, too, have a close link with effective financial management. A broad view of financial management, rather than a narrow one, is likely to produce the best returns.

4 Given the importance of feedback to the system, good management

information is essential. Financial information in most schools is still very primitive. It mainly records the exchange of funds into human and physical resources; it is insufficiently designed for planning or evaluation. Good-quality non-financial information is equally important.

5 Financial management has two faces – money management and cost management. Money management, centred on the first component, is the easy bit – although often it does not seem easy. How should we spend our money? How should we control it? (Remember Mr Micawber's ill-kept axiom: 'annual income twenty pounds, annual expenditure nineteen pounds nineteen shillings and sixpence, result happiness; annual income twenty pounds, annual expenditure twenty-one pounds, result misery!')

Cost management is more difficult, less pressing but in the long run far more important. Cost management is not just identifying costs and reducing them, valuable though this is, but also costing time utilisation, the educational process and its outputs, and alternative educational strategies. You will only be a really effective financial manager if you can both plan and balance your budget – the money side – and cost your operation, its outcomes and alternatives. (In industry this division is reflected professionally by two groups of accountants: financial accountants who are responsible for company finances, and cost and management accountants who monitor production, sales and profitability.)

The remainder of this chapter surveys the context for financial management and then grapples with concepts of costs and examines some of the key principles for effective financial management. It concludes with some definitions of terms.

■ The context for financial management

School financial management does not operate in a vacuum. It is greatly affected by its context, as figure 1 suggests. In systems that are still strongly centralised, those responsible for managing schools will operate in an Alice in Wonderland situation where, although they are said to be managers, they do not really know what their school's costs are and are in no position to manage them. They will tend to see finance for their school as coming from some magical external source, and so not really their business (except to complain!). Such managers will often accept this bizarre situation as normal, so strong is the effect of dependency, although their counterparts in industry and commerce would find it unthinkable – and they would find it unthinkable too in their everyday lives. (However, it should be said that, although there is a strong trend worldwide away from this situation, some of the school systems that appear to be very effective – such as in Japan and Germany – are still administered centrally.)

Where substantial delegation occurs there can still be marked variation. Worldwide, delegation schemes differ enormously. Some are driven principally by ideas of *managerial efficiency*, delegating decisions to the lowest level to increase local accountability and create flexibility to respond to local needs. Edmonton, Alberta, the longest running delegation scheme, fits this description, and so do developments in Australia, Belgium, The Netherlands, and the earlier 'pre-LMS' schemes in the UK. Others, particularly in the USA, are driven more by the idea of *empowerment*, freeing teachers, parents and community to run their schools. Here financial delegation is likely to be only part of more general restructuring.

Others (England and Wales since the 1988 Education Reform Act is the leading example) are centred upon the creation of a *market economy* for schools, based on a belief in the superiority of free markets to deliver services efficiently to consumers and provide them with choice. In this situation the school will be concerned to attract students and the funding that follows them, and so will lay more emphasis on marketing, public relations and 'customer satisfaction'. There are, however, important issues of equity in this context which are discussed in Chapter 8.

In all three types of scheme, much depends on the spirit behind them and the detail of implementation. In some schemes, particularly in the USA, administrators have still retained considerable control through regulations, and in many schemes regulations are still often inconsistent with the underlying intention. In England and Wales some LEAs have remained paternalistic and supervisory in attitude, for example in the returns that they require and in regulations for community use of premises.

The environment for school financial management will also be deeply affected by current political, social and economic conditions. Although school managers cannot control these, they can at least anticipate them or perhaps attempt to influence them. Politically there is a marked trend in many western countries towards decentralisation (but with national definition of goals and monitoring of outcomes) and privatisation. Socially the trend seems to be towards greater participation and 'consumerism'. Economically, trends are much more difficult to foresee, particularly fluctuations in the level of economic activity. However, there does appear to be pressure on the welfare state in many countries, partly caused by the growing numbers of elderly people and the increased costs of technological advances in health and other care. Education itself will compound this as costs grow with increased use of new technology, rises in participation rates and expansion of higher education and training.

These three types of delegation scheme all give schools control over *expenditure*, but not over *supply* of funds. Even the 'market economy', with open enrolment and funding based largely on a per capita formula, gives them influence over the *volume* of funding – but not its per capita level. Only income generation allows schools to increase the *level* of funding. Is the ultimate logic that schools, to manage their own destiny, will want more control over the level of funding – including parental quasi-fee contributions – or will political and equity implications prevent this? Recently this has occurred in South Africa. In April 1992, 'White' schools were invited to become 'Model C' schools, taking responsibility for all non-salary costs and for raising the funds for them. They will now be legally entitled to charge fees – initially estimated at 500–1000 rand annually per student, if they wish. This *cost transfer* arrangement is clearly a fourth category of delegation, different from those described above. (Of course many schools in developing countries are already in this situation.)

The nature of costs

A definition

A working definition for 'costs' is: *resources foregone to acquire other human or physical resources to achieve an objective*. It needs some elaboration. The resources foregone need not be financial. They could be a diversion of people, premises or other resources from one purpose to another (for example, switching the duties of a secretary from administration to support for teaching staff, or converting a cloakroom to a store). They could be greater wear-and-tear on buildings and equipment (although ultimately this would be translated into maintenance and so need financial resources). The resources could be time, either within the school day or personal time. At the extreme are the intangible resources like morale, health, motivation and energy of teachers, students and others.

Examples of non-financial costs

Teachers' time Each teacher sets a limit on the amount of time he or she will devote to the job. Time spent on one activity may prevent time being spent on another.

Students' travel A long journey uses time that could be spent in more useful ways, and may reduce school efficiency.

Students' earnings foregone – a very real cost to families with older children at school. This is acknowledged when students are given maintenance allowances, and when labour economists regard it as investment to enhance later earnings.

Students' nutrition Cafeteria systems for school meals undoubtedly reduce a school's costs. But what about the nutritional costs! (Similarly, tuck-shops are a welcome support to school funds – but at what dental cost?)

Heating homes A compressed school day can reduce school heating costs, but be replaced by a less obvious cost for parents.

Vandalism This is a cost for the community, in time and environmental terms, as well as in rectification.

Often costs can involve both financial and non-financial elements.

Example The closure of a small village school is proposed. Financial costs saved include the extra teaching staff necessary for a small school, the maintenance costs of the premises and the financial return foregone on the capital value of the building – offset by some additional transport and meals costs. Non-financial costs include the effect on the community of the loss of its social centre, and time spent by children travelling – offset perhaps by educational gains of children in a larger school.

Within the definition above, 'foregone' includes both deliberate allocation of resources and allocation by default – for example by using staff inefficiently or incurring unnecessary energy costs. 'Achieve an objective' includes the incurring of costs for intangible purposes, such as enhancement of a school's image or improvement of staff morale.

Costing

The inclusion of both financial and non-financial elements within costs creates problems, because it is obviously desirable to cost non-financial resources in financial terms – the process of costing. This is far from straightforward, as John Fielden, formerly partner in Peat Marwick (management consultants), has explained:

Costing is the art of measuring the consumption of resources in financial terms. Contrary to most perceptions there can be a large element of subjectivity in costing exercises. There are often no easy ways of measuring resources use or of converting it into

money terms, and the person carrying out the costing will there-fore have to make assumptions or value judgements.

Also, costing of inputs is much easier than costing of processes or out-comes. So the latter are usually neglected in schools – although any com-mercial business has to cost both. Costing is also difficult because it is often by no means clear which resources should actually be included. Chapter 10 examines these issues more fully.

Full cost accounting

There is a convincing accountancy theory that costs should be measured at the point where they are ultimately consumed, not where they are first committed. This leads to full cost accounting – the reallocation of central overheads to operational activities. So when a hotel chain, for example, costs the letting of a room, it includes an element for both hotel and chain overheads.

For school activities we could reallocate school administrative and premises costs, LEA/school board costs, and even central/state govern-ment costs when appropriate. Although this reallocation may be on a crudely proportionate basis, it still has considerable value:

- Costs become transparent. There are no hidden costs and no 'free lunches'.

- It highlights the cost of overheads.

- It enables the 'customer' – the teacher, department or school – to assess whether these are reasonable value.

Example If the reallocated costs of the educational psychological service to one school in one year was £1000, and if the school had received only a sin-gle one-hour visit during that time, several questions arise. Is the service unreasonably costly? Could it be better provided in an alternative form? Or is the school making too little use of it? Could the amount be better used else-where – the opportunity cost – assuming that it could actually be rede-ployed? Or possibly, is the basis of allocation unsound?

The important point is that it is only through reallocation of costs that these questions are raised. Without it, the figure would probably not even be known to the school and certainly not questioned.

- It may lead to actual recharging for central services, and even pro-vision of these on a full cost recovery basis.

Example A school's photocopying costs may be hidden under a heading such as 'office' or 'administration'. But if these are separated and then allocated to users, advantages immediately flow:

— Each user will try to reduce expenditure or obtain better value for money.
— Discrepancies between users surface.
— Each user can make comparisons from year to year.

However, it is important that the 'full costs' include all the additional costs incurred; i.e. equipment (rental, purchase, depreciation etc.), stationery and materials, maintenance, electricity, possibly insurance. There will be other costs that are not seen as extra (e.g staff and premises costs) since they already exist, but *they are a resource diverted from other uses* and technically they should be included, although this may not always appear practicable (premises may have no alternative use).

Full cost accounting is most useful in school systems that retain a large proportion of expenditure centrally. But even with schools that enjoy a high degree of delegation, reapportionment of central state, local authority and school overheads is still valuable – and easy with a spreadsheet! Above all it throws up the opportunity costs of free, unpriced gifts (which are still actually bought from education funds).

Example Currently in England and Wales, grant-maintained schools opt out of local authorities and are now administered 'free' from the central DFE (Department for Education and Science). But this still creates extra costs at the centre, financed from the total funds devoted to education (and it is alleged, more expensive than the previous LEA administration!).

However, a word of caution. Full cost accounting can lead to wildly fictitious allocations. And recharging is not always appropriate – it can undermine the resourcing of valuable services (e.g. if schools choose not to 'buy' the school library service).

Opportunity costs

Every expenditure and transfer of resources has its opportunity cost – the next-best alternative use for these resources.

Example A PTA tells a headteacher it has some money for the purchase of microscopes. The head accepts with gratitude, although feeling that a higher priority would be to expand the basic equipment in one of the laboratories. This is a clear example of an opportunity cost – the 'opportunity' that a particular sum of money would buy if it was not spent in this particular way.

If the opportunity foregone appears of greater value than the opportunity accepted, then the expenditure is misconceived. Education services worldwide have been riddled with examples of this 'separate pocket' mentality.

With greater delegation to schools, this kind of opportunity cost has reduced, but many examples still lurk unseen. For example, schools are quick to see that the opportunity cost of high fuel bills is the books they would have liked to buy, but slower to see that the traditional way they have deployed teachers can often mask substantial opportunity costs for meeting students' learning needs in other ways.

■ Cost classification

Cost information is like any other data. It needs to be organised into a pattern before significance can be read into it. The cost data of a school can be arranged in numerous ways to bring out different features.

Direct and indirect costs

In commerce and industry an important distinction is often made between direct and indirect costs. The former are costs that can be easily identified with a cost centre (a cost centre may be a factory, or a department within the factory). The latter are costs that cannot be so identified and have to be apportioned (loosely called 'overheads'). So if a department has a separately metered electricity bill, electricity is a direct cost; if the bill relates to the factory as a whole, electricity is an indirect cost. This division is extensively used and has obvious value in controlling costs and setting prices.

The distinction is not very helpful for most schools. If we see the school as a cost centre, almost all school-centred costs (salaries, purchase of goods and services, many premises-related costs) will be direct, and most local authority or district costs will be indirect. Some large secondary schools with delegated budgets are, however, beginning to see their departments as internal cost centres, and here the distinction may be valid – although disentangling premises or even staffing costs for a department may not be easy.

Prime and subsidiary costs

This is a more useful distinction, between resources related to a school's prime educational function and those relating to its subsidiary administrative, transport and catering functions. The distinction is not black-and-white, and is better seen as a gradation, as suggested in figure 2. Another category, local authority/school board and central government services, could also be added.

The classification in figure 2 is distorted because over half the total will be in the first item – teachers' 'teaching' salaries. However, the division of total school costs into such categories, with a percentage for each, is important. It makes it possible to monitor the percentages over years and see if the proportionate – and actual – expenditure on the subsidiary categories is shrinking or rising. This has implications for budget format which are discussed in Chapter 7.

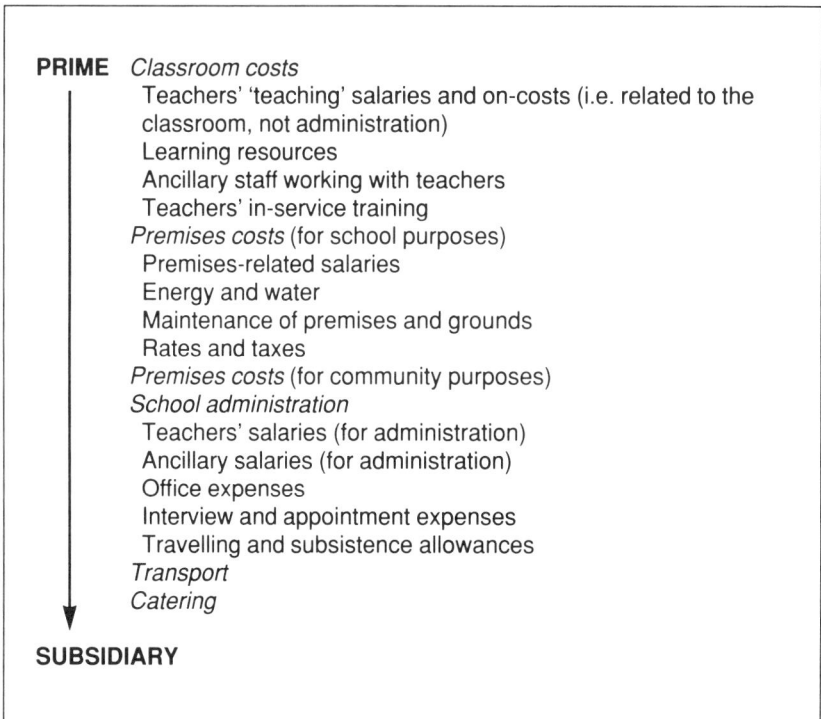

PRIME   *Classroom costs*
            Teachers' 'teaching' salaries and on-costs (i.e. related to the classroom, not administration)
            Learning resources
            Ancillary staff working with teachers
            Teachers' in-service training
            Premises costs (for school purposes)
            Premises-related salaries
            Energy and water
            Maintenance of premises and grounds
            Rates and taxes
            Premises costs (for community purposes)
            School administration
            Teachers' salaries (for administration)
            Ancillary salaries (for administration)
            Office expenses
            Interview and appointment expenses
            Travelling and subsistence allowances
            Transport
            Catering

SUBSIDIARY

Figure 2 Prime and subsidiary school costs

Variable and fixed costs

The distinction between variable and fixed costs is a very important one in the industrial and commercial field. Variable costs are those that change in proportion to the quantitative changes in the processes of the industry; fixed costs are those that remain unchanged for a given period of time, despite fluctuations in the volume of the activity undertaken.

Example In a shoe factory, the quantities of leather, thread and glue used will be directly related to the number of shoes produced, while the rent of the factory will remain unaltered whether the factory is on overtime or short time.

In industry this distinction is of great importance. Constant watchfulness is needed to keep fixed costs as low as possible and to increase the volume of activity so that they are spread more thinly upon each item of production. Fixed costs are not, of course, fixed in the other sense. They will vary from time to time – rates and rents may go up, for example, but this variation is related to external factors, not to internal changes in the volume of production.

Schools are a different type of organisation and their costs do not rapidly reflect fluctuations in volume of students. However, the distinction is still important. It is particularly important at a time of falling rolls, when a number of costs may remain completely or relatively fixed, even though the number of students may fall dramatically, and so squeeze the finance available for variable costs. This issue is discussed more fully in Chapter 6.

Although the concept is important, its use in practice is more difficult. Once again, black-and-white shades into grey. At one extreme we find costs that clearly vary in exact proportion to the number of pupils. A good example is stationery, whose use is closely related to the school's population. An equally close relationship to student numbers will be found attached to examination fees, free school meals, and uniform and maintenance allowances, although these of course may be affected by other external factors as well. At the other extreme, the best examples of fixed costs are loan charges (on capital expenditure) and telephone rentals. In between, we find some costs that respond broadly in line with pupil numbers but with some lag – for example, teachers' salaries, books and equipment; others that are considerably affected such as transport costs; others that are affected to some degree such as heating and lighting; and others that may be affected to some extent, but probably only after a substantial change in numbers and after a considerable time-lag – for example, premises maintenance and administrative costs.

In one sense no costs are totally 'fixed'. Even loan charges, for example, are only fixed as long as that particular school building is still in use. If it is possible to amalgamate two schools and to sell one of the buildings, then at that point they become a variable cost. So costs that appear fixed may over a long time-scale be open to variation.

Controllable, sunk and idle costs

Who controls costs? The question is not as simple as it sounds. In accounting convention, costs are normally managed by those who hold budget responsibility for them. So a manager is responsible for all his or her budget costs except those that are completely fixed during the period in question. Budgetary responsibility is aimed at identifying the person who has the most effective cost control over the item concerned.

In schools to which little financial responsibility is delegated, the situation is not so clear. Obviously the head or principal has virtually no control over local authority or district expenditures, although he or she may have influence over them. On the other hand the local administration may have little influence or control over many areas that are technically its budgetary responsibility; for example, energy costs or staff deployment. One of the main arguments for maximum delegation to schools is that it prevents this blurring of responsibility and makes schools responsible for what they can control.

There will be some school costs that still appear not to be controllable – such as rates or taxes related to the premises. But there is no objection to these remaining part of school managers' responsibilities – they cannot do any harm there! At least it makes managers aware of them, and perhaps keener to do something about them.

Other costs may not really be controllable because expenditure cannot be reduced or recovered – 'sunk costs'. For example, an expensive piece of equipment or a facility like a swimming pool which the school does not feel able to close, but for which the costs are more than the school would like to spend. Or costs may not be fully controllable because premises or other resources are underused – 'idle costs'.

Unit costs

Unit costs are the most powerful but most under-used weapon in the financial manager's armoury. What are unit costs? At first sight . . .

$$\text{Unit costs} = \frac{\text{total costs}}{\text{number of units}}$$

This is broadly correct – but in practice unit costs are more complicated. For example, total costs are not self-evident and it will often be a matter of contention as to exactly what costs should be included. Studies into school unit costs may not be comparable because each takes a different cost base. Often total costs should be disaggregated; for example, comparing unit costs per student in two schools may be of limited value if one school has a much higher proportion of older students. It is sometimes necessary to subdivide totals according to age of students, type of activity etc.

Similarly, the divisor-units show equal variety. We can choose input units (£s, space, etc.) or output units (students, examination passes, etc.). We can choose historic cost units, standard units (equivalent to the standard costs used in industry), or modelling units ('what happens if . . . ?') Units can be students, or classes, or schools; meals, journeys, or courses; they can be units of time, hours, or lessons, or days; or any other useful unit. They give insight, often dramatically. Try waving three £10 notes in front of a pupil who is thoroughly idle – the cost of his or her week's education – and ask if the ratepayers have had their money's-worth this week! They are also very useful for comparisons – between schools, for example, or over a period of time.

Unfortunately such unit costs lack dynamism – they suggest a static total divided by a static number of units. In real life student numbers rise or fall, buildings close, meals shrink and buses fill. If one unit is added at the margin the extra costs (usually referred to as the *marginal* costs) of that extra unit will often be less than the previous average unit cost. For example, an extra student joining a school may mean extra learning resources, but the effect on the cost of heating, lighting, postage, non-teaching staff, administrative costs, etc., will be minimal. Also, additional students do not increase costs evenly – just one additional student at a critical point may trigger the need for an additional teacher or classroom. So we look less at the cost of one extra unit than at the group of extra units implied in any change. This is the *incremental* cost – the cost of the group of units added by growth; or for those subtracted by contraction, the *decremental* costs. The dynamics and use of unit costs are explored more fully in Chapters 7 and 10.

■ Cost characteristics of schools

P.H. Coombs and J. Hallak in *Managing Educational Costs* (1972) drew on extensive Unesco experience of schools worldwide. They pointed out that the behaviour of costs is strikingly similar in all educational systems, over-riding differences of development or regime. A number of features characteristic of school systems in many countries can be identified.

1 Most schools are 'non-profit' organisations. In maintained schools the profit motive is largely absent – and, more important, the profit measure. In a profit-orientated organisation, profit provides a single measure of efficiency of performance; it relates benefits (expressed

in income and profit); it assists comparisons of efficiency between different centres and different types of activities. Non-profit organisations, lacking the profit measure, have inherent problems in performance measurement:

a There is no single objective criterion to use in measuring or comparing performance, or in assessing alternatives.

b There is no easy way of estimating the relationship between inputs and outputs, or judging the effect of particular expenditure.

c A realistic pricing policy is not necessary, nor the discipline of cost control that goes with it.

Some independent schools are profit-orientated, making profits for their proprietors. The majority are not profit-seeking in that sense, but they do have to adopt a realistic pricing policy and avoid making a loss. They are profit-conscious, although not profit-orientated.

2 Schools are service organisations and perform a social as well as an economic function. This makes measurement and costing of their output difficult. We can estimate the cost of teaching pupils mastery of skills in metalwork, or the achievement of an examination pass in physics. But it is quite impossible to cost the school's efforts in promoting good citizenship or desirable social qualities. Given the very variable nature of the human material schools deal with, it is very difficult to cost many of their 'outputs'. Measuring productivity, and improving it, is very difficult. And services cannot be stored – another obstacle to efficient organisation.

3 School cost structures are very stable. This reflects primarily the stability of educational technologies and practices. Technological change in education is very slow. It also reflects the stability of assumptions on which schools are based. Education is the only industry where all employees and all customers (parents) have had their assumptions moulded by prolonged first-hand involvement in the process. So schools are very conservative institutions.

4 Schools work within a very slow cycle. They are geared to an annual rhythm. Once the school year begins, the costs for the institution are more or less committed, apart from unforeseen changes because of inflation, etc. Indeed any attempt to reduce costs *during* the school year causes a lot of disruption, and often creates damage out of proportion to the savings made. Beyond that, students usually spend several years in a particular school, and many changes have to be introduced slowly and phased over a long period so that education is not damaged. Schools cannot be amalgamated or closed like factories without ignoring students' long-term needs. So introducing substan-

tial changes in schools is a little like turning an oil-tanker – it can be done, but it takes a long time.

5 School unit costs tend to rise when education becomes more technical and science-centred, when it deals with older students, and when there is greater concern for quality. So in most countries of the world school unit costs are rising in real terms.

6 Schools are very labour-intensive. For example, the Chartered Institute of Public Finance and Accountancy (CIPFA) Education Statistics 1990–91 Estimates records nearly two-thirds of LEA expenditure on primary and secondary schools coming from teacher salaries, and over 70 per cent from all salaries. Catch 22 now surfaces. The conventional labour-intensive service industry invests in improved technology to reduce labour costs. Hospitals speed the turnover of patients; restaurants automate the cooking; shops convert to self-service. But if schools do this they increase the student/teacher ratio, and thereby increase class size, narrow the curriculum, and loosen social control.

7 School calendars cause high costs. The traditional school day, school week and school year lead to heavy under-use of premises. Schools are seldom used for more than 55 per cent of the year, often less. On the 190 to 200 days that they are open in most countries, school proper only lasts for six or seven hours (and usually only four and a half to five hours of this is 'education'). For over 80 per cent of the hours in the year the typical classroom lies unused and undisturbed save by the occasional cleaner or classroom ghost.

8 Schools are constrained by legislation, regulations, policies and attitudes that have often developed without consideration for costs, and yet which considerably affect them.

Key concepts for effective financial management

(The following section is quoted, by permission, from my contribution to the module 'Managing the Resources' in *Management in Education* published by Henley Distance Learning Ltd)

"The UK Audit Commission had adopted the Three Es as the foundation of good financial management – Economy, Efficiency and Effectiveness.

Economy can be defined as careful use of resources, frugality and good housekeeping. It implies the avoidance of expenditure above a reasonable minimum or of a speculative sort.

Examples Repair of equipment rather than a new purchase; a drive to reduce peak hour telephone bills; purchase of equipment only after thorough survey of the market and negotiation of discount; effective arrangements for stock-taking and investigation of losses.

It is a useful and familiar concept, but limited in that it only relates to expenditure, and not to its use.

Efficiency is the fullest possible attainment of specific objectives or standards.

Examples A heating system which brings all rooms to the desired temperature; a security system which detects intruders effectively; a clerical system which collects payments for hire of school premises promptly; a timetable which deploys staff fully, teaching appropriate subjects, with a contact-ratio comparable to good practice in peer group schools.

Cost-efficiency relates efficiency to its cost. X is more cost-efficient than Y because it achieves greater efficiency at the same cost or the same efficiency at lower cost.

Examples A new boiler which provides the same heat more economically; reduced expenditure on an administrator rather than a teacher to administer school examinations; preventive maintenance of buildings which avoids long-term maintenance costs; purchase of slightly more expensive equipment which stands up better to wear.

Effectiveness is the fullest possible attainment of the goals and objectives of the school.

Examples Improved performance, possibly against performance indicators, such as improved examination results or test scores (but only if this is not caused by some external factor such as improved quality of student intake); improved student attitudes and behaviour; better parent and community relations; improved school environment.

Cost-effectiveness relates effectiveness to the cost incurred – greater effectiveness for the same or low additional cost, or the same effectiveness at lower cost.

Examples Expenditure on promotion of the school brings increased enrolment; purchase of a minibus brings expansion in educational visits and off-campus learning; an increase in size of A-level classes (i.e. lower unit costs) brings no deterioration in examination results; peer-tutoring improves student performance with little extra cost.

The three Es can be in conflict. Economy may reduce efficiency or effectiveness ('false economy' or diseconomy); obsession with efficiency can reduce effectiveness.

Examples A tightly controlled system for issuing stationery in a school may reduce expenditure (economy) and reduce waste (efficiency) but if it prevents pupils doing the required amount of written work it is not cost-effective; using the cheapest paint may be economical but not cost-efficient.

Also note that such judgements are not solely quantitative. In any consideration of efficiency and effectiveness, quality is equally important. So judgements of a more subjective kind are inevitably required."

Cost/benefit analysis goes a step further, attempting to cost ultimate benefits of the system.

Productivity is not a comfortable term for educators – it sounds too industrial. Yet the concept of increasing outcomes for each unit of input (e.g. £s, teacher hours or student hours) is important. Higher school productivity, however it is measured, implies one of the following:

- Cheaper education, the same for less cost. Cheapness should not be derided. There is no advantage in a process being more expensive than it has to be. If it is, it blocks the opportunity costs that would have been freed by a cheaper process.

- Increased education, more for the same cost. Any increase in educational outcomes for the same cost speaks for itself.

- Speedier education, the same in less time. This would free time for additional curriculum – perhaps at last the quart could be squeezed into the pint pot.

Productivity is an important issue for school financial management and perhaps likely to be the central issue in the future. At present there is little evidence that school productivity has improved. Outcomes have generally improved in terms of standards of performance and quality of curriculum, but inputs have increased. There is little evidence that children learn a standard process like using percentages or reading at a specified level more cheaply or more quickly than previously. (These issues are explored more fully in Chapters 10 and 11.)

Closely linked with productivity is the idea of *value added*. The development of multivariate analysis of examination and test results is beginning to make possible assessment of the value added to a student by his or her experience in the school, i.e. achievement detached from socioeconomic factors. This can obviously be costed against inputs. It will also encourage schools to look at alternative, cheaper or more cost-effective strategies for creating added value (see Chapter 11).

Value for money (VFM) is a common-sense idea familiar in our everyday lives which is a useful yardstick for school financial management. Simple questions like 'How much does this cost? Is it good value for money?' help to deter those unreal attitudes which can creep into public finance. As an industrialist once said to me: 'Always ask yourself – if this was *my* business, would I spend *my* money like this?'.

■ Some operational principles

Their money or my money?

There are two sorts of money circulating in schools: their money and my money. 'Their money' has a magic quality: it trickles down like manna from heaven, and with any luck there will be plenty more where it came from. ('Them' can be the government, LEA or school board, or the school management team or governing body.) So it should be spent with a light heart, free from tedious concern with opportunity costs, value for money and cost-efficiency. 'My money' is quite different. It is normal money, just like my own personal housekeeping, to be jealously guarded, saved and spent with great care and thought.

One of the arts of financial management is to convert 'their money' to 'my money', at every level.

Maximum delegation

The important Coopers & Lybrand report *Local Management of Schools* suggested in 1987:

> **The underlying philosophy of financial delegation to schools stems from the application of the principles of good management. Good management requires the identification of management units for which objectives can be set and resources allocated; the unit is then required to manage itself within those resources in a way which seeks to achieve the objectives; the performance of the unit is monitored and the unit is held to account for its performance and for its use of funds.**

This approach also has in-school implications. Not only should there be maximum delegation *to* the school but also *within* the school; i.e. from headteacher or principal to classroom teachers, departments, caretaker etc. It should be assumed that those closest to the point of use are likely to know best, unless proven otherwise.

It is also important that such delegation of responsibilities occurs within an appropriate framework. Budget holders should not require authorisation from a higher level except for specified exceptions, should not be unduly restricted by regulations, and should be free to switch expenditure from one heading to another.

Budget holders must however be clearly accountable. If there are any restrictions on their scope for action – for example a maximum sum for any single expenditure or for virement (see below) without requiring additional authority – this should be clearly spelt out. Any expenditure should be clearly authorised by the person responsible, and so traceable to the authorised budget.

▇▇ Definition of terms

Gross and net Gross expenditure is the total money spent, before any allowance has been made for income offset against it, at which point it becomes net expenditure. Similarly gross income is total receipts, before allowance for any expenses incurred reduces it to net income.

Capital/revenue Capital expenditure usually refers to major durable items, such as buildings, land, large items of equipment, and often including major renovative or enhancement programmes. It also usually includes the 'kitting out' of a new building with equipment and furniture, and sometimes a large order for related equipment such as a set of computers.

Because these are major one-off expenditures, they are normally excluded from the annual budget since they would distort it. They can also be regarded as bringing forward into one year expenditure which should be seen as stretching over the life of the item. However, the distinction between capital and revenue is not a black-and-white one. Smaller capital items can be financed from revenue budgets, or payments made from the revenue budget into the capital budget or fund ('revenue contributions towards capital outlay'). Also, capital expenditure is commonly financed by borrowing, which creates annual 'loan charges' or 'debt charges' which can be paid from the revenue budget, similar to a householder's mortgage. Capital items can also be acquired by leasing, again with charges paid from the revenue budget.

Virement is the authorisation to switch ('vire') expenditure from one budget heading (probably underspent) to another (possibly overspent or needing extra funds for an additional purchase).

Cost centres Industrial and commercial firms, in an effort to establish management accountability, commonly identify various forms of responsibility centres: revenue centres; mission centres (directly related to the organisation's objectives and functions); service centres (subsidiary to and supporting those centres carrying on the main business); profit centres (where each centre is given its own profit target); and where profit is not appropriate, cost centres. A school can be seen as a natural cost centre, but there may be other cost centres on the site – for example if it has a community education, sports or youth centre. And larger schools can possibly think of their departments as internal cost centres. The essential characteristics of a cost centre are that it is responsible for its own budget and that all expenditures incurred by it are debited to it. It should also have its own objectives or targets against which its performance can be judged.

Prices create problems because, in an age of inflation, they are not constant. It is always necessary to establish which price base is being used (e.g. in April 1993, or in the financial year 1993–94). The second example implies a price base at the start of the financial year. Prices can also be described as 'current' (this financial year).

Constant prices means that it is assumed sufficient addition will be made to offset inflation, so that the 'real value' of the budget etc. is maintained. *Out-turn prices* means the actual figures obtaining at the end of the specified period – so a grant of £1000 for three years at out-turn prices means that each year a £1000 grant will be made, even though in the second and third year the grant may be reduced in real terms by inflation.

* * *

Theory should be used, not just read or talked about, so it is hoped that this short excursion will encourage those managing school finances to reflect on what they are doing – perhaps seeing finance working within the school as a system; looking beyond money management into cost management and analysis; being alert to changes in the external environment; being aware of the '3 Es' and concerned about productivity; and being sensitive to value for money – in short, thinking about the underlying implications of what they do as well as the practice.

2 Plans and priorities

In everyday life, the household that can look ahead, establish priorities and plan its activities is the one that manages its money well. A household that just lives for the day ends up in the bank manager's office! So too in schools. If you are to manage school finance effectively, you need clear longer-term plans and priorities. Financial management without them is like a house without foundations.

Plans need long-term objectives. A good starting point is a thorough analysis of the school's current performance and situation, since this will throw up needs for the future. This could arise from a 'whole school review', for which many English LEAs have developed procedures. Or it could arise from an external inspection report on the school. Otherwise a SWOT analysis will produce a useful starting point. It has the great advantage of being straightforward, practical and not too time-consuming – a school staff and governing body, properly organised, can produce a useful one in an afternoon.

For those not familiar with a SWOT analysis, it simply asks:

Strengths	What are these, currently?
Weaknesses	What are these?
Opportunities	What opportunities are likely to arise in the future?
Threats	What threats are likely to arise?

Brian Fidler suggests in *Effective Local Management of Schools* (pp. 26–30) that such an analysis needs to consider the school's environment, internal resources and organisational culture (values, attitudes, relationships, styles, politics, etc.) as well as the school's performance and outcomes.

The next step is to produce a statement of the long-term mission, goals or vision for the school. This will also bring out consideration of the school's underlying philosophy and values, which also need to be explicit and agreed. Mission statements are quite fashionable in schools nowadays. Brian Spicer, writing in 1990 from an Australian context, suggests that the key elements of a mission statement should be:

Why do we exist?
What dimensions of education will we concentrate on?
What distinctive role will we aim for?
How shall we conduct our educational enterprise? (i.e. with what
    management values and style?)

However, mission statements are not always very helpful. They tend
to state the obvious or be difficult to translate into action. Long-term
goals are possibly more practical – 'What do we hope to have achieved
here in five years time?' The best approach may be to create a 'vision' of
what the school could and should be like in five years' time. This encourages people to dream of their ideal school and so frees them from current
preoccupations and assumptions. It encourages more creative and divergent thinking. Techniques for 'visioning' are well established; for example that developed by Louis Tice of the Pacific Institute (see Addresses).

However, converting a vision, set of goals or mission statement into a
plan is not easy. Do we need a long-, medium- or short-term plan?
Strategic or operational? Development or maintenance? There are problems over time scale, terminology and function. More important, the
umbrella term 'plan' hides somewhat different approaches to the planning process.

■ What kind of planning?

■ Model A: The rational approach

Most of the school development plans produced worldwide by state or
local education departments and by individual schools follow a rational
planning model. This suggests a cycle of:

Analysis	(discussed briefly above)
Goals	(discussed briefly above)
Objectives	What is specifically to be achieved? When? With what criteria for assessment of success?
Plans	What needs to be done in practical terms to achieve these objectives?
Resources	What human, financial and physical resources are required for these plans?
Implementation	How and when are the plans going to be put into effect, by whom?
Monitoring and evaluation	How is the process going? What criteria will be used for evaluating the plan? Have the objectives been achieved?

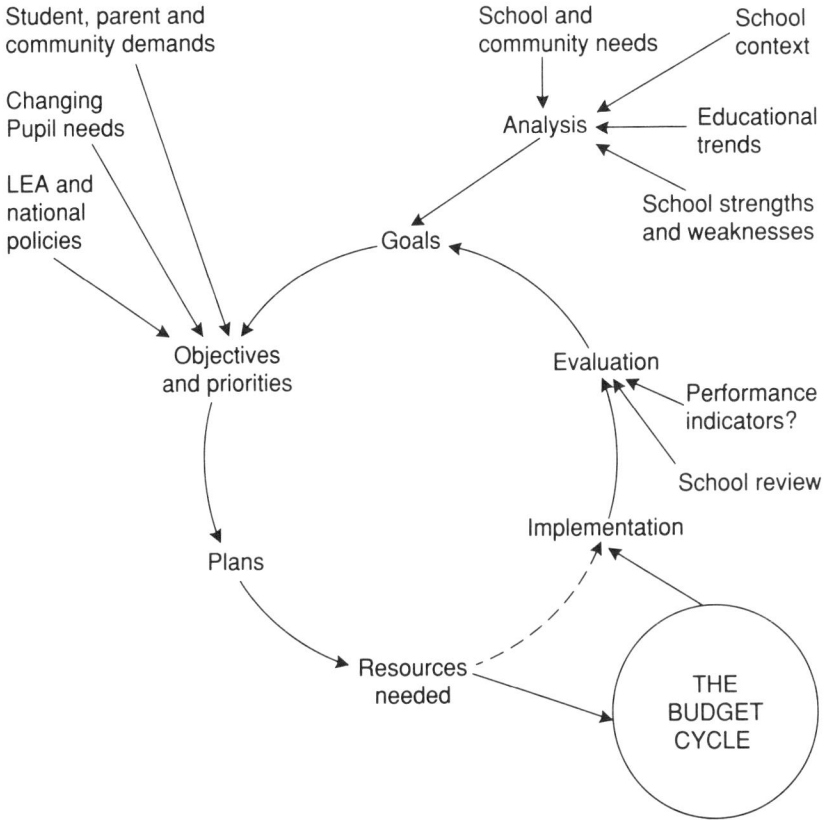

Figure 3 The management process (Source: 'The LMS Initiative' Training Package, Level 1 Module 2, quoted in Knight, B., 1989a: G1)

Figure 3 is a typical example of this process. David Hargreaves' model, set out in the DES document *Planning for School Development*, is a more refined but similar example. So too is the widely quoted model from Australia described in Brian Caldwell's and Jim Spinks' original book on collaborative school management (see figures 24 and 25 on p. 137–8).

Berkshire LEA has introduced (1989) a practical planning system for its schools. It asks them to identify a few 'global targets'.

A global target is a fairly long-term goal expressed in terms of the broad benefits or outcomes that are sought.

In identifying global targets for development it is vital not to tackle too much all at once. It is better to focus on a small but realistic number of achievable goals that are well understood by everyone. If there are too many then it is difficult to keep them all in mind and even more difficult to resource them properly . . .

A global target may be achieved within a year; on the other hand, it may take three or four years to complete. However, the fine details of a plan should only be determined for about a year ahead so that adjustments can be made if circumstances change. Subsidiary targets (shown as dots in figure 4) indicate the *concrete actions* or *practical steps* which, if taken over the next few terms, should lead to realisation of the long-term goals. Where work towards a global target is intended to continue beyond the end of the year, further sub-targets can be determined as part of the next development plan, after an annual review of progress.

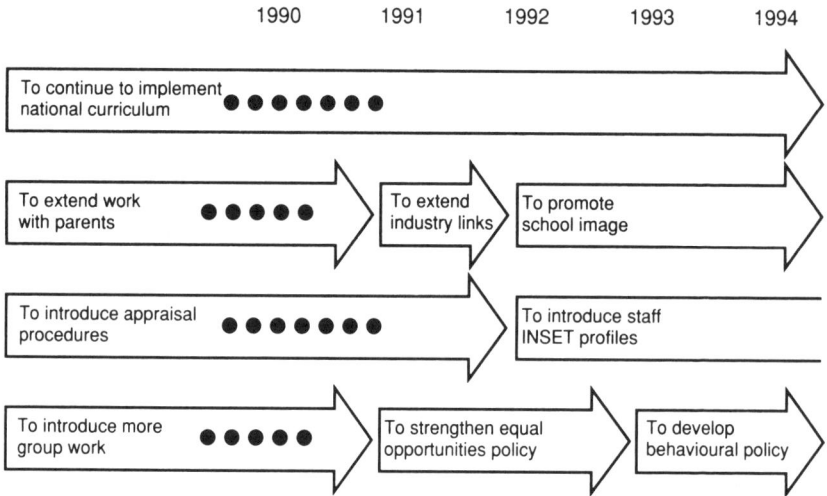

Figure 4   Berkshire LEA school development plan model: global targets
(Source: Berkshire LEA, 1989)

The diagram illustrates some possible examples of global targets spanning one or more years. The subsidiary targets are planned for one year only at this stage.

However, in practice schools seem to find development plans troublesome to use. They often find it difficult to translate them into action and to link them with their budgets. Quite commonly they remain impressive documents in a desk drawer. This rational approach to planning does not seem to reflect the reality of school life.

First, schools are not necessarily rational organisations. The extreme statement of this view was the 'garbage can' model developed by March and Olsen. Their research suggested that people in schools often have different goals, limited viewpoints and varied involvement, and so decisions are taken in a 'garbage can' of school or personal problems, ideas and preferences, participants and decisions. In other words, decisions are as much political, with a small 'p', as rational.

Second, rational planning implies a reasonably predictable and stable environment. Currently many school environments are far from stable! This is a phenomenon in most countries, and the instability seems to be increasing. Mike Wallace, in *Educational Management and Administration* (July 1991), reports an interesting case study of four UK schools that were considered to be effective in dealing with change and were using development plans. He describes graphically the pressure created by unpredictable change in central government and LEA policies and funding. He concludes (p. 182):

> **A consequence of these factors was that, although some plans were carried out as predicted, the substance of schools' development plans became less representative of changing priorities, targets and detailed plans as the year progressed and did not in practice guide ongoing development planning.**

So the rational approach to planning is logical – there is no logic in planning irrationally! – but often difficult to implement. It is best used in straightforward and practicable situations.

Example A school has identified a need to develop and improve its library. Here a methodical study – establishing objectives, plans for what needs to be done, the necessary staffing, premises, furniture, books and other requirements, the arrangements for implementation including phasing, reporting on progress and final evaluation – would be very sensible. This would clarify the finance needed and be more likely to achieve value for the money spent.

However even in this example the plan would probably need adjustment, depending on the availability of finance etc.

Rational planning suffers from a third, perhaps more serious defect: you can only plan for what you can see. Yet often a particular development may have great hidden potential which is not apparent at first sight.

Example A school which is asked by local people to run a holiday play scheme may not find the idea very attractive. It may look like a lot of work, and possibly problems, for no great return. It may appear peripheral to the school's main mission, and so not fit into a rational plan. Yet it could lead to community contacts and goodwill which may later bring great benefits to the school but which could not be foreseen at the outset.

Model B: The pragmatic approach

This seeks to overcome the problems of turbulence in the school's environment by working towards an objective in small steps, as and when opportunity arises. So the planning process identifies the objective, but leaves the steps towards it to be filled in later. This could be called the traditional approach, practised by countless headteachers and principals everywhere before development plans were invented.

Recently this approach has been endorsed by leading writers on management who have stressed the importance of the evolutionary process in organisations. Peters and Waterman in *In Search of Excellence* constantly stress the need for 'incrementalism' – experimentation and improvisation. Charles Handy in *The Age of Unreason* goes further. He sees development and innovation in an increasingly turbulent environment as *discontinuous* and not continuous. We cannot plan for an unpredictable future. Planning must be a *learning and responsive process*, learning to understand our changing environment and respond to it.

However, if such evolutionary, responsive planning is to be more than short-term opportunism, it needs a strong underlying sense of direction. Peters and Waterman stress that a strong core ethos of mission and values is essential – firm enough to control innovation, but loose enough to encourage it. Handy suggests organisations need to be like an 'inverted doughnut' – with a solid core of values and agreed tasks, and a surrounding space of risk and ambiguity.

This approach will seem more realistic and practical to many schools in their current environment. It is flexible and it builds on existing strengths. It is well suited to a complex process such as curriculum development.

Example A school wishes to improve the quality of pupils' classroom experiences. It establishes within the staff a clear and agreed set of objectives and values, and then plans to exploit curriculum opportunities as they appear – local and topical events, appearance of new materials, involvement of the local community – with appropriate in-service training. Here finance cannot be planned in advance, but rather allocated to a reserve which can be drawn upon as needed.

This lacks the clarity of objectives of the rational planning model. It is prone to 'short-termism'. It may easily become conservative unless the ultimate vision is strong. And it still does not look further than one can see, or search widely for alternatives (compare Model B of figure 5 with Models C and D). It tends to respond inadequately to sudden or sweeping change or opportunity.

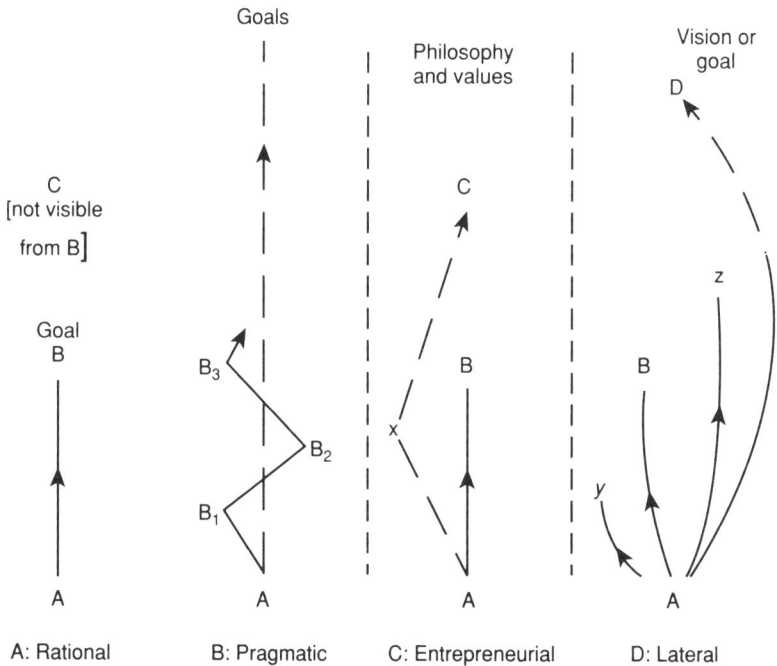

Figure 5 Different planning approaches

![] Model C: The entrepreneurial approach

Rational planning and small step advances are not the hallmarks of the entrepreneur. Essentially the entrepreneur is an exploiter of opportunity.

So entrepreneurial planning requires a positive search for opportunities and the availability of resources to exploit them as they occur.

Example A school hears that a local training organisation wishes to develop attitudes and skills appropriate for modern industry in schoolchildren. It immediately contacts the organisation and suggests an innovative programme, with development of the school's curriculum and facilities resourced jointly by the organisation, the school (it has reserve funds available) and its PTA. This new development is then publicised extensively in the media, leading to further opportunities.

At first sight this hardly looks like planning. But it does require a coherent philosophy and set of values, so that opportunities falling within them can be readily identified and others excluded; a management and financial system geared to quick response; and the development of a rich network of contacts. If you like, 'planning for opportunity'. It does not exclude rational planning and small step advances as well, but is not dependent on them. It does imply restricted consultation processes, as these inhibit quick response.

An excellent example of such an approach is given in the book by Goodchild and Holly about Garth Hill School, Bracknell. This describes (p.25) how Stanley Goodchild as the new headteacher of a failing school rapidly developed a broad strategy to respond to the immediate situation, but also to exploit it. So changes in school uniform and the appearance of the school were used to bring positive publicity. Subsequently he identified computer technology as the core of the school's development. A series of innovations followed – a new computer centre, a business office, electronic mail, a new hi-tech library, links with industry. Many tapped industrial sponsorship, and all produced national and even international publicity.

Many good examples can be found in community education, where frequently one development will open up quite unexpected new opportunities. This entrepreneurial approach is illustrated in Model C of figure 5, where a plan that allows seizure of an opportunity 'x', which initially appears tangential to the main thrust to point B, actually opens up an unexpected opportunity to reach point C.

■ Model D: The Lateral approach

The fourth and least common approach to planning rests on a visionary statement of future goals and identification of the full range of possible routes by which they could be achieved. So in-depth analysis, brainstorming and divergent thinking are required. Model D of figure 5 suggests a plan which explores several routes, two of which prove abortive, but one which leads to a long-term objective D.

Example A school considering development of its library decides that more fundamental planning is required. It obtains advice on the latest developments in information technology, data retrieval and library organisation. Questions are asked such as:

— Is a school-based library worth its cost?
— Are books other than reference needed in a school library?
— What should be the role of distance learning?
— To what extent should school library resources be available for external users?
— Should the library be the totality of the school's total learning resources, wherever situated?

The school then explores a combined library with other schools ('y' in figure 5, found to be impractical), a joint-use library with the local community ('z' in figure 5, politically difficult and so abandoned), and a combined school/community/industry development of a multimedia information and distance-learning centre networked throughout the school and to other users (point D in figure 5).

This is an example of lateral planning where divergent thinking about possible developments uncovers an objective that may not otherwise be identified. Good examples can often be found in vocational education, where different approaches to 'training' are often considered. TVEI (the Technical and Vocational Education Initiative) in the UK often encouraged this lateral approach to planning. It is likely to become more important as new technologies and methods open up alternatives to classroom learning. It is perhaps better used at intervals. Annual brainstorming can be exhausting.

■ Which approach is best?

There is no single answer. Each school and management team needs to adopt the approach best suited to its situation. In practice two or more approaches can be combined. Mike Wallace, in the article referred to earlier, suggests (p. 188):

> . . . it will be more profitable to consider flexible planning as a
> dialectical process, with planning activity varying at times
> between relatively extensive planning exercises specifying action
> well into the future and rapid, informal planning activity in
> response to unanticipated events.

Stanley Goodchild clearly followed an entrepreneurial approach, but
supported by more immediate planning of both the rational and pragmatic variety (Goodchild and Holly give many examples, e.g. p. 75).

It seems likely that as financial delegation spreads to schools, particularly in a market economy situation as in England and Wales and New
Zealand, schools will be led to differentiate, some of them even tempted
to become 'magnet schools' with a distinctive curricular orientation. For
this, entrepreneurial and lateral planning will be more helpful. Bob
Smilanich has noticed this differentiation occurring in Edmonton,
Alberta (p. 11):

> With parents having an open choice of schools, schools are more
> aware of the need to offer quality, relevant programs. For example,
> although there are regional schools for the gifted, all high schools
> and the majority of elementary schools now offer programs for the
> more able. The challenge for staffs to develop programs that will
> 'keep their kids at home' and thus increase their allocation and
> school viability is recognised. In a few instances, the complete
> nature of a school has undergone a program emphasis change. In
> response to 'market demand', a centrally located vocational school,
> for example, has made the successful transition to a fine arts orien-
> tated school.

In practice the choice will often depend upon the personality and mind-
set of the senior management team. Conservatives may prefer the pragmatic approach, radicals the lateral, etc. Whatever you do, you need to
feel comfortable. Taking liberties with Alexander Pope: 'Let fools for
plans of management contest; Whate'er is best administered is best'.

Many prestigious UK public schools have developed perfectly well in
the past without any written plan at all – but they have had a very strong
ethos and implicit goals, and an intuitive pragmatic plan in the minds of
the headteacher and senior staff. (For capital development they have
produced written plans, usually of the rational type.)

The underlying point remains: you do need a clear purpose and set of
priorities, produced in whatever way seems comfortable, directed to
your school financial management. Also, the actual process of planning
can itself bring great benefits in terms of participation and involvement,
improved understanding and shared values etc., which will assist effective financial management.

▰ Linking plans to the budget

Producing a plan for the school is one thing. Actually linking it to the budget is another. This linkage is technically quite difficult, for various reasons.

▰ Time scales

School development plans need a long time horizon, ideally three to five years; a budget only covers twelve months. Figure 3 above suggests this, with the cycle of the development plan moving on a different time scale from that of the budget. Similarly, a development plan need not be firmly fixed to dates; a budget has to operate from the start of the financial year.

The problem can be solved quite easily if we think of a plan as comprising:

- a long-term strategy, say 4–5 years;
- a medium-term strategy, say 1–3 years;
- operational planning – the current school year and the start of the next one, i.e. 0–1 year.

Only the operational planning needs to be linked to the budget, although the medium-term strategy ideally needs some budget forecasts. (However, in many state schools worldwide, forecasting budgets more than a year ahead is currently very difficult owing to national budget uncertainties. This makes a mockery of planning.)

It is useful to visualise a development plan as a paper landscape that is rolling forwards. The distant landscape is only lightly sketched in; the middle ground more firmly pencilled in; and the foreground inked in. Next year the landscape will roll forward: the foreground will drop into the limbo of history; the nearest part of the middle ground becomes the foreground and can be inked in; the old background becomes clearer as it rolls forward, and behind it new distant land comes into faint view.

This little mental model has the virtue of showing how planning depends upon its time horizon, and how only the operational planning element can be at all firm. But even here there is a technical problem. Much school planning needs to be done by academic years, and often these do not coincide with financial years. The UK has a troublesome arrangement, with the financial year beginning on 1 April and the academic year at the start of September. Figure 6 demonstrates that planning for academic year 2 has to begin early in academic year 1, with any

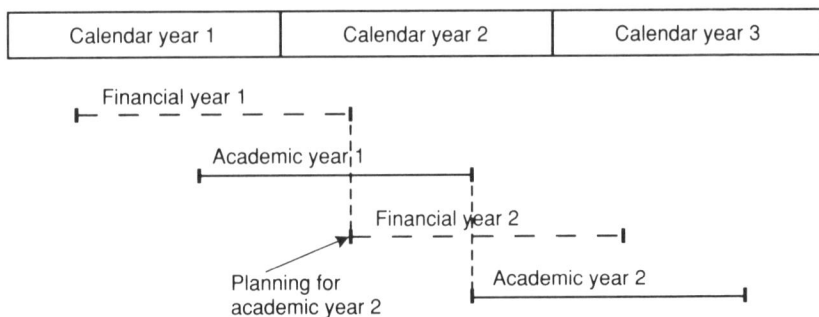

Figure 6   Non-coincidence of academic and financial years (example from the UK)

financial requirements settled mid-way through the year, before the start of financial year 2. It also means that the first five-twelfths of financial year 2 (April–August) are completely committed to the earlier academic year.

This disjunction extends the operational planning operation unnecessarily. It restricts changes of spending from one academic year to another (since the first seven months of a new academic year are funded from the existing financial year). It also makes the construction of a budget much more complicated. However, it has one beneficial side-effect: it cushions the financial impact of any changes within an academic year. On the whole it is a nuisance, and to avoid it Edmonton School District has moved its financial year into line with the school year. Happiest of all is Australia where calendar, academic and financial years broadly coincide.

▉ Integration of different elements

Any plan is likely to combine various elements. It could include a curriculum plan; a plan for human resource development and an in-service training programme; a plan for premises and grounds; a plan for public relations and/or marketing; a community education programme; or perhaps a plan for a major project. These can easily originate from different quarters – particularly where governing bodies have a staffing or premises sub-committee, or where working parties have been set up. Coordinating several different programmes, particularly in a large school, needs care.

▓ Constraints

School planning operates within a straitjacket of constraints. Few schools are comparable to a commercial company, which can plan to close or expand a factory, change a product line, increase prices or sales or raise capital at any time. Schools are locked into an expected (and largely statutory) function, with buildings and staff not easily altered, curriculum externally imposed, and all manner of other constraints imposed by external regulations or community expectations. Only where schools provide community education can they enjoy the planning flexibility and responsiveness of their commercial counterparts. (Further education colleges enjoy similar flexibility.)

So you need to be realistic about your real room for manoeuvre.

▓ Development – or maintenance?

One problem with development plans is that they encourage development. They create an expectation of expansion. Yet unless the school's budget is growing in real terms, there can be no place for development that requires additional funding unless something is displaced to make room for it. So planning needs to distinguish between *maintenance* and *development*. Most of a school's budget will always be committed to maintenance of the ongoing operation. Nevertheless there can be real scope for discretionary planning at the margin. (The Audit Commission 'base-budget' concept discussed in Chapter 7 focuses on this committed/discretionary divide.) However, schools that have a budget which is falling or even constant per pupil in real terms, or where falling rolls reduce the per-pupil funding available for variable costs, may have no scope for any development that requires funding, only scope for a reduction in activities. Also, developments often create maintenance costs in following years.

So you may need to safeguard against expectation of growth. Several of the budget construction methods – such as the limited plan (p. 132) and base budget approaches (p.132) and zero budgeting (p. 138) – will do this. Also, it is worth stressing that many features of a development plan will have little or no financial requirement, and these can be encouraged at no cost to the budget.

▓ Establishing priorities

Unless your school has more funds available than it needs – which seems unlikely – it must draw out of its plans clear priorities for spending. It will be more satisfactory if these are established against published criteria.

Jim Spinks quotes Granville Secondary School in Australia (in *Managing Schools Today*) as establishing priorities for areas of learning as follows:

Category 1: Critical areas of learning requiring change and development to the curriculum

Category 2: Important areas of learning but no immediate change and development required

Category 3: Desired areas of learning if inclusion within the resource cap is possible

---

Examples
- Maintenance of the delivery of the curriculum at the resourcing standard of last year (category 2).
- Development of group activities and residential experience to meet the recommendations of the Student Personal Qualities Report (category 1).
- Improvement of maintenance of the premises in accordance with the Premises sub-committee schedule (category 3).

Any school can develop its own criteria, preferably related to the objectives of its longer-term plan. It may be important for the criteria to distinguish between maintenance and development, as discussed above. Wherever possible they should include some indication of the level of performance!

Linking plans and priorities to student outcomes

Most planning is concerned with inputs. The problem is to relate it to outputs as well. Referring back to the system diagram (figure 1 on pp. 2–3), how can we alter the financial inputs on the left and relate this to different outcomes on the right?

HM Treasury in the UK has grappled with this problem for years at a macro level. In former times a government department would put in a bid and after haggling receive some – or all – of it. Currently the Treasury operates a much more sophisticated system. It requires the department to state what it expects to achieve for a proposed development or activity and *how* it will know what has been achieved. Next year the department is expected to report on the development assessed against the agreed criteria.

It ought to be possible to use this approach, within limits, for school plans. For example, a proposal to increase expenditure on staff salaries in order to reduce class size and so improve student achievement could be assessed in this way. It will often be difficult to produce clear answers – but even asking the question can be salutary.

*   *   *

Good planning provides a fine starting point for financial management. But it does need thought. What type of planning fits your team and your school? And how realistic is it in your school's particular environment? And can you devise a mechanism that will relate it in practical terms to the budget, feeding in objectives, priorities and criteria for evaluation?

Just a final note of caution: 'Planning is often little more than an elaborate, symbolic exercise, robbing important person hours from other projects and resulting in only the illusion of achievement' (Craig Wood, 1986). But not in your school, of course.

3 Roles, responsibilities and systems

Devolution of financial management to schools increases the importance of decisions to be made and the quantity of work to be done. Schools do not always identify the shift in roles and responsibilities or the training and systems this requires. In practice these will depend a great deal on the personalities of the people and the culture of the organisation, but we can see some general principles.

■ General principles

Figure 7 sets out in a simple form the relationships involved in financial management. It makes a distinction between *management* decisions and *administration*: the former broadly comprising definition of objectives and policy, strategic allocation of resources, motivation and team-building, creation of systems, coordination and evaluation; the latter processing of decisions, operation of systems, recording, monitoring and reporting of information.

Figure 7 is inevitably simplified and cannot show all the linkages. It shows finance descending to the school from external sources who make decisions about its level. The school can also try to increase some of this funding. The responsibility is shown as shared between the strategic decision-making group and the delegated budget holders, some of whom often directly initiate fund-raising or generate income. Decisions are then made by the strategic group on the retention of central funds, the placing of external contracts and allocation of funds between budget holders, and then by the budget holders themselves on allocation within their delegated budgets.

The strategic group may be just the senior management team and the governing body, with consultation with other staff; or may, in a fully collaborative model, be the staff and governors as a group, working collegially. In large schools the financial administrators (bursar, administrative officer, finance clerk or school secretary) will also be

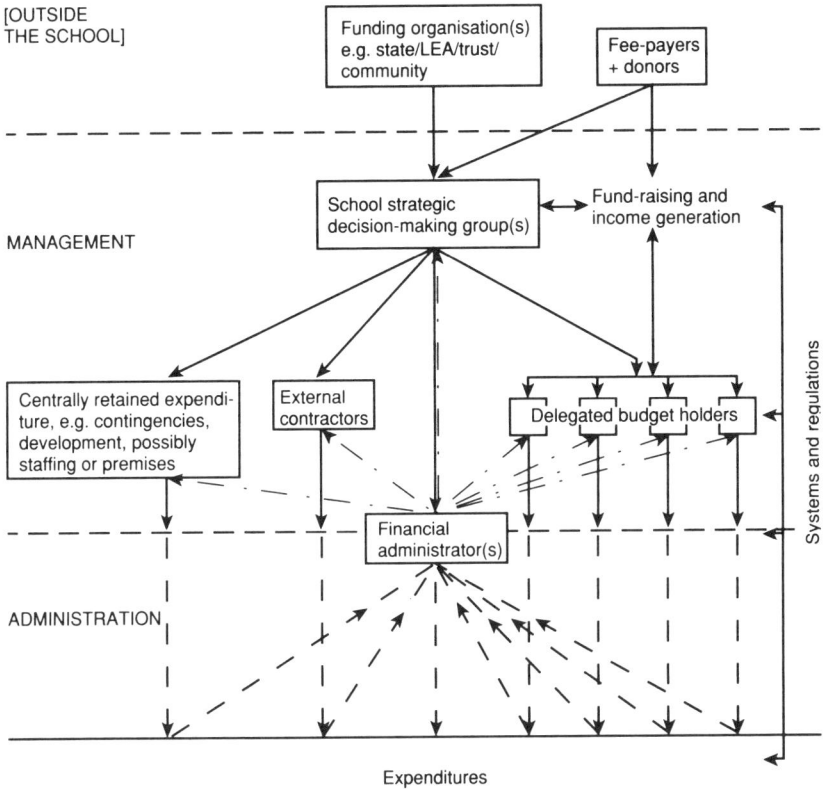

Figure 7   Financial management: relationships

involved. Budget holders can be school departments; staff responsible
for sections such as lower school or year-groups; individual teachers
with their own budget; and staff responsible for premises, office, reprographics, etc. or any special project.

Once these allocation and spending decisions are made, administration takes over. Orders are placed, goods checked, invoices certified and
paid, contracts completed. The diagram shows some of the administration carried by the budget holders and some by the financial administra-
tor(s). Information is then reported back to the budget holders and
central group, where it may require further decisions. The whole is held
together with systems and regulations, shown on the right hand side of
the diagram. Various principles can be seen.

The influence of size

Roles depend on the scale of the operation. The system shown in figure 7 is theoretically the same for any school. But the larger the funds, the more important the decisions and the greater the administrative work. So the roles depend upon the degree of external delegation, the scale of fund-raising and fees, and the size of the school. Small schools – say with five or fewer teachers – face particular problems with their restricted number of role-players, and are discussed separately on page 52.

Sources of funding

Roles also depend on the sources of funding. In a trenchant article, Guilbert Hentschke (1985) suggests that US school district administrators oscillate between the roles of public manager and 'private manager'. His ideas can equally be applied to headteachers, senior teachers and members of the governing body. He suggests that where they receive funds as largesse from above (e.g. in schools, budgets delegated from an LEA or school board or regular grants made by trusts, churches or communities) they behave as 'public managers'. In this capacity they will seek to maximise the largesse, and once the maximum limit has been established, provide the quality of service that it will bring for the number of pupils in the school. So the level of funding determines the level of service. However, when they receive fees, raise donated funds or generate their own income, they act as 'private managers' and behave quite differently. Here they seek to maximise their income by providing the best mix of quality, volume and range of services, and where appropriate raising or lowering fees or charges or requests for donations. So in this private role the level of service determines the level of funding.

This Janus-stance of headteachers etc. adopting both public and private management roles will be familiar to anyone involved with a community school. Here the role can switch several times in a day as the headteacher deals first with resourcing a 'normal' school, and then community activities. However, headteachers now regard 'student-led' funding in a similar light to fees and so are acting more like 'private managers'.

Internal delegation

Roles also depend upon the scale of internal delegation. The more management decisions are delegated downwards to budget holders and financial administrators, the more roles will alter. Figure 8 illustrates this.

In areas A and B, the degree of external delegation is low (for example in schemes where salaries, teaching or non-teaching, or premises-related costs are not devolved) and/or the school is small. In A, what is dele-

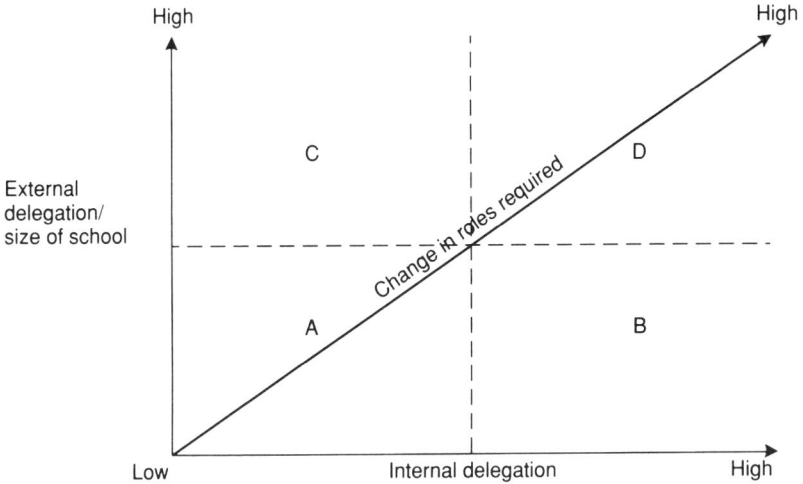

Figure 8   Changes in roles with financial delegation

gated is still controlled by the headteacher, and so there is some role change for him or her but little for others. In B, more responsibility has been delegated to internal budget holders, and so there is more role change. In C, much more has been delegated, and/or the school is larger. Management is still centralised, but as decisions are more important, other people besides the headteacher are affected. In D, with maximum external and internal delegation and/or in larger schools, all groups are substantially affected.

The layering of responsibility

Financial responsibility is distributed in layers. Strategic decisions are normally taken by the central group, others at budget holder or financial administration level, others at the operational level (individual teachers or non-teaching staff). Responsibility will be for decisions but also for administrative action; e.g. control of resources. At each level responsibility should be coupled with authority to take decisions, and accountability, to answer for them.

Example The headteacher and possibly governors are ultimately responsible for the cleanliness of the school. But primary responsibility lies with the caretaker (or with the manager of any organisation contracted for the cleaning), and operational responsibility with the individual cleaner. At each level the responsible person will be taking decisions within parameters established, explicitly or implicitly for that level.

Multiple job roles

One person may fill more than one role. A particular person may operate at different levels in the organisation. For example, a headteacher will be at the centre for strategic decision-making, but might in a smaller school retain personal responsibility for premises or office expenditure. In this case he or she is really acting as an internal budget holder, accepting delegated responsibility (from himself or herself!) for a separate budget-head. A school bursar might operate at several levels: member of the central decision-making group, budget holder for premises or office expenditure, and financial administrator.

Clarity of role

Clarity of role is important. For example, just taking one group – say governors – we can ask what are the financial matters that they …

> must decide;
> must approve (e.g. a proposal drawn up by others);
> must participate in (i.e. give an opinion with the understanding it will gain strong consideration);
> must be consulted about (i.e. give an opinion, along with others);
> must know about;
> should know about;
> may know about;
> do not need to know about;
> must inform others about;
> can inform others about;
> do not need to inform others about?

We can ask the same questions for …

> headteacher/principal;
> deputy/senior staff;
> other teaching staff;
> bursar/administrative officer;
> finance clerk;
> premises manager/caretaker;
> other non-teaching staff;
> students;

parents;
community, local employers.

The clearer the answers to these questions, the less chance of role ambiguity or conflict. However, it is not possible to think out all the answers in advance; many need to be resolved by trial and error.

Systems and regulations – within reason – certainly help to clarify responsibilities, tasks and roles. They do not always need to be written down. A responsibility clearly understood is better than a written statement never referred to. Reporting will also be more effective if each person reports mainly to one individual or group – what the Edmonton School District calls the 'one-boss-rule'.

Role overload

Avoiding role overload is important. Increased financial management in schools means more work. Unless extra staff hours are provided for this additional load, some existing staff will need to work longer, more intensively, or more efficiently – unless an equivalent amount of other work in the school is eliminated in some way. So it is important that every effort is made to reduce other tasks, and to increase efficiency by adoption of time-saving systems and procedures and making the fullest use of information technology.

The load can also be spread by increased delegation of responsibilities downwards. This has the additional virtue of increasing understanding and involvement in the staff as a whole – though it does also require some additional time for the consultation and reporting required.

Intangibles

Roles are affected by intangibles that cannot be shown on the diagram, like:

Ethos	*'What we believe in'*
Culture	*'How we do things here'*
Climate	*'How we feel about this place and these people'*
Relationships	*'How we treat each other'*

There is a risk that financial management leads people into adopting mechanistic, uncaring systems, laden with formal regulations, bureaucratic procedures and 'damned statistics'. Like any other area of management, it will be much more successful if people work as a team, identifying with the enterprise and caring for each other. But there can be a conflict between shared decision-making and clear accountability. The arrangements for participation or consultation need working out carefully, with *ultimate* responsibility clearly identified.

■ Specific roles

■ The headteacher or principal

Published studies of financial devolution worldwide show general agreement that the role of the headteacher or principal is enhanced. He or she is seen as more important, more of a manager and the key figure in the school. Headteachers themselves talk of being more in control, better able to steer the ship or alter course.

However, each headteacher needs to take decisions on his or her specific role in the light of the principles suggested above, and particularly on the scale of involvement. This will depend partly on his or her view of the role as a whole – whether teacher-educator, professional leader, or chief executive. But it will also depend on his or her affinity with the world of accounts, fund raising and resource management. In part it will be a personality response and will depend on the other pressures upon the headteacher's use of time. So the role will vary from the 'minimiser' to the 'maximiser'. A parallel would be the situation in secondary schools where some headteachers have only minimal involvement in the timetable, while others are heavily involved in its construction.

Whatever the definition of the role, it will still involve extra tasks – and for maximisers, many of them. So headteachers do need to ask themselves whether they already have slack in their personal time management available for this (unlikely!), or if not, what other tasks they need to shed. It may help to look critically at the areas of financial management and the tasks involved, as in figure 9.

Many of the areas in figure 9 could well be delegated to other teaching or non-teaching staff. Similarly the diagram suggests that within those areas where the headteacher still retains responsibility a number of tasks can still be delegated. For example, he or she might retain responsibility for deployment of teaching staff, but delegate professional development and in-service training or management of non-teaching staff; or retain responsibility for the use of premises, but delegate energy conservation or premises maintenance to a sub-committee. Of course in a small school there are few people to delegate to – and this is discussed on page 52 below.

The other possible role change concerns style. Extension of financial management makes it more difficult for headteachers to be autocratic. They need to work more closely with their governing body and to win support from their staff. They will usually be driven to delegate more, and communicate more with staff, parents and students.

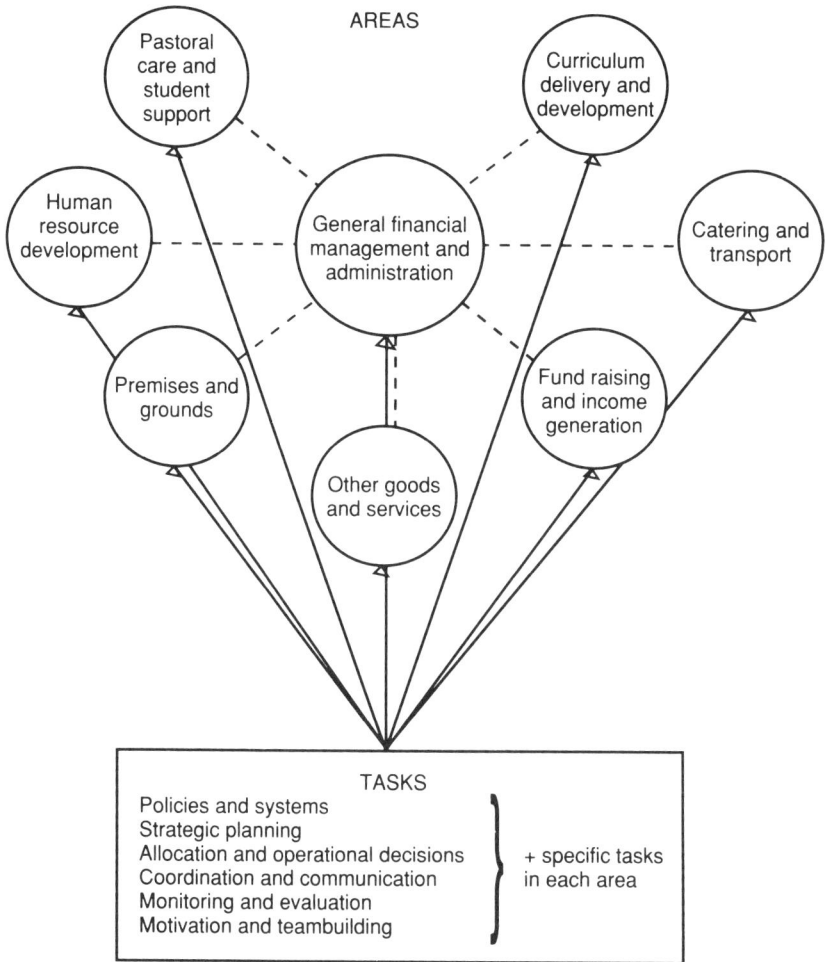

Figure 9   Areas and tasks of financial management

Deputy headteachers, vice-principals and senior staff

Their role will be the mirror image of the headteacher's. If the head-teacher minimises his or her financial management role, senior staff will maximise theirs – and vice versa. In many ways financial management and its associated areas is well suited to delegation to a deputy or senior teacher: the boundaries are clear; it need not coincide with class teaching time (there are some exceptions, such as premises maintenance which can take a deputy away from a class); and it provides development of management skills for the person concerned. Also the deputy is often closer to teaching and non-teaching staff and so finds informal communication and trouble-shooting easier.

In primary schools, deputy headteachers are often given insufficient responsibility, and delegation of financial responsibility can redress this.

▉▉ Members of governing bodies

Financial management significantly enhances the role of governing bodies. The risk is that they will be tempted to do too much just because it is an area more comfortable for most lay people than, say, curriculum or teaching methods. Governors need to ask exactly the same questions as headteachers, to define and limit their role. They need to be even more sensitive about time management, because they have less time to give.

Governors need to identify their key tasks, i.e. the tasks they must do statutorily, or which if they fail to do will not be done, or done as well, by anyone else. These will probably involve strategic decisions over fund raising and fund allocation, evaluation, and reporting to parents, and interest in specific tasks in areas such as premises and human resource management. But they must avoid being dragged into everything.

Many governing bodies have created committees for finance, premises, personnel etc. to spread the load. This has the merit of enabling each governor, through his or her committee, to obtain greater mastery over one area while still retaining an overview of the school. It also allows co-option of outside specialists. But it is not a panacea: it demands more time from the chairperson and headteacher; it requires careful coordination; and it increases the flow of paper.

Governing bodies need to think carefully about the composition and terms of references of their committees, and about their own standing orders. They also need to pay particular care to demarcation of responsibilities with the headteacher and senior staff (as suggested by the checklist on p. 44).

▉▉ Teaching staff

Budget holders will find their roles extended with financial devolution, particularly in the minority of schools that have delegated downwards the responsibility for items such as non-teaching salaries, maintenance or heating of premises, furniture and furnishings. So will classroom teachers who are given a specific budget. But often teachers will not see the need, or have the time, to become involved in the financial management of the school, except at times of controversy such as cuts in staffing.

Some will wish to become involved for career development or personal reasons, or to be involved in a specific area such as energy conservation.

Gradually, however, teachers are likely to be drawn in more fully. Sometimes this will be a response to an invitation to participate. Sometimes it will arise from the logic of financial devolution – where previously they would say 'We need an extra teacher' and expect a fairy godmother to provide one, now they can possibly provide one themselves *if* they are prepared to accept changes elsewhere.

■ Administrative staff

Bursars

School financial management has brought the role of bursar, administrative officer or business manager to the fore. There is a strong argument that many of the areas of financial management in figure 9 – finance, premises, goods and services, catering and transport, non-teaching personnel, and possibly fund raising and income generation – are better managed by a person with commercial and administrative rather than teaching experience. It is sometimes argued that a bursar is too heavily involved in decisions affecting children's education for the role to be filled by a non-teacher. This seems a weak argument, particularly as independent schools have traditionally had bursars of this type, as have most further education colleges. However, such a bursar does need thorough induction into this strange new world.

The main argument arises over cost-efficiency. Does the additional efficiency from a full-time administrative officer cost more or less than the part-time involvement of a deputy headteacher or senior teacher, and can it be afforded from the budget? The larger the school, the greater the likelihood of a positive response. Probably many schools would like to have a bursar, but are not able to afford one. There are a few examples of group bursars, serving a cluster of schools. French schools operate in this way.

Even when bursars are appointed, there is some variation in the role. The full specification can comprise the following:

Financial administration of both 'official' and 'unofficial' school funds
Fund raising and income generation, within limits
Premises and grounds maintenance, cleaning, heating and lighting
Furniture, furnishings and equipment
Office management
Reprographics
Purchasing advice and policy

Management of all non-teaching personnel
Community use of premises
Catering
Transport and vehicles

Some schools have narrowed the role to finance, office management and purchasing, but this seems to reduce the justification for it. Some have given higher priority to fund raising and income generation, sometimes under the role 'development officer', but here there is a risk of too large and diverse a task for one person. Similarly, community use can become too large or important to be a part of the bursar's responsibilities.

Other administrative staff

The 'finance clerk' is affected substantially by extension of school financial management. If there is no bursar, he or she will fulfil more of the bursar's duties. In any case there will be additional tasks, and more high-level tasks, and much more use of information technology. So financial management upgrades the role (though not always in practice the salary).

The role of the caretaker is also upgraded, sometimes symbolised by a new title of 'premises manager' or 'plant engineer'. This is particularly so where schools take responsibility for energy management and premises management, or where community use of the school is extended.

Parents

Parents as a whole do not seem very excited by the financial management of their children's school, except in crisis situations. If all is going well they can rest happily. This is equally true of fee paying and state schools. Of course a minority will be interested, and in state schools it can be argued that parents are taxpayers and stakeholders should at least be kept informed of the outline of the school budget. However, presenting this in a user-friendly way is not easy.

The only exception appears to be occurring in South Africa, where parents of 'white' state schools are now being asked to cover all non-salary costs by fund raising or fees. Since these schools were formerly free, this new 'tax' is causing widespread parental interest in the schools' finances.

A minority of parents may be interested in another way, to volunteer their services. Some schools have gained appreciable net contributions in this way for grounds and premises maintenance, redecorations, catering and clerical support, as well as classroom aides and of course fund raising.

■■■■   **Students**

Students have a role, much underrated, in school financial management. Apart from their obvious value in fund raising and income generation, and as volunteers, they are the direct consumers of all the school's resources – human, premises, supplies and services. So they bring the experience and attitudes of consumers.

The most obvious area of involvement is premises management. Some schools have been very enterprising in involving students in energy conservation, reporting of defects, planning maintenance and improvements.

Example Norham Community School, North Tyneside, has involved students in planning the refurbishment of the school sports hall and redesign of the playing fields. It has also given year-groups small sums of about £200 to plan and provide improvements to the school environment.

Some secondary schools have developed maintenance, redecorating or grounds teams (common in independent schools), and linked school finances to business studies or economic awareness.

■■■■   **Local community and employers**

Worldwide the evidence suggests that increased financial devolution expands community involvement in the school. Places for community representatives are being found on governing bodies; schools are making more efforts to raise funds from their communities, and in return they open their premises more to them. If this community involvement and use of facilities becomes extensive, the needs for role clarification and development of good systems arise, similar to those discussed above. Problems arise where there is not a readily identifiable community, or where a community is served by several schools – and worse still – schools that draw students from several communities.

Employers and business people may be co-opted to help the school with their expertise. Here role problems can arise if the person concerned tries to introduce industrial or commercial practices and ideas without being fully sympathetic to the school context. Others are likely to be involved in sponsorship and fund raising as discussed in Chapter 5.

◼ Roles in small schools

In some ways financial management in small schools is easier. The budget is much smaller and less complex; buildings are smaller; there are fewer staff. Decisions are fewer and of lesser magnitude; communication is easier, informal and face-to-face. But . . . there is much less room for financial manoeuvre, and there are many less staff to share the same spread of tasks indicated in figure 9, albeit of smaller scale.

In schools with up to, say, five teachers, inevitably the headteacher has to adopt a multi-purpose role. He or she may often be the central decision-maker, the financial administrator (with the school secretary), purchasing officer, premises manager, personnel officer, public relations officer, and internal budget holder. Poo-bah would feel at home: 'It is my . . . duty to serve . . . as First Lord of the Treasury, Lord Chief Justice, Commander-in-Chief, Lord High Admiral, Master of the Buckhounds, Groom of the Back Stairs, Archbishop of Titipu, and Lord Mayor . . . all rolled into one.'

However, there are some possibilities for improving the situation.

1 Financial management can be made a whole-school affair. Because the number of staff, teaching and non-teaching, will not exceed eight people, say, and because the governing body will be smaller, it is quite feasible to involve everyone in the school as one large decision-making group. Audrey Stenner, when headmistress of Buckden Primary School, Cambridgeshire, used this approach very effectively – albeit in a larger school; she described it in Ian Craig's *Primary School Management in Action*. A smaller sub-committee can still be created if necessary to administer the budget, premises etc. in detail. The same intimacy of the small school also makes it much easier to involve parents and students.

2 An audit can be made of the special strengths and expertise of the people working at or involved with the school. It is possible that some will have some special interest or experience in areas like energy conservation, premises maintenance, fund raising, and would take on specific responsibilities there.

3 The role of the deputy headteacher should be sharply examined. The previous arguments for delegating most or some financial management to him or her are even stronger in a small school.

4 The scope for delegation to class teachers should be explored – certainly for classroom items including furniture. Schools with two buildings may be able to delegate redecoration or energy costs to a section of the school.

5 Cooperation with other schools can also be explored, to share facilities or expertise, combine for activities such as INSET or premises maintenance, or purchase goods and services jointly with reduced cost or effort.

Systems

Management of information

Information is a resource that can and should be managed, just as much as finance, human resources, premises etc. Figure 10 sets out a simple model for a management information system.

The model distinguishes between data – raw facts not yet usable for a decision process, such as in files, records and reports – and information, data that has been arranged to provide the knowledge and understanding necessary for decision-making. Schools are awash with data, much of it already recorded. The challenge is to reduce it and select what management needs, and to present this information in a form that is easy to interpret and interrogate. This implies well thought out procedures for selection and presentation. So, for example, information needs to be aggregated and simplified for the needs of each user. A particularly useful device is 'management by exception', where information is only presented when it falls outside specified parameters. For example, this would identify internal budget holders that are under- or overspending beyond a defined percentage of their budget.

One current problem with school data is that it is too insular. There is not sufficient comparative data nationally and from peer schools to facilitate full understanding (this issue is discussed more deeply in Chapters 7 and 10).

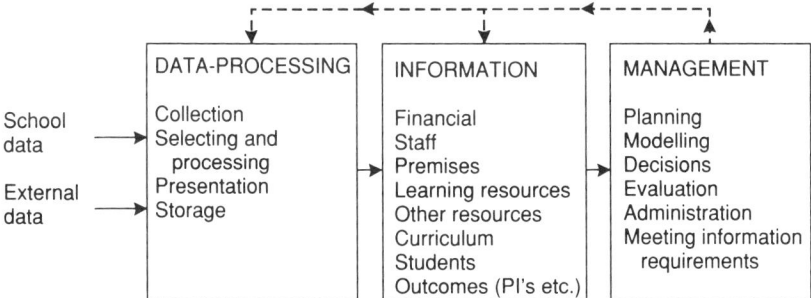

DATA-PROCESSING	INFORMATION	MANAGEMENT
Collection	Financial	Planning
Selecting and	Staff	Modelling
processing	Premises	Decisions
Presentation	Learning resources	Evaluation
Storage	Other resources	Administration
	Curriculum	Meeting information
	Students	requirements
	Outcomes (PI's etc.)	

School data →
External data →

Figure 10   Model of a management information system

Information required is not just financial. Most management information relating to the school's human or physical resources, its curriculum and organisation, its students and its outcomes, can be useful for financial management. For example, information on outcomes is directly relevant to financial evaluation and to consideration of alternative budget strategies.

Constructing a good management information system is difficult. It requires clear thinking about the key management processes in the school, their requirements for success, and the information needed as well as good technical advice on software and hardware. So not surprisingly many systems have tended first to computerise existing clerical tasks and to concentrate on administration rather than management. Even within the management area, systems tend to be used for the more routine aspects, such as budget construction, rather than more advanced uses such as modelling alternatives and exploring 'what if' situations.

The new generation of software is filling this gap. For example, the Phoenix *School Management Portfolio* (see Addresses) contains modules on school development planning, budgeting and project management. A 'windows' graphics interface system allows the user to model, map, project, prioritise, phase, construct graphs, import data, switch activities etc.

An information system can be no better than the questions it is asked. It needs intelligent management and so fits one of the recurring themes of this book, that school managers need to think deeply and reflectively about their role. Also, as David Lancaster has commented:

> ... **headteachers and other senior staff of schools need to ensure that they use information systems and financial systems to assist them in their core activity of delivering effective learning rather than being diverted from that purpose and managing the school to too great an extent on the outputs of an information system, however sophisticated that system may be.**

Communications

Figure 7 suggests that a complex flow of communications is necessary for financial management. Fortunately this communication is linked to the budget and planning cycles and so can be predicted. So it is straightforward, but important, to organise a calendar of meetings and reports that provide efficient communication for financial management.

▉ Procedures and regulations

For similar reasons, financial procedures should mainly be predictable and easily defined. Efficient, simple, easily understood procedures, clearly explained, can contribute a great deal to efficient financial management. For example, minor procedures like obtaining a receipt for all petty cash expenditures or the signing of all invoices by a responsible person as 'goods received and approved for payment', can prevent errors or abuse – and save everyone's time! A minimum of regulations are also essential; for example, standing orders for the governing body about declaring a financial interest, awarding of contracts etc.

▉ Training

In most schemes that have been introduced worldwide, there has been strong criticism of the training provided, its quantity, quality and timing. This apparent failure seems to arise from a lack of good *needs analysis:*

Which groups of people need training?
What training does each group need?
How much time does this require?
How many people are there in each group?
What would be the most cost-effective form of delivery of this training to this number of people, for this amount of time?

As a result, the daunting logistics of delivering training on such a large scale are not sufficiently exposed. Also there has been a tendency to concentrate on the technicalities of financial management rather than the general management principles which underpin it.

However, inadequacy in initial training for financial management is a one-off problem that headteachers, governors and others have to overcome as best they can, often by learning 'on the job' and teaching themselves. There will be a recurrent need for initial training for new headteachers and, particularly, for new governors, but once financial devolution is established existing personnel should be able to provide this.

The more enduring problem is the provision of training for strategic and reflective financial management, dealing with the kind of issues discussed in this book. At its heart is a question that has not yet really been examined. To what extent is it possible to train managers to be more self-critical, more questioning, more divergent in their thinking and more visionary? Or to select managers with such qualities? Can such a frame of mind be learned – or is it cast in the personality of the manager? Nurture – or nature?

4 Delegated funds and their allocation

Schools manage finance from four sources:

Delegated tax-borne or trust funds, or similar
Fees
Fund raising
Income generation

This chapter deals with the first of these, particularly the principles underlying the delegation process and the alternative strategies available for delegation to schools, and within them. The final section deals with capital funding.

■ The principles of fund delegation

Funds trickle down through various levels of the education system until they finally irrigate the classroom. At each level of delegation there is a 'donor' who delegates and a 'beneficiary' who receives. A simple model is set out in figure 11.

In practice the process is often more complex. For example, in England and Wales for LEA maintained schools it would currently be:

Taxpayer → central government → local
authority → LEA → school → (Faculty in large school) → budget
holders

A school may receive some funds from one level and some from another (e.g. from LEA/school board and direct from central/federal government). Or it may receive funds from more than one government source; e.g. in the UK from the Training Agency or TVEI programme (Technical and Vocational Education Initiative). Funds may also flow to more than one beneficiary on the school site; e.g. a youth wing, community education centre or arts centre.

This trickle-down process occurs because the donors at earlier stages

Donor	Taxpayer	Trust benefactor/church or community member
↓ [1st transfer]	↓	↓
Beneficiary and donor to next stage	Government/school boards etc	Trust fund, church or community
↓ [2nd transfer]	↓	↓
Beneficiary and donor to next stage	School, educational or similar institution	School, educational or similar institution
↓ [3rd transfer]	↓	↓
Beneficiary	Internal budget holder	Internal budget holder

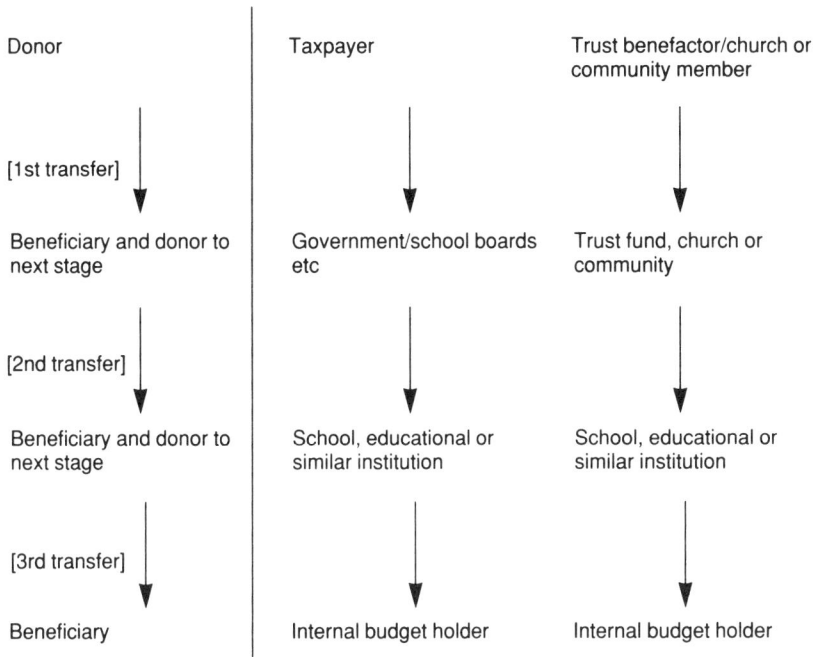

Figure 11   Delegation of educational funds

cannot manage the expenditure themselves. A central government cannot run thousands of schools from one office; a headteacher cannot personally select textbooks or equipment for a range of classes. The span of control is too wide. But increasingly the process is also seen as good management.

Two recent examples

'The Commission considers that more delegation of authority and responsibility to the local level will result in better value for money and avoidance of waste.' (UK Audit Commission, 1984)

'.... the efficiency and effectiveness of the system can be improved only if schools have sufficient control over the quality of education they provide . . . . To maintain a system of education which responds to changing Government and community priorities and which can use Government funds most efficiently, individual schools must become the focus for the administration and delivery of education.' (Western Australia Ministry of Education, 1987)

The key feature in this trickle-down is the transfer from each donor to each beneficiary. It is an important and delicate process – particularly for the donor. Uneasy sleeps the head that wears that crown. It may be more blessed to give than to receive, but it is certainly more fraught with problems.

■ Problems with delegating funds

Donors at any level the world over are tormented by this transfer problem. What is the best way to delegate funds with the maximum effectiveness and the least hassle? Actually there are three separate decisions:

- the total sum to be allocated;
- the allocation process;
- the distribution mechanism.

This is the same anguish that torments any parent doling out 'pocket money' or personal allowance to children, although the sum involved is perhaps a little smaller.

First, the sum:
How much should I spend on my children?
How much can I afford?
How much of this should be pocket money?
Secondly, allocation:
How much does each of my children need?
What for?
How does this compare with my other children, and my child's friends? Is it fair?
Thirdly, the distribution mechanism:
Shall I give a straight handout? Or make conditions? Do I expect anything in return? Does it matter what it is spent on, or how wisely it is spent? Do I keep some back? Give cash, or credit?

Parents everywhere search for the best delegation strategy. So do all other 'donors'.

■ Criteria for delegation

Donors select strategies against a set of principles, which may be explicit or intuitive. (Actually this is giving them more credit than they deserve.

Many do not really choose at all, they just carry on as they have always done.)

Effectiveness

The donor is unlikely to delegate funds to a beneficiary who cannot or does not wish to achieve the donor's own objectives. Of course this does imply that the donor has a set of clear objectives in mind.

Effectiveness also requires that donors provide sufficient funds for the job, what US writers have termed 'adequacy'. There is always a risk that donors will shirk their responsibilities and then blame inadequacies on the beneficiary – what the UK Audit Commission has called 'abdication of blame'.

Efficiency

No donor likes to see money or other resources wasted. Also, donors prefer arrangements that are easy to set up, simple to operate, and predictable for both parties.

Equity

Donors dislike unfairness in allocation because it troubles their conscience, or creates hassle from the unfairly treated, or undermines effectiveness. Equity is examined more fully in Chapter 8. It can be horizontal (treating similar schools or students the same) or vertical (treating schools or students differently so that funding reflects their actual needs).

Accountability and political legitimacy

Since public money is involved, donors feel it is important that allocation and distribution decisions are made publicly and within the democratic process, beneficiaries are accountable, and reasonable precautions for financial probity are made.

Examples of effectiveness criteria
- A state government wishes to see schools use funds to make education more vocationally relevant.
- A school management team are hoping to see classroom teachers spend more on student-centred learning resources.

Examples of efficiency criteria
- A school board wants its schools to deploy teachers more efficiently.
- A headteacher wishes to improve budget holders' stock control.

Examples of equity criteria

- A school board allows the same amount per student for books, materials and equipment.
- A school provides more money for science and technology classes because of their greater need for equipment.

Examples of accountability and legitimacy criteria
- A central government agency creates a set of performance indicators for schools.
- School governors establish a set of financial regulations for internal budget holders.

Unfortunately these principles often conflict. For example, equity may require complicated allocation arrangements which conflict with efficient delegation. So each donor has to resolve this conflict while solving the problems discussed above. (For a useful discussion of these issues in the UK context, see the article by Rosalind Levačić in *Educational Management and Administration*, 1989).

Delegation of funds *to* schools is examined in the next section, and *within* them in the following section. Each section examines the three problems discussed above in turn: establishing the total sum available, allocating the funds, and selecting the best distribution mechanism(s).

■ Delegation of funds to schools

■ Establishing the sum available

At first sight this looks quite straightforward, since the funds available will be determined by transfers at earlier stages as in figure 11. But at no stage is the delegated sum immutable. Each organisation, in its role of beneficiary, is likely to press its donor(s) for improved funding.

Some of this pressure will be of a political nature. But it will contain a rational element, usually centred on the notion of adequacy. A school, for example, will try to show that the sum delegated to it is inadequate for its needs, or new developments, or in comparison with others, or with funding last year, or . . . . So there is a dialogue between the beneficiary and the donor, contrasting what is 'needed' and what is available, and pressing each donor to work upwards in the chain for increased funding from earlier donor(s).

Example This process can be seen operating clearly in England and Wales, when at the 'annual spending round' in the autumn the Treasury negotiates a budget with the Department for Education, which then negotiates with LEAs, which then negotiates with schools. At each stage squeals arise which may soften the heart of a donor earlier in the chain – though perhaps not until the following year.

Once the amount available is settled, the donor needs to decide the proportions to be retained centrally and delegated. This will depend partly on political pressures and the donor's philosophy and also on rational considerations.

Allocation to schools

Strategies

In so far as allocation is a rational process it centres upon the concepts of 'need' and 'adequacy'. Both are very slippery notions. 'Need' suggests something more objective than 'wants', but it is harder to identify. Beneficiaries will know what they want, but is this what they need? And how adequate is 'adequate'? Of course allocation will not be entirely rational. There are strong political and organisational dimensions to the allocation process (for a good discussion of these, see the 1989 article by Tim Simkins – see References).

Donors can choose from a range of strategies, including:

Programme budgeting, i.e. allocating funds for specific programmes or objectives
Incrementalism, as in an LEA 'continuation' budget
Open market, inviting competitive bids from schools
Patronage/benevolent despotism
Formula funding.

Programme budgeting tends to be complex and time-consuming at this level (the principles are discussed on page 135). Incrementalism is widely used in practice. Open market and patronage is best suited for development funding. Increasingly donors resort to formula funding. The advantages of each strategy are discussed more fully below (in the section on their use *within* schools), and the checklist of questions on p. 72 is almost as appropriate for this level.

Formula funding

This is growing in use worldwide, particularly as the scale of delegation increases. It seems to resolve conflicts between effectiveness, efficiency, equity and accountability. However there are problems.

One problem with formula funding is that it conveys an impression of scientific objectivity which it does not merit. A formula automates allocation – but only after decisions have been made about the composition of the formula itself. Such a decision is so crucial that it tends to be taken because of political pressure or organisational convenience rather than rational discussion.

In theory the formula should allocate funds according to need. In England and Wales the formative DES circular 7/88 stated: 'The basis on which resources are allocated to schools . . . will need to be based on objective needs rather than simply on historic spending to ensure an equitable allocation of available resources to schools.' But how are objective needs assessed? At least one LEA has attempted to build up a standard cost model of resource needs for schools, establishing from existing data the necessary cost for each line of expenditure for a school of a given size. This operational research approach, also recommended by the UK Audit Commission (1988), still requires all kinds of value judgements (e.g. about staffing ratios) and is very time-consuming and complex. It also tends to generate higher expectations than the global sum available can support. An earlier and sophisticated 'Alternative Use of Resources' scheme was operated by the former Inner London Education Authority, using a range of indices for need including free meals, family data, parental occupations, command of English and ethnic origins. The information was, however, complex and expensive to collect.

Activity-led staffing models also attempt to establish needs-based funding (for example that set out by Dr Alison Kelly in *Managing Schools Today*, 1992). This concentrates on the 70 per cent or so of a school's budget that is spent on teacher's time. It breaks down this time under four categories:

- Classroom contact with students (built up from the teacher contact and class size, needs of different age-groups, plus additional special needs and primary specialist and support staffing).
- School-related activities (policy development and planning, external relations, supervision and administration etc.).
- Teacher-related activities (cover for absence, professional development, meetings, lesson preparation etc.).
- Student-related activities (marking, records, reports, student care, extra-curricular activities etc.).

Values in teacher hours per week or year are attached to each category for each year-group. These can then be aggregated and used to establish the staffing required and so staffing costs and budgets for different sizes and types of schools.

Meanwhile LEAs in England and Wales assess needs pragmatically for each formula element. However, comparison of their formulas shows marked variation for each element, so that identical schools in different parts of the country with identical needs receive quite different allocations. Even if a uniform national formula was imposed this would only conceal the problem. There would be no guarantee that it would 'meet needs' any better than some or most of the LEA formulas. And any attempt to establish a fully rational formula must be tempered by the need not to diverge too far from the previous historical allocation. If this divergence becomes too great, the stress for the schools affected is too severe and political opposition rises rapidly.

Probably the best approach is to ease over a period of years from the historical position to what is perceived as closer to needs. To some extent this will occur naturally as comparative information for peer-group LEAs, school boards etc. leads those authorities with allocations at the extreme to bringing them closer to the average. As rational debate about needs continues, formulas will gradually come into line. This appears to have happened in the oldest surviving formula scheme in Edmonton, Alberta, where there has been a significant shift in funds from secondary students to elementary, a reduction in the diversion of funds from the 'regular' student population to students with special needs, and simplified differention.

The Edmonton resource allocation ratios per student 1992/93 are in nine levels as follows:

1	Kindergarten, Elementary, Junior High, Senior High (General)	1.00
2	Academic Challenge, Senior High (other), English as a second language	1.27
3	Trades and services	1.55
4	Academic assistance, adaptation, opportunity	1.80
5	Learning disabled	2.61
6	Moderate physical or mental impairment	2.88
7	Behaviour disorder, further degrees of physical, visual or hearing impairment	4.40
8	Further degree of physical, visual, hearing or autistic impairment	6.41
9	Extreme hearing and visual impairment	7.89

▇ Distribution mechanisms

Donors fret about the allocation to each school. Yet once the allocation is decided they spend remarkably little time thinking about the best mechanism to distribute it so that they achieve their own objectives. Mostly they just dole out money. Yet there are a wide range of tried mechanisms available. Fifteen are listed below, each with its own characteristics.

1 Grants without strings. This is by far the most common form of funding, where finance is delegated without any conditions. Frequently this takes the form of a single block grant that can be spent by the school according to its priorities. In some systems it is compartmentalised under headings such as staffing, classroom materials etc., without the facility of virement. This appears to give the donor more control but actually runs against the logic of delegating, namely to allow more efficient local decision-making.

2 Grants with recommendations. Sometimes a grant will be provided with the stated expectation that it will make possible some improvement, e.g. in the pupil/teacher ratio. But there is no guarantee that this will occur. For example, in 1977 Shirley Williams, Secretary of State for Education & Science in England and Wales, allocated an additional £7 million to LEAs for in-service training – only to see it swallowed up without trace.

3 Grants related to outcomes. Funds are specifically linked to general and operational objectives, often with criteria by which success may be judged. For example, since the UK government's Financial Management Initiative of 1982, government departments have been required to publish objectives and targets linked to their spending proposals, often with criteria by which success may be evaluated.

4 Incentives. Here the donor builds in a condition which, if achieved, releases additional grant – or a penalty which holds some back. For example, a school board may give each school an energy expenditure budget and allow it to keep 50 per cent of all savings. Of course, many of the other distribution mechanisms have an in-built incentive, but not as explicit as this.

Incentives can also create problems. If a donor rewards successful schools, will the unsuccessful find it more difficult to succeed? Also, defining and assessing the performance required may not be easy.

5 Negotiated budgets. Here donor and school negotiate the shape and size of the delegated budget, or part of it. So there is discussion of spending relating to needs. Further education colleges have commonly been financed on this basis, as are cost centres within large companies.

6 Speculative bidding. The donor reserves funds and awards unsolicited bids. No criteria for granting funds are laid down, and there is no open competition. Sometimes the existence of the funds is not made public. In England and Wales many LEA advisers previously handled funds in this way, until LMS pared them down. This is patronage in action, with its obvious advantages and disadvantages.

7 *Earmarked grants* ('categorical funding'). These are direct grants dedicated to specific categories of expenditure with no virement allowed to other uses. Grants can be unconditional, or conditional on meeting specified conditions (the current DFE funding of in-service training falls into this category).

8 *Honeypot management.* Here the donor dangles a pot of honey to encourage the slumbering bears to dance. The donor announces the funds available, their purpose, and the criteria for award of funding, and invites submissions. The funding can be competitive (only the best dancers win the honey) or equitable (all win who meet the criteria).

For example, the original MSC TVEI scheme of November 1982 offered £7 million for the ten LEAs whose submissions for improved technical and vocational education best met the criteria (competitive). In later stages of the TVEI scheme, any LEA could gain funds providing its proposals met the criteria (equitable).

This mechanism is very useful for stimulating change. It forces the donor to clarify objectives and criteria, and the bidder to think out a good set of proposals to meet them. It targets a donor's priorities. It enables the donor to implement policy without being operationally responsible for it – a form of sub-contracting. It leaves a lot of scope for local initiative and creativity among the bidders. But . . . it is much less suited to permanent on-going objectives. It can create complaints of inequity. It can be time-consuming and difficult to monitor. And it is central direction in delegated clothing, and so subject to the danger of centrally dictated priorities overriding local needs. (For a fuller analysis see Knight, 1987).

9 *Pools.* The total available for delegation is 'top-sliced' to provide a central fund on which beneficiaries can draw for a specified purpose. This is similar to earmarked funding, but the finance is retained centrally and so provides flexibility for beneficiaries to draw according to their needs. For example, the DES previously operated a pool from which LEAs could draw funds to second teachers on long-term courses.

A pool is really a collective earmarked fund – providing greater flexibility to meet needs, but also allowing entrepreneurial (or greedy?) beneficiaries to draw more than their share. Pools can easily overrun unless firmly controlled.

10 *Refund of expenditure.* The donor agrees to refund expenditure for a defined purpose up to a specified level. For example, an LEA or school board may agree to reimburse teacher supply (relief) cover for staff absent on training courses. This is similar to a pool. The refunding mechanism psychologically encourages beneficiaries to feel they 'own' the expenditure – but refunding can be administratively troublesome.

11 *Tendering*. The beneficiary contracts to provide goods or services for an agreed payment. For example, a school may offer to host a district arts festival for £*x*. As in all tendering, it is important that the level of service and criteria for assessing it are clear.

12 *Purchase of goods and services*. In tendering, the donor asks 'What would you charge for this?'. In purchasing the donor says 'I will pay you X for this.' A school might receive funds for receiving student teachers in return for an agreement to provide a specified level of service to them in tutoring, support and supervision.

13 *Matching funds*. The donor agrees to provide funds for a specific purpose to match those raised by the beneficiary. The matching could be at any ratio (e.g. 1:1, 1:2, 2:1, etc.). For example, a school board or LEA might agree to double all funds raised by a school in a poor socioeconomic area (a good example of a mechanism to achieve equity). This is a useful but much under-used device that encourages local initiative and commitment.

14 *Tapering funds*. The donor initially provides 100 per cent of funds for a specific purpose, but in following years reduces this percentage, the beneficiary making up the difference. For example, a science adviser could make a grant to cover all additional costs of a new course in a school, but make it clear that over the next three years the grant would fall away to zero. Here the donor clearly hopes that the new practice will root itself sufficiently for the beneficiary to accept full costs later.

Transitional arrangements (e.g. to buffer the cost to a school of switching from an historical to a formula-funded budget) are similar.

15 *Enrolment-dependent funding*. The Education Reform Act of 1988 introduced a form of formula funding that is not just a strategy for allocation. The formula funding has a student-related element of 75 (later 80) per cent, linked to 'open enrolment' and a range of measures to provide parents with more complete information about the outcomes of their local schools. So in this way formula funding is intended not just to allocate funds but to encourage competition between schools in order to raise standards.

*   *   *

The foregoing financial mechanisms deserve further study. (See the 1992 article by Janet Ouston and others, examining their use in one large project involving several schools.) They also need care, and some need careful specification. Using too many could be administratively cumbersome and create conflict. But they can be very powerful devices to achieve a donor's objectives. At present they are grossly under-used – most donors do not even consider them. This is strange, because those who are parents already use them in everyday life . . .

'I'll double your allowance if you can come up with ideas for improving your test score.'
'I've kept some back – you can draw on it for your holiday.'
'I'm not made of money – you can't keep asking for extras.'
'If you pay half, I'll pay half.'
'I'll pay it all this time, but next time you have to contribute.'

■ Delegation of funds within the school

■ Determining the sum available

Although the bulk of a school's funds may come from an external donor or fees, the school may still be able to raise additional funds or generate income. So to some extent the sum available will depend on the school's ambitions. This relationship of income and expenditure within the budget is discussed further in Chapter 7.

■ Allocation to internal budget holders

Within most systems, in secondary and larger primary schools the budget for books, stationery, equipment and materials has traditionally been delegated to internal budget holders. With the spread of local ('site-based') financial management, in some schools this delegation now includes funds for furniture, fittings and reprographics and sometimes in-service training, supply (relief) teaching, and – where the geography of the school allows it – maintenance of premises or energy costs. But staffing is usually allocated by the school management centrally and in kind (e.g. in 'bodies', to a department or class). Exceptions – where internal budget holders are given responsibility for teacher salaries – will be rare, perhaps in very large schools.

Assessment of needs

A useful tool for planning allocation is a 'needs assessment matrix'. Figure 12 gives an example produced for the Publishers Association. This is used here for assessing the need for books and other material in a primary school, but it can be used in any type of school to assess any category of need (e.g. books, materials, equipment, IT, library/learning resources, furniture, premises, non-teaching support, teachers' in-service training needs etc.) It can be based on current provision as in figure 12, or on future requirements.

Blank matrix sheets can be completed by the headteacher or a senior

THE LEARNING RESOURCES ASSESSOR

Person completing _Sara Smith_

Class _Class Four_

RESOURCES

AREA	Readers	Classbooks	Reference books	Other printed materials	Wall display posters etc	
ENGLISH	4	3	2	3 Mostly worksheets	2	
MATHS		3 Essentials good, desirables not	2	2	2	
SOCIAL STUDIES		4	1 we need to spend a lot here!	4	4	
SCIENCE		4	3	4	3	
TECHNOLOGY		2 lot really needed	3	2	1 few available	
ART, LIGHT CRAFT		N/A	2	5 some very good design sheets	2	
			2	4 song sheets mostly	2	

THE LEARNING RESOURCES ASSESSOR

Class _C. P. School_

Person completing _Headteacher_

RESOURCES

AREA	Readers	Classbooks	Reference books	Other printed materials	Wall display posters etc	
ENGLISH	434453 3.8 ✓	343334 3.3	232213 2.2	344343 3.5	22325 2.5	
MATHS		342342 3.0	232122 2.0	234422 2.8	232212 2.0	
SOCIAL STUDIES		434353 3.6	121122 1.5	433443 3.5	433344 3.5	
SCIENCE		435443 3.8 ✓	324224 2.8	443333 3.3	323223 2.5	
TECHNOLOGY		22 n/an/a23 2.3	333234 3.0	233433 3.0	112232 1.8	
ART, LIGHT CRAFT		n/an/an/a n/a	223223 2.3	544344 4.0 ✓	2333322 2.5	
MUSIC		543445 4.2	231223 2.2	434453 3.8 ✓	233222 2.3	

Figure 12   A needs-assessment matrix (Source: Publishers Association)

teacher, or by subject or class teachers. The vertical columns need to be labelled with the categories of needs to be assessed, if necessary broken into sub-categories as in figure 12. The horizontal rows mark the 'areas' to be assessed; e.g. subjects (as in figure 12 for a class teacher), classes (for a subject teacher) or year-groups (for a department), etc.

Whoever completes the matrix assesses needs for each cell using codes and criteria designed for the particular purpose. For the example in figure 12 these were as follows:

	Essential resources	Desirable but not essential resources
5 = Excellent	In ample supply and good/ excellent condition	Good or excellent supply and in good condition
4= Good	Fully supplied, mostly in in good condition	Adequate, but some improvement in supply or condition desirable
3 = Reasonable	Fully supplied, possibly with minor exceptions. Condition reasonable, occasionally poor	Only partly adequate supply. Condition good to poor
2 = Mediocre	Not fully supplied (some sharing) and/or condition rather unsatisfactory	Inadequate supply, and/or condition poor
1 = Unacceptable	Poor supply (extensive sharing) and/or very poor condition	Few supplied
N/A	not applicable	

The completed assessment sheets can then be compared – to highlight differences of needs between departments, subjects, year-groups, class teachers etc. – or collated and averaged as in the lower example of figure 12 to show whole-school needs. Where sheets are completed by different people, some moderation between optimists and pessimists may be needed. Finally, a summary of 'action required' is needed.

This needs-assessment matrix is a useful 'quick and dirty' tool. It quantifies qualitative judgements, and does not require much time for its completion. It is particularly useful for identifying areas that are under-resourced.

Alternative allocation strategies

Benevolent despotism. Here funds are allocated by a central arbiter, usually the headteacher but possibly another senior teacher responsible for finance or a bursar. He or she discusses with budget holders how last year's funds were used, the needs of the coming year, and the purpose of any new proposals. Judgement is then used to adjudicate between rival claims and make a final allocation, sometimes kept private but more commonly published.

This strategy varies considerably in practice. It can be formalised by the request of standardised 'bids'. It can be a very open or very private process. It depends a good deal on the philosophy and judgement of the despot. At one extreme it can be very sensitive to budget holders and school needs, at the other almost arbitrary, with the headteacher using school funds like some war-chest to finance personal preferences.

Properly managed this approach is quite effective. It can be gratifying to the participants. It involves some crude evaluation of cost-effectiveness, and can be very flexible for new needs. But it is time-consuming and is very much open to prejudice on the part of the arbiter, or special pleading and lobbying on behalf of the recipients. It is better suited to small schools and is likely to come under pressure if delegated financial management requires headteachers to be more consultative.

Open market allocation. Each budget holder is invited to produce estimates for the coming year, both for maintaining the status quo and for development. Estimates can be requested under various headings, and/or in priority order. Objectives can also be requested, and budget holders may be asked to present and justify these requests. A full programme budgeting system may be used. (The original collaborative management model of Caldwell and Spinks (1988, Chapter 7) is of this type.)

The advantage of this approach is that it is better structured and more open, with thorough examination of requests, often by peers. It lends itself to closer scrutiny of the status quo, even to the use of a zero-based approach. But it does encourage budget holders to inflate their estimates, and undervalues modest and realistic departments against the pushy ones. The final decision may be taken by the headteacher or by the budget holders collectively. In either case the process tends to be time-consuming, because the total estimates will usually exceed the total available. Paring them down can be difficult and is often done on a proportional basis.

Incrementalism. This assesses the percentage increase in the total school budget available and then raises last year's quota for each budget holder by that proportion. It has the advantage of being simple, time-saving and low in political conflict, and for these reasons is more common than schools like to admit. However, it only perpetuates the historical situation and so does not allow for new developments or for any change in the responsibilities or relative importance of budget holders. In situations of falling rolls or cuts in school funding it can, of course, be 'decrementalism', although any increase in funding from inflation will often mask this.

Formula allocation. The needs of each 'academic' budget holder are determined by two factors: the number of weekly student-periods that they teach, and a weighting factor for the level of expenditure that they need for each student-period compared with other budget holders. The first is logical. If a subject or a primary class teacher has 10 per cent more, or less, student-periods, then he or she has a prima facie case for a 10 per cent increase, or decrease, in funding. Actually this may only be approximate, since some of the budget holder's spending may be on fixed costs which will not alter much with fluctuation in student-periods. But in broad terms it does adjust for any change in the relative spending needs of budget holders.

Some schools weight student-periods by age of the students, assuming that students of one age cost more per period than another. (For an actual example see Boulton, 1986, p. 32.) Of course, for some budget holders a student-period allowance is not appropriate (e.g. library, IT, audiovisual, office or premises expenditure), although a modified version linked to student numbers and the proportion of their spending that is fixed or variable is still possible.

The weighting factor, to reflect the greater cost per student-period of say Science compared with English, is more troublesome. How much more expensive is one subject than another? The author is not aware of any conclusive published studies, and indeed the differential will vary according to the age of the student and probably from school to school. In one school a subject may be under-resourced and need supplementing; in another it may be limited by poor accommodation or staff, and so need less; in another it may have a particularly high profile – at the extreme, the leading subject of a magnet school.

Comparisons between schools are also difficult because the actual items delegated to budget holders may vary. For example, they may include or exclude stationery, reprographics or furniture. Nevertheless a rationale for a differential between subjects can be constructed, based on differences in needs per student for expenditure on books, stationery, major equipment, minor equipment, consumable materials, and other items. One way of introducing this is to calculate the existing weighting of subjects (dividing each of their existing allowances by their current total of student-periods) and comparing these. They can then be matched against subjective judgement of how adequate each weighting appears to be at present, perhaps using the needs-assessment matrix described above, and then adjusting accordingly.

Hybrid strategies. Many schools combine two or more of these approaches. It is a common and logical practice to separate funds for *maintenance* of the status quo, adjusted for changes in volume, from funds for *development* (e.g. in one school, 80:20). The latter is obviously not suited to incrementalism or formula allocation, and increasingly some form of open market negotiation seems to be used. But it is important to confine the development budget to genuine developments, either whole-school or of a scale beyond the scope of an individual budget holder.

For the maintenance budget, schools commonly adopt a hybrid strategy, for example combining open market bids with despotic decision.

A suggested approach

Tim Simkins (1986) from his research suggests that schools' allocation strategies contain four different dimensions:

- Information gathering – from informal to systematic and quantitative.
- Openness – from restricted to full information and open consultation.
- Criteria – incremental, judgemental or formula.
- Decision-making – either headteacher, senior team/governors or collegial.

Any school designing a system for internal delegation of funds could test these dimensions with questions like the following:

Have you separated allocation from 'development' and 'maintenance'? (the latter adjusted for changes in volume).
If so, you will need to work through the other questions separately for each.

Is your information base and needs analysis sound?
Do you have useful information on previous years expenditure? (and attainment of objectives?)
Are requests systemised and written?
Is each budget holder's requests prioritised?
Do requests have to be justified? With objectives clarified?
Is the 'status quo' challenged (not every year?) with zero-based thinking? ('What would happen if we didn't spend money on this?')
Is there a systematic needs analysis? (see matrix above)

Is there open communication about allocation?
Is communication top-down, bottom-up, or preferably both?
Do budget holders see, and scrutinise, each others' requests?

Are the final discussions, and the finished outcomes, public?

By what criteria will decisions be made?
By reference to last year's expenditures? If so, are the limitations of incrementalism recognised?
By qualitative judgement? If so, how objective and informed is it?
By formula? If so, on what basis are the subject and other weightings established?

How are the final allocation decisions made?
By headteacher? Senior management team? Governors?
Committee of budget holders? Or a combination?
Is the approach collegial and consensual? If so, how are unresolved decisions made?

▐ Distribution mechanisms within schools

The same mechanisms discussed earlier are available to managers in schools. You may wish to refer back to the earlier explanations. Those most commonly used are the least effective. Some of those least used, operated judiciously, could be a powerful tool to achieve school objectives.

Grants without strings. This is the normal method of funding in schools, used uncritically. It gives budget holders freedom, but does not relate spending to school objectives or create any accountability.

Grants with recommendations. These have no teeth, as discussed earlier. For example a headteacher may grant extra funds to a department with the suggestion of improving its book stock, only to find it is spent on equipment.

Grants related to outcomes. These look more promising. Enhanced spending on special-needs students in a school can, for example, be linked to objectives and possible expected advances in performance.

Grants with incentives. These can encourage economy. Classroom teachers in a primary school can be given a budget for reprographics and be allowed to keep any savings. A headteacher can warn department heads that in future excessive damage to furniture will be debited to the department concerned.

Is there a place for incentives to improve outcomes? Stephen Hoenack in a provocative article (1988) argues:

> **Considering how closely overall value incentives [i.e. incentives linked to monetary gain] and successful invention and entrepre-**

neurial activity have been historically, it would be most surprising if these relationships did not hold in education. . . . It is unlikely that productivity in schools will ever increase appreciably in the absence of appropriate incentives for teachers and students.

Hoenack suggests a complex and probably unrealistic scheme linking incentives to 'outcome based instruction', but he raises important issues.

Tim Simkins suggests, in correspondence, that we can categorise incentives as:

	Personal	Systemic
Effectiveness incentives	E.g. performance related pay (see Chapter 9), bonuses	Capital programme awarded to over-subscribed schools
Efficiency incentives	[no major examples?]	Block grants to buy in reprographics, furniture, etc.

Negotiated budgets. These are useful for cutting out low-priority expenditure. A headteacher is, for example, able to show an internal budget holder where money could be saved or used to better effect.

Speculative bidding. Not the ideal mechanism! A headteacher may keep a fund under his or her personal control, allegedly for contingencies but actually open to special bids.

Earmarked grants. This is useful for focusing expenditure, although it conflicts with the spirit of maximum delegation. For example, a school allocates additional funds that can only be spent by budget holders on IT (unconditional). Similarly, budget holders may have to show that they have a clear IT policy and have received adequate training before the grant is payable (conditional).

Honeypot management (see p. 65). This is seldom used in schools, but can be very effective. In secondary schools it is often difficult to persuade all departments that they should take 'English across the curriculum' or equal opportunities seriously. Honeypot funding could avoid this (but see the limitations discussed earlier). For example, a school management team can make funds available for student-centred learning, either for the best proposal submitted, or for all departments making proposals which meet set criteria.

Pools. These have some use, but can be wasteful. A school might set up a pool for fieldwork expenses, to encourage fieldwork, the teachers carrying out the most fieldwork gaining the most benefit. A school creating a pool for reprographic costs, allowing users free or subsidised use, is a poor arrangement, likely to encourage waste.

Refund of expenses. This can have a useful incentive effect. For example, a cross-curricular coordinator for environmental awareness may agree to refund expenditure by departments or classteachers on environmental studies.

Tendering. A special-needs coordinator previously concentrating on students with learning difficulties might offer to provide services for gifted children for an agreed sum, payable to his or her budget.

Purchasing. This is similar to tendering, but in this case it is the headteacher etc. who makes the offer. A school could offer a department or classteachers £X if they agreed to organise a group of parents or children to redecorate some classrooms.

Matching funds. This is another incentive mechanism. For example, a teacher asks the headteacher of the school if a piece of equipment can be bought from central funds, and receives an offer to pay half.

Tapering funds. This is similar to matching funds, but not a permanent commitment. A school management team may wish to encourage educational visits and suggest paying, from central funds, 100 per cent of all costs in year 1, 75 per cent in year 2, 50 per cent in year 3 and 25 per cent in year 4 (the remainder being paid by budget holders).

▄▄ Capital funding

In many countries in the 1990s, constraints upon central and local government expenditure are likely to tighten, often as schools are acquiring more responsibility for their own finances. In this situation it is probable that state schools will be tempted to fund minor and middle-order capital projects themselves, rather than wait for funds to trickle down.

Schools raising their own capital face a series of decisions, as figure 13 suggests.

Needs assessment

Schools need to ask some hard questions. First, is the proposed capital facility really necessary? (For example, some proposals to add specialist facilities or additional rooms could be avoided if schools designed their school days more effectively – see p. 177.) Could it be scaled down? Or phased, or deferred a year or two (to help accumulation of funds)? What is the reasonable life of the capital item? What is the maximum period for

NEEDS ASSESSMENT

Total capital sum required
(and phasing etc.)

Maximum years
possible for
repayment

Estimate of
future
inflation

Funds available at time of
payment
i.e. Sale of assets
    Capital reserve fund
    Transfer from revenue a/c
    Project appeal

+

Loan requirements
Interest-free
low-interest
commercial rate
leasing, short-term,
rolled over

Annual repayments
Debt charges (paid from revenue
    a/c)
Sinking fund (revenue a/c)
Income or cost reduction from the
    capital project
Further fund-raising

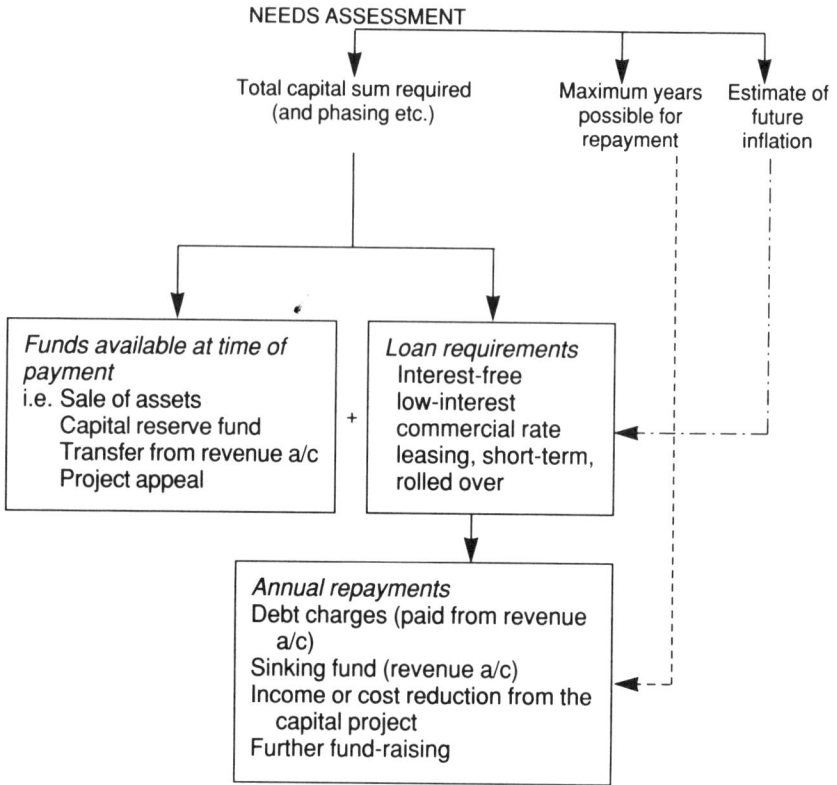

Figure 13   Decision path for capital funding

loan repayment (most schools, as opposed to government or municipal bodies, cannot easily raise long-term loans). What about depreciation? Will this require the item's replacement at the end of the loan period? How about the inflation prospects?

Funds likely to be available, other than loans

What finance, other than loans, is likely to be available by the time payment is needed? There are a number of possibilities:

- Sale of assets, e.g. unused land, buildings, plant or vehicles. These may belong to a higher authority and so sharing of the spoils may need to be agreed.
- A capital reserve fund built up in anticipation.
- Transfer from the revenue account (particularly if there is a surplus

from previous years, or slack in the budget) or from other accounts.

- An appeal fund for this project (see the next chapter, on fund raising.)

Loan requirements

Any additional sum will need to be raised as a loan. The maximum possible is determined by the length of time available for repayment and the amount that can be repaid each year. Loan possibilities include:

- Interest-free loans, from parents and friends of the school.

- Low-interest loans, from the same sources.

- Commercial loans, from banks and finance houses, municipalities etc.

- Leasing – commonly used in industry and commerce to acquire capital assets (but the overall rate of interest is high).

- Short-term borrowing 'rolled over'. The rate of interest can be lower, but there is more uncertainty and hassle.

Guarantee arrangements for loans are necessary. For smaller loans parents or friends may be guarantors; for larger loans underwriting by an LEA, or school board or similar organisation is needed, unless the loan can be backed by collateral of school buildings or land. Small loans could be backed from the school contingency or reserve funds.

Example The New Zealand Government has already foreseen this possibility. *Tomorrow's Schools* suggests (paragraph 1.1.31): 'The Board (of Trustees) will be able to borrow money commercially if they so desire. Because of this, it may be necessary to create a general liability – held to a specified limit of the (delegated) grant funds – as security for lenders.

Annual repayments

Again there is a range possible:

- Annual loan repayments from the revenue account ('debt charges').
- A sinking fund; i.e. a separate fund fed by annual payments from the revenue account and building up at compound interest, to pay off the remaining part of the loan. This is only worth considering if loans are at low or nil interest, and so serviced at less interest than that paid on the sinking fund.

- Extra income created by the new capital assets (e.g. funding for additional students, fees or charges for use) or reduced expenditure from greater cost-efficiency.
- Proceeds of future fund raising (but donors prefer giving for a project in the future rather than the past!).

All these are problematical, so estimates need to be cautious.

Allowance for inflation

What is inflation likely to be during the loan period? The higher it is, the better to be a debtor since repayment will be reduced in real terms and so easier to make (assuming the school's income generally rises at the rate of inflation).

Example For a loan repaid over five years with 10 per cent annual inflation, the repayments by the middle of year 5 would be only 66 per cent of those in year 1 *in real terms.*

Inflation also affects the savings you make. The value of any reserve or sinking fund will depreciate annually by the rate of inflation, in real terms, though offset by the compound interest paid. So your main concern here is the real rate of return on investments; i.e. the difference between the rate of interest paid and the rate of inflation.

Examples

- 10 per cent interest on reserves, with 8 per cent inflation, gives a real return of 2 per cent.
- 8 per cent interest, with 10 per cent inflation, gives a *negative* return of 2 per cent on investment.

Discounted cash flow

A gift of £100 today is worth more than such a gift in five years' time. Apart from any question of inflation, we can have the use of the £100 for five years. If we borrow the £100 now, the interest we pay is the rental for its use. So when you are looking at fund raising schemes, you need to bear this in mind.

The payments from the later years of a deed of covenant are worth less to the recipient than those of earlier years, even if there is no inflation.

* * *

This is a very sketchy review of capital funding. Space has not allowed discussion of the complexities of capital and interest repayments or discounted cash flows. Any school embarking on substantial capital funding should obtain professional financial advice.

5 Fees, fund raising and income generation

All the sources of revenue discussed below – whether fees, donated money or goods and services, voluntary help, or income from goods and services marketed by the school – depend on the principle of exchange whereby each party feels that what is received is of more value than what is given up. Nobody simply gives money away – we only donate it if we feel the transaction is worthwhile.

Fees and obligatory payments

In independent (non-government) schools

In theory, independent schools operate like any other seller of goods and services, charging the maximum that the market will bear. Or do they? Many independent schools are non-profit-making and so do not necessarily charge the maximum possible, although clearly they must break even. Moreover in economists' terms the 'supply' of a school is not very elastic: any increase in numbers beyond a certain point would require building extensions and perhaps a change to the school's character. Also the 'market' is very imperfect. Once children have entered a school parents are unlikely to take them away if fees rise.

Schools fix fees against a mix of six factors (see figure 14):

- The number of students enrolled.
- The minimum break-even fee, i.e. the unit cost per student (including a contingency element for market uncertainties).
- Total income.
- The efficiency of the school in converting income into education.
- The quality of education provided.
- Customers' perception of the quality of education provided.

Student numbers and the unit cost per student determine the total income available, and this sets a ceiling on the quality of education that

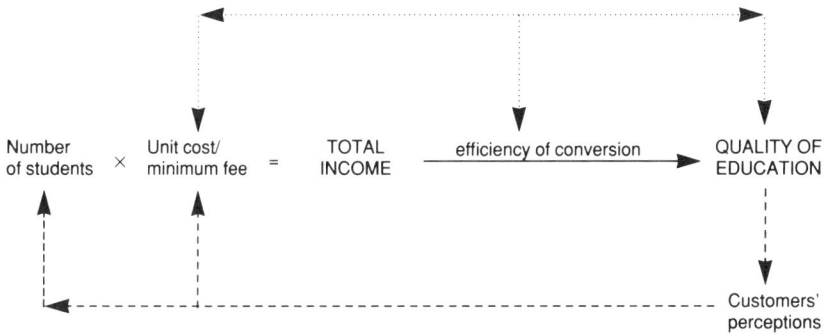

Figure 14   Factors determining level of school fees

can be planned (e.g. student/teacher ratio, learning resources). The actual quality of education provided will also be affected by the school's efficiency (e.g. the teacher class-contact ratio, curriculum or quality of teaching). However, parents' perceptions of the quality of education may or may not reflect its actual quality, and it will be these perceptions which feed back into their willingness to send their children to the school (student numbers) or pay fees of a given level. The school may decide as a result to alter the planned quality of its education, or its fees, or efficiency. It may also survey what parents believe are the components of quality, and the extent to which it can provide these within the limitations of its fee income.

Of course, independent schools do not work out their fees in this theoretical way. In practice they look at the income from current fees and enrolment, and the quality of education this provides, and if the combination seems satisfactory and broadly in line with similar schools, they maintain this fee level. They may feel that their enrolment or perceived quality allows them to charge more – but as non-profit schools they will do this mainly to enhance quality further. So the fee level is a trade-off between the desire of governors and staff to improve the school and their wish not to increase financial pressure on parents. Figure 15 illustrates this adjustment process.

---

1 A school generates fees sufficient to cover its fixed costs, shown here as 20 per cent of the total costs when student numbers are at their maximum (N_m), and variable costs. The line CC shows how total cost/income rises as student numbers increase. The level of income for enrolment N_1 allows the school to provide education of quality Q_2.

2 If the school's fees are seen as average for schools of this perceived quality, and if there is sufficient parent demand, this situation is sustainable. If the **perceived** quality is higher than Q_2, fees could be raised to the line $C_1 C_1$. This would then allow provision of quality Q_1.

3 Even if the school's quality is Q_2 it may gamble that raising fees and so increasing income to $C_1 C_1$ will allow it to raise quality to Q_1, and so make these higher fees sustainable.

4 If perceived quality is at a level below Q_2, fees will now be seen as too high.

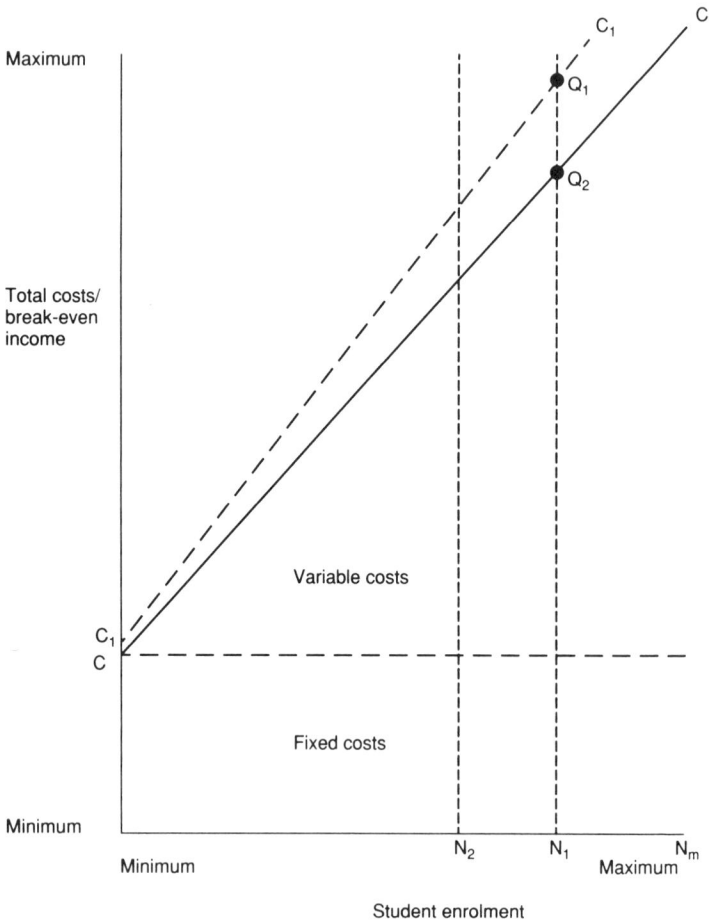

Figure 15   The effect of changes in enrolment and customers' perceptions of quality upon fee income: Q_1, Q_2 etc. represent customers' perceptions of quality

Either enrolment will fall (e.g. to N_2) or fees will be reduced – unless the school can improve the customers' perceptions of its quality. Reduced fees will, however, lead to reduced income, and so to a cost/income line below CC. This implies reduced quality and so possibly a restoration of the fee–quality gap.

5 If there is a reduction in enrolment (from N_1 to N_2) then some increase in fees will be required, because the school is working at reduced capacity. This is because the school's fixed costs do not fall when numbers fall, and so the cost per student rises, as explained in the next chapter.

Schools will also seek to improve the 'acceptability' of fees because this may make a higher level possible, using devices such as 'extra' charges, differentiation by age, discounts and easier payment arrangements.

Crucial to fee setting is accurate cost accounting. In Australia, Ross Harrold (1988) has developed a tool for non-government schools to establish the break-even class size for the whole or any part of the school, or any subject. The procedure requires detailed data collection, but the principles are easily explained.

Harrold strips out any non-tuition outlays such as boarding, but attributes all other expenditure to the teaching service the school provides. So 'the basic unit of recurrent cost incurred by the school is outlay per face-to-face teaching period and the fundamental unit of financial return is the notional income per pupil period (in each week/teaching cycle).' So the analysis focuses on the extent to which the average class

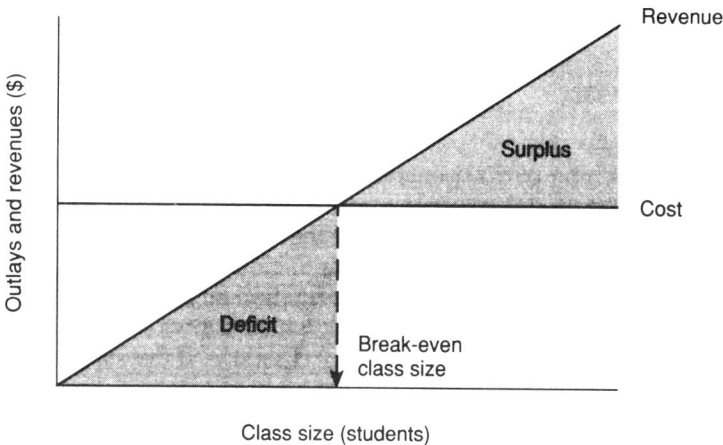

Figure 16   Revenues and outlays for a class taught in a timetabled period
(Source: adapted from Harrold, R., 1988)

Total expenditure attributable
to teaching periods

|
divided by
↓

Total teaching periods per ←——————→ Total teaching periods per
week/teaching cycle   week/teaching cycle (c)

| |
equals |
↓ |

(a) expenditure per teaching period |

↓   ↓

BREAK-EVEN CLASS SIZE   AVERAGE CLASS SIZE
(a ÷ b)   (d) ÷ (c)

↑   ↑

(b) income per pupil period

↑

equals

total pupil periods per ←——————→ total pupil periods per
week/teaching cycle   week/teaching cycle (d)

↑
divided by
|

Total income from pupils' fees

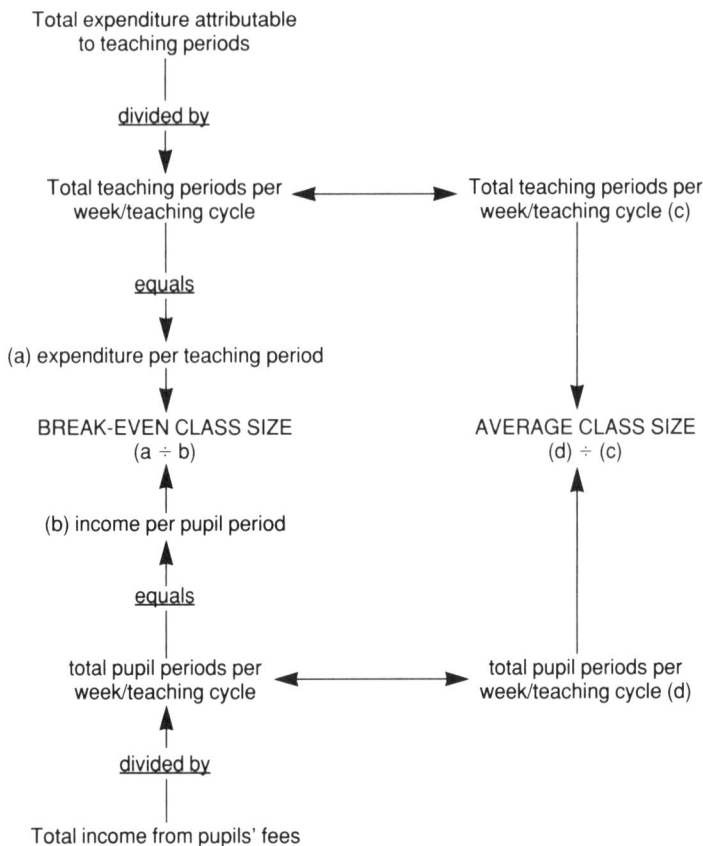

Figure 17   Calculation of break-even and average class size (Source: adapted from Harrold, R., 1988)

size for each teaching period generates sufficient income to break even (see figure 16). The model assumes, reasonably, that the great bulk of the costs of each teaching period are fixed for the duration of the school year (i.e. a reduction in class size makes little reduction in class costs).

The model then translates financial information on income and expenditure into terms of class size (figure 17), which allows the break-even class size to be compared with the average class size. If the average class size is greater, a surplus is generated. So it highlights the relationship of finance and curriculum organisation. Harrold uses this technique to identify those areas of a school's teaching activities that are subsidising other areas. This enables a fee paying school that is in financial difficulties to modify its timetable so that it is more cost-effective.

███   **In government schools**

School fees are widespread in the government schools of many developing countries. However, there is a strong feeling worldwide that charges for basic education are not 'right'. Mark Bray in *Community Financing of Education* points out (Chapter 4) that the United Nations Declaration of Human Rights states:

> **Everyone has the right to education. Education shall be free, at least in the elementary and fundamental stages . . . [Article 26]**

However, he comments that it is not clear why education has this privileged status, and not health or housing. Perhaps education is seen as closer to justice, a service that should be equally open to all and therefore free. This issue of equity is discussed further in Chapter 8.

There are other arguments against fees in state schools. One is the dislike of cost transfer from the government to parents. Flat rate fees are seen as an education tax and a regressive one. Other objections centre around the practicalities of collection, especially in developing countries – its cost, particularly for fees imposed by the government as opposed to the local community, and the risk of theft or embezzlement.

Yet fees are still very common in developing countries. The main reason is a very practical one: education is very expensive and developing countries with exploding populations often cannot afford free universal education. So fees create extra revenue that creates extra, or better, school places. Bray points out it can be argued that fees can improve education, quoting World Bank officials:

> **When resource transfers between levels of education and from other sectors are impossible . . . increased user charges for primary education could increase efficiency within schools, especially if that revenue stays with the school where it was raised.**

It can also be argued that they can extend equity. Bray writes:

> **To those who suggest that the fees infringe a basic human right, the communities would reply that denial of an education . . . is a much more serious denial.**

Whatever the ethics, government schools setting their own fees face the same factors in setting them as their private counterparts (see figure 14 above).

In developed countries fees for compulsory education were abolished mainly in the last century. However, in recent years pressure on school budgets has elevated parents' voluntary contributions to a quasi-fee status in many countries. Some English school PTAs now suggest a rate for 'expected' parental contributions. In Australia, schools impose levies for textbooks, library, transport and even charges for reference and photo-copied material. Parents and Citizens Committees also raise a levy on parents for other amenities. These are not compulsory, but there is strong pressure on parents to pay, and inducements such as acceptance of standing orders or credit cards. Payments in Western Australia are reckoned to be made by at least 80 per cent of parents.

This drift towards quasi-fees seems likely to continue, as welfare budgets come under increasing strain, and with a growing trend towards privatisation and a 'user pays' philosophy. So the South African 'Model C' development, whereby parents are obliged to take responsibility for all non-salary costs (schools charging fees if they wish), may not prove an isolated one.

Logically quite a strong case can be made out for fees in state schools of a 'top-up' sort; i.e. meeting part but not the whole per student cost:

1 The total amount of money available for education is likely to increase. Even if the government or other funding body scales down or underestimates its contribution, for various reasons it is unlikely that such reduction could equal or even come near the increase contributed by fees. So there would be a net gain in funding to schools as a whole.

2 'User pays' charges can be seen to be fair, in that families that gain from their children's education in increased future earnings and other benefits pay for them to some extent.

3 Such charges increase parental commitment and sharpen schools' accountability. This process is already occurring with the parental levies in Australia.

4 The ability to set the level of fees would enable schools to manage not just expenditure, as now, but also supply. So schools would not be limited to funds trickling down from above, plus some fund raising; they could expand their activities or improve their quality, financed from the fees that parents would be willing to pay for this. This assumes that each school decides its own top-up fee rate. It could, for example, offer them the flexibility to expand new technology, develop curriculum areas, improve premises or introduce performance-related pay.

5 Collecting fees is more cost-efficient than fund raising, which can be a major distraction – although it can also contribute to 'esprit de corps'.

6 The gap between state and independent schools would narrow.

But ... fees would create horrendous problems of equity, both for individual parents unable to pay or faced with hardship, and for schools serving poorer areas. However, a government really interested in overcoming inequity could develop mechanisms to avoid these. Poor families could receive remission of fees or bursaries (although this would need careful treatment to prevent a poverty trap). Poor area schools could receive a block grant, ideally with some kind of incentive mechanism as suggested on page 66.

School fees in state schools raise complex philosophical and political issues. They are emotive and almost unthinkable, yet they could offer advantages *provided* the equity issues were overcome.

■■ Fund raising

School fund raising the world over is enormously varied and ingenious, and space does not allow discussion in detail. Many schools operate on a 'traditional' basis with a large collective effort and well-tried methods to produce funds, fun and satisfaction. For raising big money a more systematic approach is helpful. Peter Drucker in *Managing the Non-Profit Organisation* (p. 41) suggests:

> **The purpose of a strategy for raising money is . . . to enable the non-profit institution to carry out its mission without subordinating that mission to fund raising. This is why non-profit people have now changed the term from 'fund raising' to 'fund development'. Fund raising is going about with a begging bowl, asking for money because the need is great. Fund development is creating a constituency which supports the organisation because it deserves it. It means developing . . . a membership that participates through giving.**

■■ A systematic approach

Audit

As in any planning, it is worth standing back and analysing your present situation. A SWOT analysis is an easy way to start:

1 How much did you raise last year – and how does this compare with other similar schools?

2 What percentage of the disposable income (i.e. income available per household after tax, mortgage/rent and household expenses) of your parent body or community was donated to your school last year? Could this be increased?

Example A primary school raised £5000 last year. It serves a community of 1000 households, each with disposable income of say £20 per week, i.e. a total of £20 000 per week, or £1 000 000 p.a. So the school taps 0.005 per cent of the disposable income of its community.

---

3 What are your school's strengths in fund raising; e.g. people, ideas, methods, organisation, commitment?

4 What are your weaknesses?

5 Are any new opportunities for fund raising likely to develop in the near future; e.g. new people, new potential donors, new needs which will appeal to donors?

6 Are there any new constraints or difficulties likely to hamper you in the near future; e.g. change in people, other demands, competition! etc?

Aim

Why are you doing this? The answer is not always as obvious as it sounds. What are your motives? Why are funds needed? Is this expenditure *really* necessary? Or is there any other way the finance could be acquired? Have you thought fully enough about what you are doing, and why?

Objective

It is much better to have a clear objective, whether a sum of money, a piece of equipment or a building. It gives people something to work for. But how much? A large amount is more of a challenge, a smaller amount is more attainable. Generally it is better to aim high, and undoubtedly some schools grossly underestimate what they could raise.

Also, how much 'appeal' does your fund raising objective have? People are much more likely to give to something that appeals to them or which they can visualise, or which seems to offer benefit to their family or to a lot of people.

Targets

Who are the possible donors, and what scale of possible funds does each have? It is worth making a complete list, covering:

- The extended school family – parents, pupils and staff, past, present and future; friends and relations; volunteers at and users of the school; neighbours of the school; suppliers.

- The community – individuals, organisations and groups (e.g. civic, political, social, sports, recreational, arts, caring and service, churches, youth or elderly etc.)

- Commerce and industry; e.g. a list of businesses, shops, commercial organisations in your area and also in the region. Are there any national firms or organisations which might be interested?

- Official bodies – local councils, national bodies and government organisations, the European Community and other international organisations, official or semi-official bodies for sport, the arts, science, etc.

- Charitable bodies; e.g. local and national trusts.

If you wish to raise a large sum it is important to spend time researching potential targets. In England and Wales, for example, there are some useful publications to consult or organisations to contact. There will be town guides and local directories, and much useful information in local libraries or with organisations like Chambers of Commerce.

When you have completed your list of possible targets, you need to prioritise. For each of the groups or organisations on your list, try to estimate two things:

1 What would be the maximum sum that each group of people or organisation might be willing to donate charitably? (For groups you can make a guestimate based on disposable income, as in the example earlier.)

2 How well disposed is each group or organisation to your school? How likely are they to give a substantial sum – or anything at all?

However crude and uncertain your final analysis, it will be a lot better than guessing, and should certainly help your planning.

Strategies and methods

What is going to be your general strategy? Do you need a short high-profile campaign, as suggested for a capital project below; or a methodical procedure operating each year, as for the enrichment scheme below? Would you be best going for a single mega-event, or do you have several events in mind? If so, there is much to be said for linking them in a coordinated programme – it makes more impact and one event helps the next.

For actual methods, there ia a huge range of possibilities:

- Donations, whether covenanted as in the examples below, or one-off. There are also loans and legacies.

- Sponsorship of individual effort, like a sponsored walk/swim/knit-in/silence . . . etc.

- Sales of donated items, from 50:50 auctions to jumble sales and produce stalls.

- Fund raising events which provide enjoyment.

- Games of chance – lotteries, gambling etc.

- Sponsorship of an event or feature of the school by an outside firm or person – really a form of benign advertising.

Implementation

The usual range of practical issues need to be faced:

- What sort of committee or other organisation is needed? (membership, terms of reference, accountability)

- What kind of budget is required? How is finance to be handled – and safeguarded?

- Does a charitable trust need to be established?

- Is outside help desirable, whether professional consultant, seconded or retired business-person (see REACH under Addresses) or local voluntary expertise? Professional fund raisers can be very useful in contributing strategic ideas. But they are expensive – and so if you use them for the main 'donkey-work' they may not be really cost-effective.

- Are there key people who should be consulted or lobbied?

- How will the fund raising be promoted? – see the later section in this chapter.

- What timetable or phasing is required?

Finally . . . who is responsible for doing what, and when? And who makes sure that they are doing it?

A 'grand design'

There is much to be said for incorporating some of the features above into a grand published plan. Such a 'grand design' has many virtues:

1 It impresses potential donors with the scale of operation.

2 It gives clear sense of direction and purpose.

3 It inspires confidence.

4 It coordinates different people and activities.

5 It links disparate donors so that they feel commitment to something greater than their immediate interests – the whole is greater than the sum of the parts.

Example. A school wishes to improve its science facilities and launches its 'Science 2000' campaign, which includes:

- a covenant scheme for a laboratory;
- sponsorship of equipment by local firms;
- a series of fund raising events, competitions and sponsored events with a science flavour;
- a large lottery.

The combined programme has much more impact and each event enhances the others.

On the same principle, even a single event can be enhanced by a range of different activities grouped together.

Example A South African school recently promoted a 'relay-marathon'. This comprised:

- a competition for teams from local schools and organisations, each running the marathon as a relay (e.g. 27 runners running a mile each);
- a similar competition for each class of the school;
- sponsorship of each runner.

So there were hundreds of thirsty runners and even more parents and admirers on site all day, needing dozens of refreshment and entertainment stalls, sideshows etc.

■ Major capital projects

A major project – say £100 000 or more – needs a special approach which has been developed by professional fund raisers. This is centred upon the visitor technique, where a cadre of enthusiastic and well-briefed volunteers visit personally all potential donors. The technique is based on the principle that people do not easily give to causes, but give much more easily to people with causes, and that a committed visitor is worth a hundred mailshots. Donations can be covenanted over a period of years.

For the campaign to succeed, however, it needs thorough planning: establishment of a charitable trust; a survey of donor potential; a realistic 'pyramid' of donations anticipated, large, medium and small, to secure the desired sum; a persuasive 'case statement', set out in a good quality brochure to support each visit; and an efficient structure of central committee and visitor sub-committees for each group of donors, plus other committees for supporting events, approaches to charitable trusts etc.

The campaign needs to be high profile but short duration, ideally one academic year. And the 'visitor' system is vital – there is no effective substitute. There is an excellent practical manual for this approach, namely *The Fund Raising Manual for Schools*, Acorn Fundraising Solutions (see References).

Covenant enrichment schemes

A well-established pattern exists in the Bristol area of England, where the oldest established enrichment scheme in a state school, Filton High, has raised £200 000. In most of these schemes money raised is used as a capital sum, with interest devoted to 'enrichment' activities which one would not normally expect the school's budget to reach.

This approach, too, requires a charitable trust and good organisation. The scheme is presented initially to well-hosted meetings of parents, with presentations and an attractive brochure. Parents (and staff, governors etc.) are invited to covenant annual payments for a period of years to the enrichment fund, donations being augmented in the UK by 33 per cent from remission of income tax. Additional funds can be added from special events and income from investment of the capital. Each new cohort of parents can be approached each year, and this is often used to offset the effect of inflation on the real value of the capital.

Arthur Turner, senior teacher at Filton High, has described his school's experience in *School Governor*, 1990.

Sponsorship

Sponsorship is not asking for a handout. It is inviting financial or other support in return for commercially valuable advertising, publicity, goodwill or association. It may be influenced by philanthropy but it is essentially a commercial transaction. Businesses are not in the habit of throwing their profits away.

So successful sponsorship depends on careful initial analysis. What exactly are you asking firms to sponsor? What benefits are you offering, tangible or intangible? What are these benefits worth from the sponsor's viewpoint, and is this the sum you can ask from sponsorship? Remember that firms often spend huge sums on publicity, advertising, promotions or launch events – so aim high. But you will only earn large sums if you can offer large benefits.

Thorough research is needed. Which companies or businesses might be interested in this kind of sponsorship? How profitable are they? What personal contacts already exist? (A good network of contacts is often the foundation for successful fund raising.) Who will make the decisions on this kind of request? (Always go to the top.) When? (A reasonable request at the right time is better than a good one at the wrong time.)

Finally, there will be the practicalities – the actual approach to the potential sponsor, preferably in person, and the presentation. Stanley Goodchild's method of inviting industrialists to the school and then making his case is worth reading about in Goodchild and Holly (1990, p. 54ff).

▇ Grants

The quest for grants, whether from government or quasi–government bodies or charitable trusts or other sources, is similar to the quest for sponsorship. It requires good intelligence, so research will be needed. Government grants available are not always well known and European Community grants are particularly complex, especially when a grant first becomes available.

Trusts, on the other hand, are well documented. Two good UK sources are the following (see Addresses):

- The Charities Aid Foundation, which publishes the *Directory of Grant Making Trusts* – comprehensive and very expensive, but available in libraries.

- The Directory of Social Change, which produces a large number of very practical publications and mounts training courses.

Information on local trusts is often available from libraries. The problem with trusts is sheer numbers. Also, grants for schools tend to be in the range of £100–£1000, although larger grants may be available. Intelligence is needed to select carefully the trusts to approach.

The main approach has normally to be in writing, unlike with sponsorship, so the actual written submission is critical. Further research will often be needed, perhaps by telephone, to clarify the information provided by the grantor and establish if possible the thinking and priorities behind it. The core of a submission is 'the case':

1 The reason for the request; i.e. your current need or problem.

2 Your proposal; i.e. what you propose to do to meet the need or solve the problem.

3 The advantages that will flow from a grant – to students/ school/community/country/other.

It needs to be brief – preferably not more than two sides of A4 – with illustrations, and with supporting information if necessary as appendices.

Applying for grants is a little like fishing: it is an inexact art, time-consuming, with unpredictable returns. Like fishing, success comes with knowledge of your quarry, practice . . . and skill.

▉ Voluntary help

Voluntary help is really a form of donation. Most schools use it to some extent, but very few exploit its full potential. Even where volunteers are appreciated, their financial value is seldom understood. If your school was able to enlist volunteer hours equal to the total contact time of your teachers, and assuming that volunteers were paid at the market rate, their salary bill would be, say, one-third that of teachers – equivalent to about 25 per cent of the total school budget. This is worth working for, and a realistic long-term target.

Even in schools that appear to make good use of volunteer help, the total hours are seldom more than a fraction of the school's teacher hours. Now suppose some magician – a government minister perhaps – granted you an extra 25 per cent on your budget to employ a multitude of ancillary non-specialist support staff and aides, would you refuse it? Of course not. So why ignore the prospect of a similar number of volunteers?

The problem is that schools do not really take volunteers seriously. They grossly underestimate the number of potential volunteers available – parents, friends, members of the community, retired staff, staff partners etc. – potentially over a hundred for a small primary school, and many more for a large secondary. They also underestimate how they could be used. Schools are manned by teachers and a few ancillary staff, and volunteers are tacked on. But if you had this army of volunteers donated by your friendly minister, how would you organise teaching and learning then, and train teachers to adjust to this new role?

Example Thomas Estley Community College, Leicestershire, appointed a 12-hours-a-week coordinator in 1982–83, externally funded, who recruited over a hundred regular or occasional volunteers. The post terminated but the volunteer register continued.

The key to extensive use of volunteers is *management*. You cannot expect to recruit, train, deploy, motivate and monitor volunteers on any scale as some sideline of a harassed class teacher, deputy or head. Someone has to be responsible for management of volunteers as a key task, with time and a small budget.

The cost-effective solution is to appoint a part-time non-teacher volunteer coordinator, with scope to be employed longer as volunteers increase. This involves very low cost for a massive possible return. A small budget is needed for telephone and correspondence, filing facilities, 'thank-you' presents and parties, volunteer out-of-pocket expenses; and there needs to be an interview room available.

The other requirement for volunteers is *involvement*. Why do they offer their services? Peter Drucker (1990) has some strong ideas:

> **... you treat them, not as volunteers but as unpaid members of the organisation. You determine their job, you set the standard, you provide the training, and you set their sights high. That, in my experience, is the secret . . . the volunteer professionals who get their satisfaction out of their work, not the pay cheque.**

Volunteers must feel that the satisfaction they gain is more valuable than the time donated. So, proper induction, training, job satisfaction, recognition and praise are important. But many volunteers unconsciously are looking for more – for identification with the school and ultimately involvement in its development and even some of its decisions. Volunteers are not free serfs and maximum volunteer support will only come if this need for involvement is recognised. These issues and the role of the coordinator are discussed more fully in a useful article by Anne Clifford in *Managing Schools Today* (1991). Volunteers incidentally also bring other intangible benefits – community goodwill, better public relations, useful contacts.

Volunteers for management or specialist purposes are also available. REACH (see Addresses) maintains a register of retired executives willing to provide services on an expenses-only basis. BESO (British Executive Services Overseas) fulfils a similar function for developing countries. Some large companies are willing to second senior executives full-time for work in the community.

One of the greatest sources of volunteers is students themselves. Recent research has suggested that cross-age peer-tutoring is very effective, not just for the younger students tutored but for the reflected effect on the older tutors themselves. It has also been shown to be more cost-effective than computer aided instruction, reduced class size or extension of class-time (see p. 188). Yet schools use it very little. The situation is similar to that of parent/community volunteers. It is little use trying to tack peer-tutoring on to conventional school organisation. Just consider the ramifications (and the benefits) if all the senior students in your school gave one hour each week to tutoring all younger pupils. Peer-tutoring needs management, perhaps a part-time non-teacher coordinator, and some rearrangement of the school day to provide tutoring outside of class-time. This could be a small investment for even a modest improvement in learning effectiveness.

▩ Income generation

A school is often the biggest 'thing' in its area – the biggest aggregation of land and premises, equipment and other physical resources, plus the knowledge and skills of highly skilled staff and the time and energy of hordes of children and parents. This total resource has a market value which schools have often grossly underestimated. So the first step is a realistic survey of potential sources of income. The checklist below may assist this.

Sales of bought-in products – e.g. stationery or tee-shirts sold in a school shop. This category includes percentage commission on second-hand uniform or book sales, and the inescapable school photographs.
Sales of the school's own products – e.g. plants, trees, food etc., or printed materials, videos and audio cassettes.
Collection of coupons from groceries etc.
Sales of services – Possibilities include:
   Instructional services – training, coaching, teaching
   Technical sources – word-processing, translating
   Caring services – e.g. crèche, pre-school
   Research and development projects for local firms or organisations
   Consultancy and professional advice.
Sale of advertising – on 'sites', vehicles, in changing rooms or on printed material (but not so as to damage the ethos of the school).
Hire of school facilities – e.g. hall or sports facilities, other rooms, fields, vehicle(s), catering, reprographics etc. – including space for car boot sales and markets. A few schools have developed conference centres.
Promotion of activities – e.g. holiday schemes, adult classes, entertainments.
Competition entries – both competitions intended for schools and national grocery and similar competitions.

Sales of assets – i.e. unused land or equipment (strictly capital rather than revenue income).

Some of these activities can raise very large sums of money; some have a high educational content; some can be a gross distraction. To develop income generation effectively without damaging the school, a coherent policy and management system is needed.

Example Ysgol ap Iwan, an 11–18 comprehensive school in Abergele, Clwyd, North Wales, set up in 1987 as its trading arm a limited company 'Year High Ltd' with charitable status (motto: Service to People). By 1989–90, income had risen to £150 000 including gifts. There have also been important educational benefits through pupil involvement.

It is also possible to combine income generation with sponsorship.

Example Willeton Senior High School, Perth, Western Australia, has set up a 'Q Centre', originally jointly sponsored by UNISYS and the school itself. This computer and video-based learning centre, housed in new accommodation and with three staff (including a marketing manager) and a team of trainers, provides learning and training services to school students (no cost), community students (moderate cost) and business students (full cost). It currently offers about 50 courses, tutored or self paced, on site or on firm's premises, plus customised training. Any profits accrue to the school.

■ Promotion and marketing

School fund raising and volunteer-gaining activities need promotion; income generation needs marketing as well. By marketing is not meant its common loose usage of 'selling', but rather Peter Drucker's classic definition: *The aim of marketing is to know and understand the customer so well that the product or service fits him and sells itself.*

Two issues are particularly important. First, management. If the school wishes to market or fund-raise on any scale, who should do it? A number of schools have appointed a full-time marketing manager or fund-raiser, usually with car and salary but with a target of generated income. Possibly smaller schools could make part-time appointments. Schools normally, however, rely on a senior teacher, bursar or parent, or a committee, and this really does need thought and care if diffusion of energy is to be avoided.

The second issue is professionalism. Promotion requires a 'professional' use of communications, printed and audio-visual media, press, radio and TV, events and exhibitions, advertising. A practical approach to these can be found in Devlin and Knight's manual *Public Relations and Marketing for Schools.*

▮ A final caveat

Fund raising and income generation can open vast possibilities of additional funding. They also bring intangible benefits – pride in achievement, esprit de corps, more contact with the world outside, and opportunities for pupils to tackle 'real world tasks'. They can also seduce schools away from their real purpose. They can dissipate energies and gobble up time. They can also change the school into a less altruistic, more self-centred institution, and damage relationships with the local community or local businesses. So beware!

6 Maintaining the real level of funding

If we are to maintain the spending power of hard-won funds we must face up to the 'Ugly Three' – cuts, inflation and falling rolls – and to boring activities like stock-taking and insurance. This is much less exciting than fund raising and marketing, but equally important.

Cuts in funding

At first sight cuts in funding have a brutal clarity. A cut is a cut is a cut. But the situation is often far less simple.

The first problem is to establish what the cut actually is. A cut is only a real cut if it is a reduction in funding that is not justified by a reduction in the volume of activity (e.g. pupil numbers). This may not be straightforward to assess because of the effect of fixed/variable costs, and of technicalities in the case of formula-funding. It also requires stripping off any allowance, or under-allowance, for inflation, since inflation is best dealt with through a separate process.

However, if you have identified a real budget cut of x per cent (i.e. excluding changes for a different volume of activity or inflation), what does this mean in practice? A cut in funding affects different goods and services in different ways. The bulk of the school budget is spent on salaries, goods and services that are totally consumed within the financial year. For example:

Items fully consumed within the year	*Items not fully consumed within a year*
Salaries, with on-costs	In-service training*
Establishment expenses (e.g. interviews, travelling, advertisements)	Books and equipment
	Some stationery and materials
	Furniture and fittings
Stationery and materials	Premises maintenance
Reprographics	Grounds mainenance
Examination and other fees,	Vehicle maintenance

| *Items fully consumed* | *Items not fully consumed* |
| *within the year* | *within a year* |

licences, insurance and
other annual payments
Premises cleaning
Energy, water, telephone,
   postage and office expenses
Student transport

*Training is purchased within the year but not fully 'consumed' within it, i.e. it can be regarded as a form of human investment for subsequent years until the effect of the training wears off.

So, for items consumed within the year a cut only affects the *service provided for that year*. The next year, if the cut is restored, the service is fully restored (although the students of course may still suffer from the effects and there may be some other lingering disadvantages).

For the items on the right-hand side of the list the effect is more complicated. Here, even if the cut is reversed the next year, the shortfall will be carried forward until either it is offset by equivalent *additional* expenditure in a following year or it comes to the end of the life-cycle of that particular good or service.

Example Let us assume that the life-cycle of an average textbook is five years. If there is a 10 per cent cut in textbook expenditure in one year, this is equivalent to a 2 per cent reduction in the total book stock. This reduction in the book stock will carry forward until year 6, as table 1 shows.

Table 1 Effect of a 10 per cent cut for one year on stock of goods with a five-year life-cycle

Year	Number of textbooks purchased	Total stock of textbooks (5-year cycle)	Textbook stock as % of base year stock
Base year	100	500	(100)
1	90	490	98
2	100	490	98
3	100	490	98
4	100	490	98
5	100	490	98
6	100	500	100

Table 1 shows that the effect of a cut on an item that is not consumed within the year is softened, being spread over several years. On the other hand the effect of the cut lingers on, unless it is reversed, for the whole life-cycle of the item. This is particularly obvious for expenditures like building, grounds or vehicle maintenance which create a level of service. So any reduction in, say, redecoration of classrooms reduces the general level of decoration for the whole redecoration cycle.

If cuts continue in succeeding years, for items consumed within the year the effect is prolonged but not increased. But with the other items the effect builds up (see table 2).

Table 2   Effect of a 10 per cent cut for four years on stock of goods with a five-year life-cycle

Year	Number of textbooks purchased	Total stock of textbooks (5-year cycle)	Textbook stock as % of base year stock
Base year	100	500	(100)
1	90	490	98
2	90	480	96
3	90	470	94
4	90	460	92
5	100	460	92
6	100	470	94
7	100	480	96
8	100	490	98
9	100	500	100

The items listed above that are not fully consumed within the year will typically only comprise 10 per cent or so of a school's budget. But they are the very items on which cuts are most likely to fall. The 'within-the-year' items will seem more pressing; teacher staffing affects all aspects of the school and so schools tend to safeguard it; energy costs are not easily reduced, etc.; whereas a reduction in items consumed over several years can be seen just as a deferment. So cuts tend to be channelled into areas like building maintenance or books or equipment, with a gearing effect so that a small overall cut becomes a large cut in one or two areas.

■ Inflation

Inflation can be defined as the increase in price for a given 'basket' of salaries, goods and services of constant quality and quantity. It should not be confused with increased costs arising from improvements in quality, increases in volume, or changes in the items included in the basket. Underestimated inflation can be serious. It has a pernicious compound-interest effect.

■ Estimating inflation

The first task is to identify the increase in funding that has been made for inflation and compare this with the real rate of inflation. In most systems inflation is estimated in advance, often several months before the financial year. Usually the government/LEA/school board constructs a notional 'basket' for the salaries, goods and services schools need, and estimates the likely inflation for each item and its proportion of the basket. The problem is that it is difficult to project inflation to within 1 or 2 per cent, and it may be particularly difficult to predict the outcome of negotiations over teachers' pay, which is by far the largest item in the basket. A second problem is that if this inflation estimate does underestimate real inflation – and this may sometimes be a convenient means of smuggling cuts through unnoticed – there is usually no attempt to measure or redress this the following year.

To keep track of inflation, schools need an objective national equivalent of the Retail Price Index. But the RPI itself will not do. Kent Halstead (1983) developed a School Price Index (SPI) for US schools, comprising a basket of nine elements: professional salaries; other salaries; 'fringe benefits' (retirement, social security, health and other contributions); services and supplies (plant and office expenses etc.); supplies and materials (classroom, office, cleaning etc.); equipment replacement; books and audiovisual; utilities; and fixed costs such as insurance, rent and leases etc. He found that between 1975 and 1982 the SPI mirrored almost exactly the US CPI (Consumer Price Index), but only because the largest element, professional salaries, lagged and so compensated for a faster increase in other elements. From 1982 to 1986, however, the SPI rose faster. One problem seems to be that education is inevitably very labour-intensive and not amenable to increases in productivity comparable to other industries. So its costs rise more rapidly than goods and services in general.

There is no School Price Index in the UK at the present time. CIPFA publishes itemised unit costs in its annual *Education Statistics, Actuals,* but these reflect changes in provision as well as prices. The most suitable measure of school inflation appears to be the GDP (gross domestic product) deflator, a measure of domestically generated inflation produced by HM Treasury each autumn. Like the RPI it is a measure of price inflation, but it excludes mortgage interest and import prices. It is also re-indexed each year and projected for future years. Current figures are as follows:

GDP deflator (November 1992)

Year	Deflator	% increase from previous year
1987/88	75.763	5.49
1988/89	81.279	7.28
1989/90	86.622	6.57
1990/91	93.537	7.98
1991/92	100.000	6.91
1992/93	104.250	4.25
1993/94	107.117	2.75
1994/95	110.598	3.25
1995/96	113.640	2.75

Examples of use of the deflator
Calculating inflation between different years
Q What will be the cumulative inflation between 1988/89 and 1992/93?
A Inflation is estimated to be:

$$\left(\frac{104.250}{81.279} \times 100\right) - 100 = 28.26 \text{ per cent}$$

Inflating figures
Q How much would £1000 in 1989/90 be in 1992/93 prices?
A $£1000 \times \dfrac{104.250}{86.622} = £1203.50$ in 1992/93 prices

Deflating figures
Q How much would £1000 in 1990/91 be in 1988/89 prices?
A $£1000 \times \dfrac{81.279}{93.537} = £868.95$ in 1988/89 prices

The current GDP deflator (with a background note from which the foregoing examples are adapted) is available from HM Treasury (see Addresses).

The effect of underestimated inflation

If inflation is underestimated, what happens to a school's finances? Table 3 demonstrates the effect of a 1 per cent underestimate when the real rate of inflation is 5 per cent.

Table 3 Effect of a 1 per cent shortfall between a school's budget increase and costs increase over five years

1 Year	2 School costs index (5% increase p.a.)	3 Actual budget (4% increase p.a.)	4 Annual shortfall (index points)	5 Annual shortfall (as % of current budget)	6 Cumulative shortfall (index points)	7 Cumulative shortfall (as % of current budget)
Base Year	100.0	100.0	–	–	–	–
1	105.0	104.0	1.0	1.0	1.0	1.0
2	110.3	108.2	2.1	1.9	3.1	2.9
3	115.8	112.5	3.3	2.9	6.4	5.7
4	121.6	117.0	4.6	3.9	11.0	9.4
5	127.6	121.7	5.9	4.9	16.9	13.9

Column 2 shows the rise of the 'school costs index' at 5 per cent inflation, and column 3 the increase in the budget at 4 per cent. Column 4
shows the shortfall in index points (i.e. in real terms) each year, and column 6 the cumulative shortfall. Column 5 shows each year's shortfall as
a percentage of the school's current budget; i.e. the budget increase
which would be needed in any year to offset the fall in the real value of
the budget at that point. Column 7 shows the cumulative shortfall. Of
course if there were a 2 per cent shortfall the figures in columns 4–7
would be approximately double. Underestimating inflation is serious
because:

1 It creates a cut in funding in real terms, intended or unintended. So
   it has the same effect as other cuts discussed earlier.

2 It becomes more difficult to correct the longer it continues. In the
   example in table 3, a mere 1 per cent budget increase will correct
   the shortfall in year 1 (column 5) but an addition of nearly 5 per
   cent is needed by year 5.

3 It has a build-up effect on goods and services not consumed within
   the year (similar to that described in tables 1 and 2). So full restoration of the budget also requires some allowance for this, in the form
   of a one-off supplement.

4 Much of the loss can never be restored – items normally consumed
   within the year which are not purchased because of the shortfall.
   This total cumulative loss of resources is shown in columns 6 and 7.

▉ Assessing underestimated inflation for your school

A simple formula can be used (the author is indebted to ideas from
Rosalind Levačić of the Open University for this).

Let B = Percentage budget increase between two years (e.g. this could
be an annual increase from 1990/91 to 1992/92, or an increase
over some years, say from 1989/90 to 1992/93). If the numbers
of students has altered you will need to adjust the budget
increase for this factor.

Let R = Cumulative rate of inflation between the years in question
(this can be calculated from the first example for the GDP
deflator above).

Then the real value of the budget in the later year, expressed as a percentage of that in the former year, will be $100 \times (100 + B) \div (100 + R)$.

Example A school with constant student numbers receives budget funding for 1992/93 which is 20 per cent greater than that for 1988/89. So *B* (percentage budget increase) = 20. For these years *R* (cumulative inflation) was 28.26 per cent (using the GDP deflator example above). So the real value of the budget in 1992/93 is:

$$\frac{120}{128.26} \times 100$$

which is 93.6 per cent of the 1988/89 budget in real terms.

Falling rolls and operating below capacity

Falling rolls in theory

In practice, school costs do not behave as predictably as this section suggests, any more than the economy behaves as economists predict. But understanding the principles is crucial for good financial management. At first sight they may appear a little difficult, but please persevere!

The extent of fixed costs

If all school costs were fully variable, altering in proportion to any change in the number of pupils, then total costs would rise or fall exactly in line with changes in pupil numbers and unit costs would remain constant. But of course they aren't. Some costs are totally fixed and many more have a fixed element.

Example For water charges, the cost for urinals will be fixed (unless some kind of sensor is fitted); but for WCs and water taps largely variable, relating to the number of users, assuming the supply is metered. Any standing charges will be a fixed cost, as will most water costs for a swimming pool.

Most items in a school budget will have some fixed element; few are totally variable. We can aggregate these fixed elements to give an overall figure for fixed costs as a percentage of the school's total costs. This figure will vary between schools, depending on type, size, situation etc. It will also vary over time – costs that are fixed for one or two years may become variable in the third.

These fixed elements are estimated in table 4, for a typical school (if there is one) in England and Wales, with a short time horizon; i.e. the financial year in which numbers fall and the following year. Where there is a marked difference between primary and secondary schools an average figure is shown. The author has discussed these estimates with a small number of schools, and they are based on a long experience of school finance in the UK and worldwide. Nevertheless you will disagree with some of these figures in relation to your school.

In table 4, estimates of the fixed element in each item are entered in column 2. Column 3 shows the percentage which each item takes in a 'typical' school. Column 4 multiplies the percentages in columns 2 and 3 to show the fixed element for each item as a percentage of the total budget.

Example If in a typical school gas and oil is considered to be 80 per cent fixed and takes up 1 per cent of the budget, then gas/oil will create a fixed element in the budget of:

$$\frac{80}{100} \times 1 = 0.8 \text{ per cent}$$

Table 4   Fixed cost elements in a typical school budget

1	2	3	4
	Fixed cost % for each item	% of budget	Fixed element as % of budget
SALARIES			
Headteachers' salary. If rolls fall, remains fixed. If rolls rise, can increase but after a considerable lag. [The percentage in col. 3 will vary considerably with size of school. In a large secondary, only *c*.2% – in a small primary 12% or more. A headteacher with responsibility for a class should be treated like the deputyr head below.]	100	6.3	6.3
Deputy headteacher's allowance(s); i.e. salary less main-scale salary for person's years of teaching. As for head teacher	90	1.7	1.5
Incentive or responsibility allowances. Initially fixed, but will rise or fall after some lag with pupil numbers	70	4.0	2.8
'Administrative time'; i.e. non-contact time for adminis-trative purposes, as opposed to classroom teachers' preparation etc. Mainly in secondary schools. It will rise or fall with numbers, but with some lag.	50	1.6	0.8
Basic salaries (less administration time, above). The largest single element in the budget. In theory teacher numbers should vary with student numbers. In practice, with rising rolls there is often some lag in new appointments, and these also tend to be on lower than average salaries reducing the variable cost effect. With falling rolls there can be a smilar effect. The situation will vary between schools: a conservative estimate would be a 5 per cent fixed cost element (e.g. if student numbers rise by 20 per cent, teacher salaries would rise by 19 per cent). This could be more for very small schools.	5	56.4	2.8

Supply (relief) staff. Should be proportional to the number of teachers so will reflect changes in this.	5	2.0	0.1
Support staff salaries; e.g. clerical, technicians, aides. These will respond to a rise or fall in numbers, but only after a considerable lag.	70	7.0	4.9
Other non-teaching staff salaries; e.g. lunch-time or other supervisors. Closely related to student numbers.	20	1.0	0.2
In-service training and professional development. Should reflect the number of teaching staff and so follows this.	5	1.0	0.05

PREMISES

Gas, oil. Largely fixed, but some reduction if less rooms are used, doors opened less.	80	1.0	0.8
Electricity. Similar, but depending on tariff. Electric heating/air conditioning similar to gas/oil; power for equipment and lights more related to student numbers.	60	0.8	0.5
Water. Largely reflecting number of users, but some fixed element and depending on structure of charges	20	0.4	0.08
Rates and taxes. In UK, fully paid by budget, so acts as if variable. In other countries position varies.	0	3.0	–
Building repairs and maintenance. Largely fixed, student numbers have some effect on wear and tear.	90	1.2	1.08
Cleaning services. Fully fixed, unless the actual area to be cleaned or frequency of cleaning alters.	95	3.2	3.04
Grounds maintenance. Similar, with little likelihood of change from student numbers.	100	1.0	1.0

SUPPLIES AND SERVICES

Books, classroom stationery, equipment, materials These should rise or fall with pupil numbers, but there will be some fixed element, particularly for equipment.	20	3.7	0.74
Postage. Letters related to the number of teachers and pupils will alter, but 'central' postage will remain largely fixed.	50	0.1	0.05
Telephone. Similar. Possibly a smaller fixed percentage.	40	0.2	0.08
Advertising. Will change with the number of teaching and non-teaching staff. Greater with rising enrolment.	10	0.1	0.01
Furniture, fittings, 'central' equipment. Largely fixed. Student numbers have some effect on wear.	90	0.7	0.63
'Central' stationery, printing. Part fixed, part variable.	50	0.1	0.05
Examination fees (secondary only). Exactly related to student numbers, but a lag until a new size cohort moves up to the examination year. So fully fixed for several years.	100	1.2	1.2
Computer administration. Largely fixed.	80	0.1	0.08
Insurance. Largely related to number of students.	10	0.1	0.01

OTHER SERVICES

External services purchased; from private supplier or a privatised service (e.g. maintenance, school library service, advisory services). Depends on charge structure, probably part-fixed.	30	0.1	0.03
Catering. Largely dependent on number of students, but some fixed costs.	20	0.8	0.16
Travelling and transport allowances. Related to number of staff.	5	0.1	–
School vehicles. Heavy 'fixed' cost element.	80	0.1	0.08
Contingency. Can be varied with student numbers	0	1.0	–
Total fixed costs as percentage of total school costs		100.0	29.07

Table 4 suggests that 29 per cent of a typical school's budget is fixed. Of course no school is typical, and certainly not yours. However, this figure is the aggregation of 30 different calculations, of which only five are really sensitive (the headteacher's salary, incentive allowances, basic teacher salaries, support staff salaries and cleaning services). So even if you feel the figures should be adjusted, a total of something above 20 per cent will probably emerge. You can work out your own school's version of table 4 quite easily, by 'guestimating' column 2 and calculating column 3 from your budget.

The 'fixed cost excess'

The fixed costs discussed in the previous section create a 'fixed cost excess' (FCE), the crucial concept for understanding the behaviour of school costs with changing enrolment. The FCE is shown in a simple theoretical model in figure 18.

In figure 18 a school's student numbers are shown as falling from maximum capacity to zero over time, along the horizontal axis $N_m N_0$. The school's costs are measured against the vertical axis as a percentage of the total costs *when the school is at full capacity*. It is assumed that 20 per cent of total annual costs are fixed when the school is at full capacity (a conservative estimate) shown by the line $F_m F_0$. It is also assumed that variable costs fall in proportion to student numbers. As student numbers shrink, the school's total costs (ie. fixed plus variable) fall along the line $C_m F_0$.

The FCE, the deadly speckled band on the graph, is created by the effect of fixed costs. If there were no fixed costs and all costs were variable, total costs would fall along the line $C_m N_0$ (we can call these 'standard costs', see figure 18). But fixed costs only allow them to fall along the line $C_m F_0$. So the speckled area represents the 'fixed cost excess'.

It is important to understand what the FCE means:

1 The FCE is the additional cost incurred to maintain the same level of provision when a school's numbers fall below capacity. It is a mathematical certainty once some of a school's costs are fixed, and *provided the level of provision remains constant*. It cannot be avoided (although this leaves open the questions of who pays for it, or whether it can be mitigated, discussed later in this chapter).

2 The FCE can be expressed as a percentage of total costs *at full capacity*, as in shown by 4%, 8%, 12%, 16% in figure 18, and this makes calculations easier. It could alternatively be expressed as a percentage or proportion of total costs at a point below full capacity; or of unit costs; or as a monetary sum for a given budget and level of enrolment.

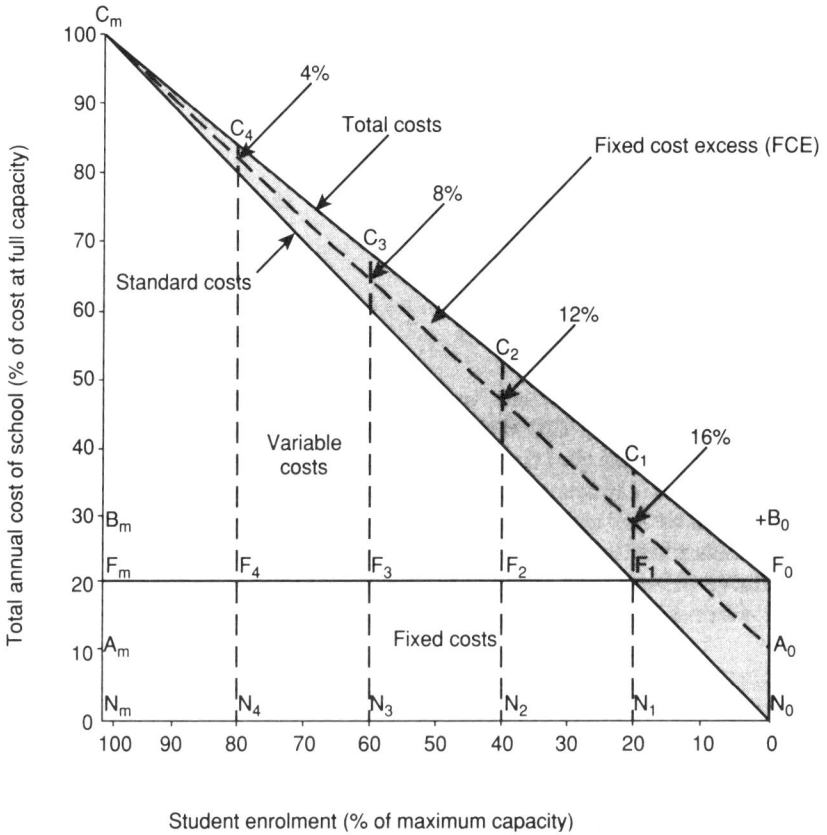

Figure 18   The behaviour of variable, fixed and total costs when school enrolment falls below capacity

3 The size of the FCE is determined by two factors:
  • The reduction in student enrolment. The graph shows that the FCE increases arithmetically as enrolment falls.
  • The extent of fixed costs. If fixed costs were 10 per cent, below A_mA_0, then the FCE would be between C_mN_0 and C_mA_0; i.e. only 50 per cent of the speckled FCE for 20 per cent fixed costs. If fixed costs were 30 per cent, below B_mB_0, the FCE would extend to the line C_mB_0; i.e., a 50 per cent increase in the speckled area.

The effects of the 'fixed cost excess'

The model in figure 18 is more complex than at first appears and deserves careful study. The main effects of the FCE are as follows:

1 *Total costs fall more slowly than they would if they were totally proportional to student numbers;* i.e. $C_m F_0$ compared with $C_m N_0$ (as discussed above).

2 *Unit costs rise as numbers fall.* For illustration, if we assume a school has 1000 students at full capacity N_m, each costing £1000, with 20 per cent fixed costs, then unit costs will alter as rolls fall:

Students	Total costs (£)	Unit cost per pupil (£)
1000(N_m)	1 000 000(C_m)	1000
800(N_4)	840 000(C_4)	1050 (5% increase on £1000)
600(N_3)	680 000(C_3)	1133 (13% increase on £1000)
400(N_2)	520 000(C_2)	1300 (30% increase on £1000)
200(N_1)	360 000(C_1)	1800 (80% increase on £1000)
100	280 000	2800 (180% increase on £1000)

(If there were no fixed costs, unit costs would be derived from the line $C_m N_0$ and would be £1000 throughout. We could call these 'standard unit costs'.) Notice that the rise in unit costs accelerates as numbers fall further below capacity. By the time there is only one student in the school, his or her unit cost will be astronomical; i.e. the school's total fixed costs plus the average variable cost for one student. For the example above this student's unit cost will be £200 800 – an increase of 19 980 per cent on £1000! This exponential rise in unit costs is shown in table 5.

Table 5   Percentage increase in unit costs when the school roll falls below capacity

Fixed/variable percentage of costs at full capacity		Student enrolment (% of maximum capacity)									
	(100)	90	80	70	60	50	40	30	20	10
Fixed	Variable										
30%	70%	(0)	3.3	7.5	12.9	20.0	30.0	45.0	70.0	120.0	270.0
20%	80%	(0)	2.2	5.0	8.6	13.3	20.0	30.0	46.7	80.0	180.0
10%	90%	(0)	1.1	2.5	4.3	6.7	10.0	15.0	23.3	40.0	90.0

Table 5 incorporates the two FCE variables mentioned earlier which affect unit costs: the proportion of fixed/variable costs and the degree to which the school is operating below capacity. Their interaction can be calculated using a formula (see formula 3 in Appendix 1 at the end of the chapter) from which table 5 is constructed.

In table 5, the exponential increase in unit costs can clearly be seen, as the school roll falls further below capacity; i.e. moving from left to right. Also the additional rise in unit costs if the element of fixed costs increases can be seen from the differences between the 10 and 20 per cent lines, or 20 and 30 per cent; i.e. moving from the bottom row upwards.

The middle line of figures from table 5 has been used to construct the graph in figure 19. This highlights the difficulties of schools that are well under capacity. It demonstrates vividly how, when numbers fall (i.e. moving from left to right on the graph), unit costs rise at first slowly but then ever more steeply.

3 *Variable costs are squeezed as enrolment falls.* This can be seen by studying the situation in figure 18 when enrolment is 100 per cent of capacity (N_m), 80 per cent (N_4), 60 per cent (N_3), 40 per cent (N_2) and 20 per cent (N_1).

The proportion of variable costs (C_4F_4, C_3F_3, C_2F_2, C_1F_1) to fixed costs falls as student numbers fall, as the following ratios show:

N_m (100% capacity)   variable 80 : fixed 20
N_4 (80% capacity)   variable 64 : fixed 20
N_3 (60% capacity)   variable 48 : fixed 20
N_2 (40% capacity)   variable 32 : fixed 20
N_1 (20% capacity)   variable 16 : fixed 20

So fixed costs drag more heavily as student numbers fall, putting pressure on the funds available for variable costs.

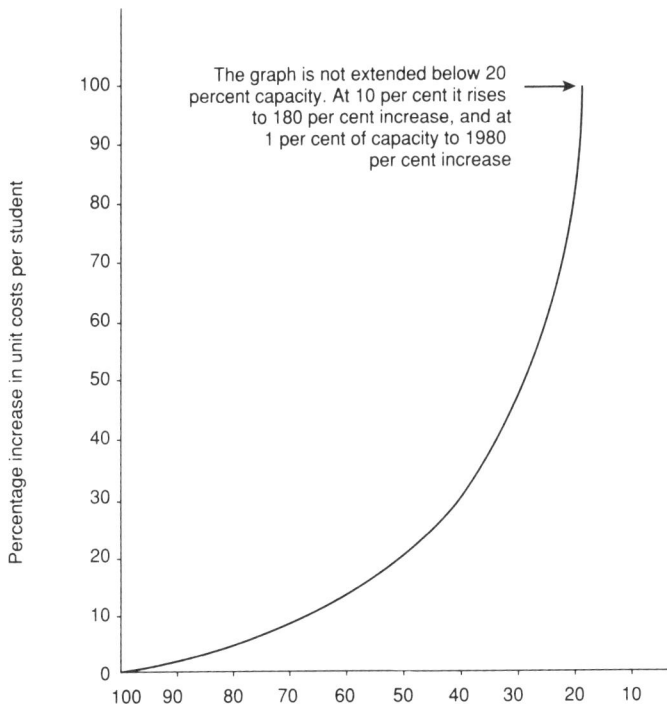

Figure 19   Percentage increase in unit costs when school enrolment falls below capacity

4 *When student numbers rise, the force of fixed costs works in the opposite direction.* For example, if the 'time direction' of figure 18 is reversed, as numbers climb from N_0 towards full capacity at N_m:

- Total costs rise more slowly than they would if they were proportional to student numbers.
- Unit costs fall.
- There is a greater proportion of the budget available for variable costs.

The same is true of figure 19. If the 'time direction' is reversed, as numbers rise (from right to left) unit costs fall fast at first, but then more and more slowly. So if a school gains extra students, each additional student is slightly less 'valuable' in reducing unit costs until the last student makes virtually no difference.

To sum up, the effect of the fixed cost excess on costs is as follows:

If numbers rise	If numbers fall
Total costs rise more slowly than they would if they were proportional to numbers	Total costs fall more slowly than they would if they were proportional numbers
Unit costs per pupil fall, but at a decreasing rate	Unit costs per pupil rise,at an increasing rate
Fixed costs decrease and variable costs increase as a proportion of total costs	Fixed costs increase and variable costs decrease as a proportion of total costs, and so variable costs are squeezed

■ Costs of changing enrolment in practice

The effect of marginal costs and time horizons

In practice costs do not change as smoothly as the graph in figure 18 suggests. For example, suppose there is one student more (or less). This may make virtually no difference to total school costs. Two? Three? Four? . . . But at some point – say the twenty-fifth student – a change in organisation is triggered and an extra teacher is employed (or shed). There may even be a point at which fixed costs change; e.g. when buildings are extended (or mothballed) or an extra deputy headteacher appointed (or not replaced). So it is these *marginal costs* – the extra cost, or saving, of one student more or less – which are so important for the school budget. Schools need to be more sensitive to these – they sometimes hold the simplistic belief that each additional student brings additional funding. Sometimes one particular student, like the proverbial straw on a camel's back, will trigger substantial extra costs, far exceeding any additional funding he or she brings. Also, as explained earlier, the value of each marginal student will be greater the lower enrolment falls below capacity.

Also important is the time horizon. It may be possible to convert a fixed to a variable cost in four years but not in two. This may enable the school to make savings with falling enrolment which were not previously possible. (The theory of this is interesting. By reduction of fixed costs at this point, the FCE is reduced and so its effects on total school costs.)

So costs rise or fall in an uneven and even stepped line, as in figure 20.

Estimating the financial cost, or gain, from the 'fixed cost excess'

At a general level the concept of the FCE developed in this chapter should give you a feel for how your costs change as enrolment changes. It is helpful to visualise the graph in figure 18 as a kind of sliding scale, where a vertical column representing the total cost of the school moves along the horizontal axis, reflecting falling student enrolment. As it

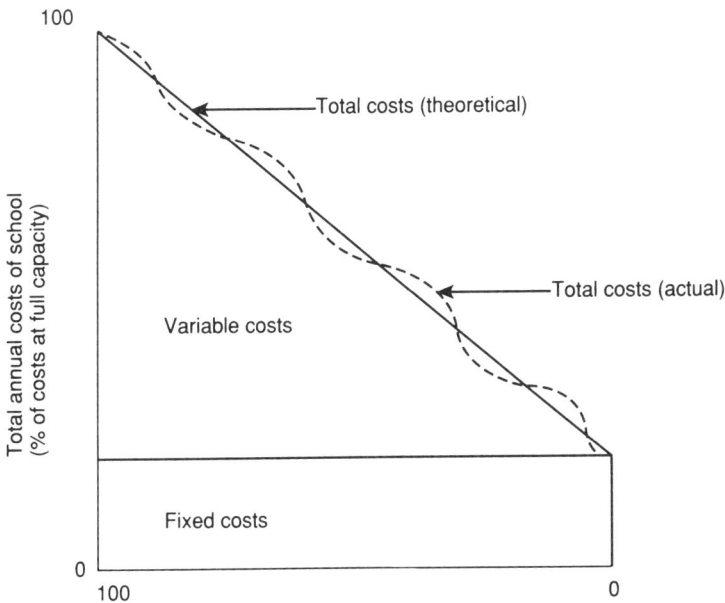

Figure 20   A model for the behaviour of school costs in practice when enrolment falls below capacity

moves, the length of the column shrinks, the FCE portion of the column grows, unit costs rise, and variable costs are squeezed (or the opposite if enrolment rises). If you have this model in your mind you should have a feel for the financial pressures your school may experience.

It is possible to produce firm theoretical figures for the additional, or reduced, costs created by changes in the FCE. The calculations are not difficult, but they need a little time and are set out in Appendix 2 at the end of the chapter. Just two warnings. First, these will be theoretical figures: the actual figures may be different as suggested above because of the uneven way in which costs rise or fall. Second, these are figures for costs which *someone* has to pay for if the level of provision is to be maintained (or can save, if enrolment rises). But your school probably will not lose – or gain – all of that figure.

As your school roll falls or rises your budget will alter according to your funding formula and this will include some factors which are not student-related. Some may be constant elements such as an allowance for small schools or for large or costly premises. So some of the FCE costs will be paid (or saved) by your LEA/state/school board. You can calculate your school's share from Appendix 3. (If your LEA paid for 50 per cent of the FCE this would be represented in figure 18 by the line C_mA_0, with the LEA paying the FCE on one side of the line and the school on the other.) If the school is funded by a formula which is fully student-related, funding per student would be constant. For such a school, operating substantially below capacity would be very difficult. Of course schools depending entirely on fees have to pay all the FCE.

The alternative approach is the pragmatic one of estimating the marginal costs likely to be created by x fewer, or more, students. You could use table 4 as a checklist to assess the financial implications for each item of expenditure. Look out for the triggering of shedding or appointing new staff or using less or more plant – and don't underestimate the incidentals!

Mitigating the financial effects of falling enrolment

While extra FCE costs may be inevitable, extra expenditure may not be. Whoever faces this additional cost – the LEA/school district etc. or the school, or both together – has four choices:

1 Make savings by increased internal efficiency and so reduce total costs.

2 Reduce the level of provision by cutting items of lower priority and so reduce total costs (but remember all savings have to come from your variable costs).

3 Raise additional funds so that you can increase expenditure (i.e. accept the higher unit costs created by the FCE).

4 Enrol more students (but watch the marginal costs).

In practice a combination of two or more of these is likely to be adopted.

The financial pressure of the fixed cost excess is permanent and inherent for any below-capacity school. At 80 per cent capacity the additional cost may be still quite small – and may indeed be worth paying for the luxury of free space and reduced pressure. Below 80 per cent, life becomes increasingly uncomfortable.

■ Maintaining assets

The remainder of this chapter identifies some additional tasks. To avoid overload small schools could seek to have some or even all of these carried out by governors or parents.

■ Depreciation and capital replacement

Depreciation is the economic concept of the decline in value of an asset over time. For example, furniture bought in year 1 may last for ten years, and so may be thought of as being *consumed* over that period until it needs replacement. Depreciation requires an accounting convention for *writing off* the book value of capital assets on a balance sheet, often on a proportional percentage basis. However, most state schools do not yet produce balance sheets (an exception is the Charter schools in New Zealand, which account annually for their assets with allowance for depreciation), and schools still have to pay totally for an item purchased in year 1 (unless they lease it or borrow for it). So the accountant's approach to depreciation may have little appeal at present, although it can be argued that it highlights the true operating cost of the school and is a useful managerial tool. It seems likely to be used more widely in the future.

Even if depreciation is recorded on a balance sheet, this does not provide the funds needed for replacement. In the past, as major capital items wore out in state schools cries of anguish would soften the hearts of the LEA or school board. This happy situation is unlikely to continue. First, as LEAs etc. delegate extensively to schools there is little left in central coffers. Second, in some systems many state schools are becoming quasi-independent (e.g. the City Technology Colleges and grant-maintained schools in the UK and the Charter schools in New Zealand) and so thrown back on to their own resources. Third, schools are becoming much more capital intensive. Computers are a good example: many UK schools stocked up in the 1980s with BBC computers, and now find themselves with a heavy replacement bill.

Science Department: Local Comprehensive School ....

Item	(a) Quantity	(b) Cost	(c) Total Cost (a×b)	(d) Life from New (years)	(e) Date Bought	(f) Life Left (years)	(g) Mean Life Left ($\Sigma f/a$)	(h) Annual Replac. Cost (c/g)
Television	1	£250	£250	8	1985	4	4	£62.50
Video	1	£265	£265	10	1986	7	7	£37.85
BBC Computer	1	£350	£350	10	1986	7	7	£50.00
OHP	2	£200	£400	15	1979	5	5	£80.00
Microscopes	15	£300	£4500	20	1975	6	6	£750.00
Microscopes (advanced)	10	£350	£3500	50	1960	31	31	£112.90
Top pan balance	3	£1000	£3000	10	1980	1	2	£1500.00
					1981	2		
					1982	3		
Water baths	4	£420	£1680	15	1975	1	$\frac{37}{4}$ =9.25	£181.62
					1984	8		
					1988	28		
Rabbit skeleton	1	£20	£220	50	1949(?)	0	0	£220.00
Oscilloscopes	5	£400	£2000	15	1980 × 3	3 × 6	$\frac{34}{5}$ = 6.8	£294.00
					1982 × 2	8 × 2		
Centrifuge	3	£200	£600	20	1980	11	= 6.3	£95.00
					1975	6		
					1971	2		
Ripple tanks	14	£130	£1820	20	1980	11	11	£165.45

TOTAL ANNUAL REPLACEMENT COST   £3,549.32
Note: columns b and c should be calculated at current replacement prices

Figure 21   Assessing annual replacement costs of science equipment (Source: Enfield LEA)

First then, schools need to estimate the extent of likely capital replacement. Some study of the capital assets for which the school is responsible will be necessary, perhaps using the capital assets inventory discussed later. These are likely to include information technology, office and audio-visual equipment; reprographics, science, technology, music, art and physical education equipment; furniture, furnishings and fittings such as blackout; school vehicle(s) and other major items. Some schools will also be responsible for the fabric of their buildings. The problem is worse in secondary schools, because they are more capital intensive. Also, in primary schools the sums involved may be more within the scope of PTA or other fund raising.

One LEA in England has produced a systematic pro forma for assessing annual replacement costs of science equipment (see figure 21). This is a rational approach which could be applied to some or all of a school's capital assets. It identifies the scale of the problem and the annual replacement costs at current prices. There is a risk that it could magnify the problem if unrealistically short 'lives' are set, though in this example they seem quite realistic.

Identifying replacement needs is one thing; funding them is another. There are several possible strategies:

1 Include a sum in the budget for the total capital replacement needed during the year. This is fine if the budget is buoyant, but in difficult years capital replacement may be starved. Also some expensive replacement items (e.g. a computer suite) may be too expensive for one year's budget.

2 Create a capital replacement fund, fed with annual sums corresponding to the average annual replacement cost (as in column (h) of figure 21). This averages out demands, and so makes them more manageable. But it is only feasible if the school can invest the fund and so gain interest to offset inflation and preserve the fund's real value. There is also the risk that such a fund could be raided when finance is short.

3 Just living from year to year, coping with each demand on an *ad hoc* basis. This is what many schools do currently. It has the merits of involving less work and setting capital replacement against other priorities. But it can lapse into Micawberism, hoping something will turn up.

An illuminating illustration of the problem has arisen recently in the UK, where the City Technology Colleges argued strongly with the DES (now DFE) that provision for depreciation of buildings and equipment should be included in their annual grant. This argument was pressed by the CTC's commercial sponsors who were already accustomed to allowance for depreciation and to the practice of independent schools who typically allow for depreciation either on a full cost basis within their accounts or by an adjustment to fee levels. But it cut no ice with the DFE, who have been accustomed to financing immediate expenditure demands and not capital replacement. Grant maintained schools have raised a similar argument, equally in vain.

The author's own view is that, because schools are becoming much more capital intensive, they do need a system for capital replacement. Internal budget holders should be made responsible for financing minor or middle-size items from their own funds (e.g. a science department might finance most or all of the items in figure 21), but this does imply that their budget should include a realistic element for this. Making internal budget holders responsible for most capital replacement converts 'their money' into 'my money' – always a healthy process. But this still leaves central items like furniture, and major items too large for an internal budget holder. For these a dedicated 'capital replacement fund' is a good idea, but only if it earns interest. If this is not possible, an annual budgeted sum as in the first strategy above will be necessary if 'management by astonishment' is to be avoided.

Stock management and control

Inventory control is tedious but valuable. Two kinds of inventory are needed: for large and durable capital items, and minor items that are not really capital but which will last for several years and need controlling. The capital-assets inventory is becoming increasingly important with the spread of electronic equipment (with a tendency to go walkabout) and with the need for a capital replacement programme discussed earlier. The minor-items inventory is equally valuable – it can often save 5 to 10 per cent of a school's expenditure on books and minor items.

A minor-items inventory should require the internal budget holder to list all items that are not consumed within the year – books, minor equipment, software, video/audio and other audio-visual aids, etc. Once a year new acquisitions should be entered, and a check carried out to assess the number of each item in stock. Discrepancies with the previous year's total should be shown as either lost or written off (e.g. discarded because worn out or obsolete).

Stock-taking is time-consuming and unpopular, so a senior member of staff needs to be responsible for receiving inventories annually, each with a summary sheet showing numbers of lost or written-off items. Primary school classrooms and specialist secondary rooms really need one inventory each. Efficient stock-taking has many merits:

1 It identifies the scale of losses.

2 It encourages budget holders to track down lost or misplaced items.

3 It leads budget holders experiencing losses to be more vigilant in future.

4 It flags up items not being used, and encourages transfer to others or resale.

Risk management

'Risk' can be defined as the possibility of loss of assets, whether goods, premises, or money – and including the loss of funds by a successful claim against the school. The aim of risk management is to minimise risk to an acceptable level at an acceptable cost.

The first need is systematically to identify risk, both for severity (i.e. scale) and probability. The former is much more important. A large but improbable risk is much more serious than a small but likely one – and perceived risk is not the same as actual risk. So an inventory of physical assets will be needed, perhaps using the capital-assets inventory discussed above, as well as an assessment of claims for which the school might be liable. Then you need to decide the amount beyond which you cannot afford to suffer loss.

There are then four strategies open to you:

Avoid the risk, by removing the item or stopping the activity. This is seldom feasible or desirable, but may sometimes occur. For example, a school that is frequently burgled may decide not to use certain equipment.

Reduce the risk, by improving security systems and anti-vandalism measures, fire precautions, removal of hazards, staff training and awareness. This could include a security audit or a health and safety review.

Retain the risk, in whole or part. In other words the school agrees to insure itself, or to accept some risk by allowing deductibles (the first part of any loss). Normally risk is retained if:

● the school cannot avoid or transfer the risk;
● the probability of risk is so high that insurance costs are prohibitive;
● losses are frequent but small.

Transfer the risk, normally to an insurance company, but possibly by sub-contracting the activity to another organisation who will take up the risk involved. The golden rule for insurance is always . . . buy on cover, not on price.

Some management issues arise. Who is responsible for risk management (i.e. who manages it)? Ideally this should be a senior member of staff, responsible also perhaps for health and safety, or buildings, or finance. In small primary schools, of course, it will often be the long-suffering headteacher. Whom will he or she report to, and when? Ideally there should be a brief annual report summarising and evaluating existing provision, listing losses during the year, identifying new risks and any changes needed. It is particularly important that risks on new activities or equipment are foreseen. Finally, what kind of insurance? This may also involve collective insurance or security with other schools, because in risk management the 'law of large numbers' is important; i.e. spreading risks across more than one school.

■ Appendix 1: Explanation of formulae

Formula 1 – To calculate the FCE for a given level of enrolment, as a percentage of total costs at full capacity (table 6, p. 122)

By inspection of figure 18, the FCE percentage is a proportion of the (20 per cent in this case) fixed-costs percentage. This proportion is determined by the percentage fall in enrolment. For example, with a 20 per cent fall in enrolment (from 100 to 80 per cent, to N_4), the FCE is 20 per cent of the (20 per cent) fixed-cost percentage; i.e. 4 per cent. Similarly, with a 40 per cent fall to N_3 the FCE is 40 per cent of 20 per cent; i.e. 8 per cent. So the FCE percentage is:

$$\frac{\text{Fall in enrolment (\%) from maximum}}{100} \times \text{fixed costs (\%)}$$

$$= \frac{100 - \text{current enrolment (\%)}}{100} \times \text{fixed costs (\%)}$$

Example FCE percentage for 70 per cent enrolment, with 25 per cent fixed costs:

$$\frac{100 - 70}{100} \times 25 = \frac{30}{100} \times 25 = 7.5.$$

Formula 2 – To calculate the cost incurred or saved from changes in rolls

By inspection of figure 18, at any level of enrolment total costs (C_4, C_3, etc.) can be expressed in 'units' of the percentage equivalent of total costs at full capacity; i.e. the vertical axis. These total costs comprise two elements:

1 The speckled FCE element, already expressed in units (and stated for all levels of enrolment in table 6, page 122).

2 The remaining portion of total costs which we can call 'standard costs', i.e. the costs that would occur if all costs were variable and total costs fell along the line $C_m N_0$. Since this line is directly proportional to enrolment, any point on it at a given enrolment percentage will be exactly equivalent to the same percentage of total costs at full capacity; i.e. units on the vertical axis.

Example A school at 60 per cent enrolment will have total costs comprising (a) an FCE of 8 units, and (b) standard costs of 60 units. So this school's current costs are equivalent to 68 units (i.e. 68 percent of total costs at full capacity).

Therefore the value of the extra costs created by the FCE will be the FCE's proportion of total current costs, i.e.:

$$\frac{\text{Current FCE}}{\text{Current FCE} + \text{standard costs}} \times \text{current costs}$$

i.e.
$$\frac{\text{Current FCE (\%)}}{\text{Current FCE (\%)} + \text{current enrolment (\%)}} \times \text{current costs}$$

This can be developed into formula 2 to assess the cost of any *change* in enrolment:

$$\frac{\text{Difference of original and changed FCE (\%)}}{\text{Original FCE (\%)} + \text{current enrolment (\%)}} \times \text{current costs}$$

For an example, see page 124.

Formula 3 – To calculate the percentage increase in unit costs when enrolment falls below capacity (table 5)

$$\text{Unit costs} = \frac{\text{total costs}}{\text{student enrolment}}$$

If all costs were variable, total costs would fall as standard costs along the line $C_m N_0$ exactly in proportion to the fall in enrolment, and unit costs would be constant. However, costs fall along the line $C_m F_0$ because of the FCE. So for a given enrolment the increase in total costs, and so in the unit costs derived from them, will be exactly the proportion of the FCE (in units) in relation to standard costs (also in units, as discussed for formula 2 above). So formula 3 is therefore as follows:

Percentage increase in unit costs for a given level of enrolment
$$= \frac{\text{FCE (\%*) for that level of enrolment}}{\text{standard cost(*) for this enrolment (\%)}}$$

(*) expressed in percentage 'units' of total costs at full capacity.

Example A school at 60 per cent enrolment will find its unit costs increased by:

$$\frac{8 \text{ (FCE\%)}}{60 \text{ (standard costs for 60\% enrolment)}}$$

$$= 13.3\%$$

■ Appendix 2: Calculating changes in costs created by changes in enrolment

The key factor in these calculations is the fixed cost excess (FCE).

Calculating the FCE percentage

The FCE for a given level of enrolment is provided in table 6, derived from formula 1. For example, a school with 70 per cent enrolment and 20 per cent fixed costs has an FCE of 6.0 per cent. Remember always that the FCE is expressed as a percentage of *total costs at full capacity*. This makes other calculations possible.

Table 6 Fixed cost excess (FCE) for a given level of student enrolment expressed as percentage of total budget at full capacity

Student enrolment as % of school capacity	Fixed costs as % of total school costs at full student enrolment					
	5	10	15	20	25	30
100	nil	nil	nil	nil	nil	nil
95	0.25	0.5	0.75	1.0	1.25	1.5
90	0.50	1.0	1.50	2.0	2.50	3.0
85	0.75	1.5	2.25	3.0	3.75	4.5
80	1.00	2.0	3.00	4.0	5.00	6.0
75	1.25	2.5	3.75	5.0	6.25	7.5
70	1.50	3.0	4.50	6.0	7.5	9.0
65	1.75	3.5	5.25	7.0	8.75	10.5

Student enrolment as % of school capacity	Fixed costs as % of total school costs at full student enrolment					
	5	10	15	20	25	30
60	2.00	4.0	6.00	8.0	10.00	12.00
55	2.25	4.5	6.75	9.0	11.25	13.5
50	2.50	5.0	7.50	10.0	12.50	15.0
45	2.75	5.5	8.25	11.0	13.75	16.5
40	3.00	6.0	9.00	12.0	15.00	18.0
35	3.25	6.5	9.75	13.0	16.25	19.5
30	3.50	7.0	10.50	14.0	17.50	21.0
25	3.75	7.5	11.25	15.0	18.75	22.5
20	4.00	8.0	12.00	16.0	20.00	24.0
15	4.25	8.5	12.75	17.0	21.25	25.5
10	4.50	9.0	13.50	18.0	22.50	27.0

Calculating the total extra cost incurred (or saved) by changes in school rolls

1 Decide on your school's 'full capacity'. This is the maximum number of students you could reasonably take before screaming 'no more!' and without adding extra accommodation. This may or may not be the same as your standard or designated maximum admission number.

2 Estimate the percentage of total costs that are fixed *when your school is at full capacity* – probably at least 20 per cent – and choose the appropriate column in table 6. (If in doubt you may wish to repeat the calculations for a second column for comparison.)

3 Estimate (a) your school's 'original' enrolment (enrolment before your roll rises or falls) and (b) the 'changed' enrolment (the actual or envisaged enrolment after your roll changes), *both as a percentage of full capacity*. Mark the two rows in table 6 for these percentages, and read off the two FCE figures at the intersection of these rows and the column chosen in step 1 above. For example, if your school estimates its fixed costs at 20 per cent, and has been at full capacity, but has now dropped to 70 per cent of capacity:
    'Original' enrolment (100%) has an FCE of 0
    'Changed' enrolment (70%) has an FCE of 6

4 Calculate the extra cost incurred or saved using formula 2 (derived in Appendix 1).

Two examples

1 A primary school with a maximum capacity of 200 has a budget of £168 000, with 20 per cent estimated fixed costs at full capacity. Its enrolment is likely to fall from the present 160 to 120. The additional costs incurred as a result of this fall from 80 to 60 per cent enrolment will be:

$$\frac{\text{Difference of 4 (original FCE\%) and 8 (changed FCE\%)}}{\text{80 (original enrolment \%) + 4 (original FCE\%)}} \times £168\,000$$

$$= \frac{4}{84} \times £168\,000$$

$$= £8000$$

Note that this will be an extra burden on its reduced 'changed' budget, not its 'original' one.

2 A secondary school currently with a 600 roll (75 per cent capacity) expects to rise to full capacity of 800. It estimates 25 per cent fixed costs at full capacity, and has a current budget of £1 000 000. The costs saved from the rise in enrolment will be:

$$\frac{\text{Difference of 6.25 (original FCE\%) and 0 (changed FCE\%)}}{\text{75 (original enrolment \%) + 6.25 (original FCE\%)}} \times £1\,000\,000$$

$$= \frac{6.25}{81.25} \times £1\,000\,000$$

$$= £76\,923$$

Appendix 3: Calculation of the school's share of changed costs created by changes in enrolment

1 Calculate the unit costs per student for your 'original' enrolment:

$$\frac{\text{'Original' budget}}{\text{Number of students ('original' enrolment)}}$$

2 Calculate the total costs for your 'changed' enrolment with the same unit costs:

$$\text{Step 1 unit costs per student} \times \frac{\text{number of students}}{\text{(changed enrolment)}}$$

3 Calculate the actual budget for your changed enrolment from the LEA formula.

4 Calculate the difference between step 2 and step 3. This is the LEA's share of the FCE costs.

5 Subtract the step 4 figure from the total extra cost figure you calculated from Appendix 2. The remainder will be the school's share of the total extra costs (FCE) incurred or saved by a change in enrolment.

7 Budget analysis and construction

The budget process normally lasts for nearly two years, with four main phases:

1 Preliminary analysis	Strategic	Before financial year
2 Budget construction	Operational	Before financial year
3 Control and monitoring of expenditure	Operational	During financial year
4 Evaluation	Strategic	After financial year

The first two phases are discussed in this chapter, the others in the next.

Inevitably there are linkage problems between the phases. As figure 22 suggests, phases 1 and 2 have to be completed for year 2 before phase 3 is complete for year 1; whereas phase 4 for year 1 can only affect phase 1 of year 3.

There are other linkage problems, particularly with the school development plan and its longer time scales, and also with information on student numbers, level of funding, prices etc. Schools in those unhappy systems where academic and financial years do not coincide have further problems.

It is not surprising that schools find the budget process troublesome. Most seem to cope reasonably well with operational aspects such as control and monitoring, but deal much less effectively with preliminary analysis, strategic budget planning and final evaluation. Indeed these processes are often quite superficial, sometimes invisible.

This chapter therefore stresses the importance of school managers clarifying the *purpose* of the budget process, choosing the best *strategy*, and improving the budget *format*. However, there is a marked difference in the needs of schools. Primary school budgets are simpler and more easily related to school objectives as a whole, but less easily focused on delivery of aspects of the curriculum. Secondary school budgets are the opposite, dispersed across departments and timetable subject allocations. Small primary schools should find the principles of this chapter relevant though they may need to prune away the detail.

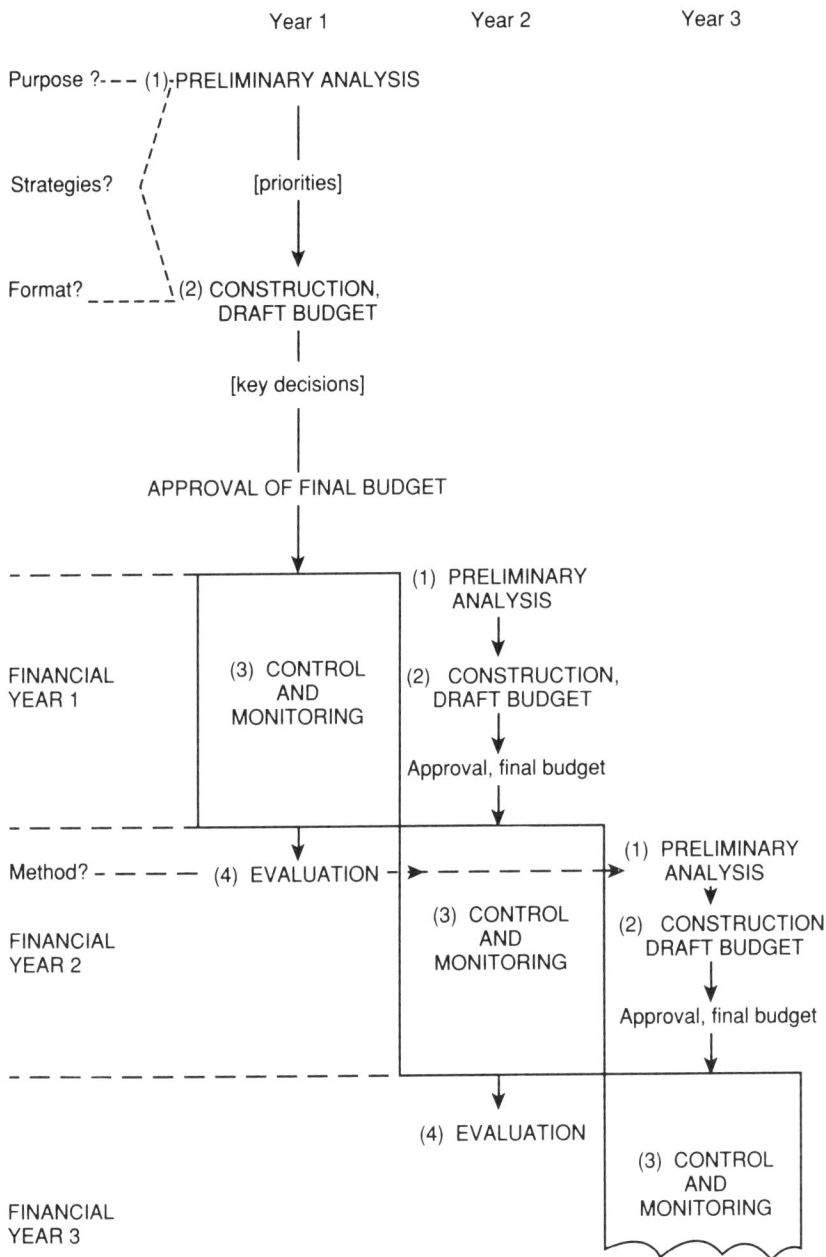

Figure 22   The budget process

Preliminary analysis

The purpose of a budget

A budget is not a balance sheet, or even a financial statement of projected expenditure. It is, or should be, a management tool for planning, implementing and evaluating. A workaday definition would be: 'A plan for the allocation and expenditure of resources to achieve the objectives of the school'. This definition emphasises the focus on planning, and the need to relate expenditure to the achievement of objectives, rather than the more familiar instrumental function of authorising and controlling expenditure.

A budget has two faces – income and expenditure. In state schools the former tends to be taken for granted, almost as an act of God. However, as schools become more entrepreneurial we can expect them to identify their resource needs first and then seek the funds for them. So the budget's supply side will become increasingly important. A budget does not necessarily involve finance, although that is our interest here – it can equally take the form of a manpower or time budget. But it always needs a time-scale – usually a year, but possibly longer or shorter, particularly for a special project.

Writers on financial management have identified a range of functions for a budget:

Planning
Forecasting
Matching income and expenditure
Establishing priorities
Comparing diverse activities through common financial denominators
Implementing plans
Coordinating activities of the school
Allocating resources
Authorising expenditure and activities
Communicating objectives and priorities to personnel
Motivating personnel by delegating responsibility
Controlling and monitoring expenditure
Strengthening accountability
Obtaining value for money, economy
Matching outcomes against inputs, assessing cost effectiveness.

Given such a diverse range of functions, it is unrealistic to expect that all or most can be executed from just one type of budget statement. Schools really need to think of three different sets of budget documents:

1 Preliminary analysis – discursive, narrative, speculative and presenting alternatives.

2 The budget statement, for both construction and control phases, quantitative and systematised.

3 The evaluation process, largely qualitative, linked to objectives, criteria and indicators.

At each stage we need to ask: 'What are we trying to do? What exactly do we hope to achieve with this document or process? And who is the audience?' So, for example, the format of any financial statement for stage 2 may need to be completely modified for stages 1 or 3.

■ Alternatives and priorities

Any initial analysis will have two starting points: the school's current objectives, ideally derived from a development plan; and an early prognosis for the coming financial year about the likely level of funding, student numbers, prices and any major financial commitments. Such an analysis should begin early, long before final funding figures are known. It will obviously be very tentative at the beginning. But the problem is not so much clarity as creativity.

Many schools are locked into a narrow and blinkered view of the alternatives open to them. Admittedly schools with constrained finances – budget losers, in the current parlance – have, or feel they have, very little room to manoeuvre. Admittedly schools work within a framework of social and legal constraints, but the alternatives examined are often unduly limited.

Example A school identifies, as a major objective, improvement of the writing and reading of the weakest 20 per cent of its intake. The alternatives examined are:

Increased teacher staffing for extra in-class support.
Ditto, for withdrawal of students from classes in small groups.
Ditto, to improve the teacher/student ratio.
Provision of an incentive allowance and special funds to a teacher to improve the choice of books and materials for these students in all subjects.
Improved funding for the school library.
Funds for extra computers and other learning aids.
INSET for all the school's staff on more effective learning for such children.

At first sight this seems a broad range of alternatives. But consider what else might have been included:

Payment of an incentive allowance and expenses for a teacher to improve home–school liaison.

An extended day programme; e.g. an after-school or twilight clinic.

Regular individual coaching, out of school.

An adult literacy type programme; i.e. informal and with activity and timing determined by the client.

An 'intensive burst' holiday scheme.

Extra support for at-risk students in feeder schools.

Peer tutoring from older students.

Peer tutoring provided by under-performing students to at-risk students in feeder schools.

Personal counselling to improve self-image.

Financial incentives, to reward individual students for progress.

The foregoing is a hypothetical but not unrealistic example. Few schools with this objective would raise, let alone consider seriously, such a wide range of alternatives, yet rationally they should do so. Why do schools limit their options in this way?

First, history rules: last year's budget is always the greatest determinant of this year's budget. This may simply reflect the continuity and unavoidable commitments involved in managing a school – but it partly reflects a conservative perpetuation of the past pattern of expenditure.

Second, the finality of figures. Once figures are written down – and even more, typed or printed – they acquire a finality to which words never aspire. '66%' is more definite than 'two-thirds'. Somehow figures gain a scientific, authoritative aura of permanence.

Third, a darker reason. Most of the alternatives in the first list above are teacher-centred, while in most of the second list the teacher's role is more peripheral. But it is teachers who will largely determine, through the 'political process', the shape of the budget. Even where there is an autocratic head or masterful governing body, there is a limit to the extent either can risk alienating the teacher body.

Whatever the reasons, schools do not generally relish fundamental re-examination of the relationship of the budget to their objectives. Just look at strategies such as improved home–school liaison, parental involvement in reading, improvement of self-image through coaching or counselling, peer-tutoring – all with strong evidence of cost-effectiveness, but with marginal or non-existent funding in most school budgets.

So if your school wishes to consider a wide range of alternatives, what should you do? Somehow you have to create a brainstorming environment where wild ideas float free and are tolerated. You can then assess each for probability of likely effectiveness, and come up with a guessti-mate of likely cost. It is also possible – though certainly not essential – to use a technique to sharpen such decision making:

1 Decide criteria to assess the alternatives.

2 Give a weight to each criterion for its importance.

3 Grade the alternatives against the criteria.

4 Adjust the gradings in step 3 for the weighting, and aggregate these.

Table 7 illustrates this, using some of the alternatives from the earlier example.

Table 7   Example of multi-criterion budgetary decision-making (figures are mainly for illustration)

	Grading for criteria			Weighted grading			Total	Likely cost £
	A*	B*	C*	A†	B†	C†		
Increased in-class support	6	7	5	36	70	40	146	6 000
Improved choice of books/ materials	3	5	3	18	50	24	92	3 000
Home–school liaison	8	6	4	48	60	32	140	7 000
Computers/learning aids	4	6	3	24	60	24	108	12 000
INSET	3	4	4	18	40	32	90	1 500
Peer tutoring	7	7	3	42	70	24	136	500
Financial incentives	5	7	5	30	70	40	140	1 200

* Criterion A: Improvement to self image and confidence
  Criterion B: Improvement to reading skills
  Criterion C: Improvement to writing skills

† Weighting for criterion A: 6
  Weighting for criterion B: 10
  Weighting for criterion C: 8

This method is not very time-consuming. It is quite difficult to decide on grading and weighting – very subjective – but the process does help you to think more rigorously and objectively. Notice that there are two stages: determining the weighted criteria, and then choosing the best alternatives. These can then be matched against likely costs. In table 7 the last two alternatives seem to be the 'best buy'.

Once you have narrowed the choice you can refine the costing and model the effect on the budget. In fact computer modelling, using some of the friendly programs now available, is important in the later stages of analysis. Also at these later stages it is important to use comparative data (unit cost, percentages, comparisons with past years or between schools) as discussed later in this chapter. By the end of this preliminary analysis you should have produced a clear set of priorities.

Budget construction

There are several different ways of approaching this.

Budget strategies

Incremental

This involves adjusting the previous year's budget with increments for any changes in volume (or in the case of decrease, with decrements). It is difficult to justify because it involves no thinking analysis, planning or linking of the budget to objectives and priorities. But it still lurks more commonly than is acknowledged.

Pragmatic

This is a down-to-earth approach, particularly useful when schools first take responsibility for their budget. It firmly bases the new budget upon the old one, and so is low-risk and economical in time and effort. But it does attempt to improve the previous budget and make savings that can be redeployed elsewhere. These savings may be treated as a windfall, to be shared out at the year's end, or planned for and so reallocated during budget construction. This approach was clearly described by Peter Downes in *Local Financial Management in Schools* (1988, pp. 24–26).

Limited plan

Like the pragmatic approach, this is rooted in the previous year's budget and uses the timetable plan (i.e. allocation of teachers and their time) as a major instrument of resource allocation. However, it also includes a more overt but limited planning element, drawn pragmatically from changes that seem necessary or desirable but within the parameters of what seems likely to be financially practicable. There is no attempt to produce a grand design if only limited resources are likely to be available. Such an approach is set out in figure 23.

A detailed account of how to use this approach is set out in the author's *Local Management of Schools*, Extensions G3 and G4. This kind of strategy is still low-risk and relatively uncomplicated, but it does not encourage long-term planning or consideration of a broader range of alternatives.

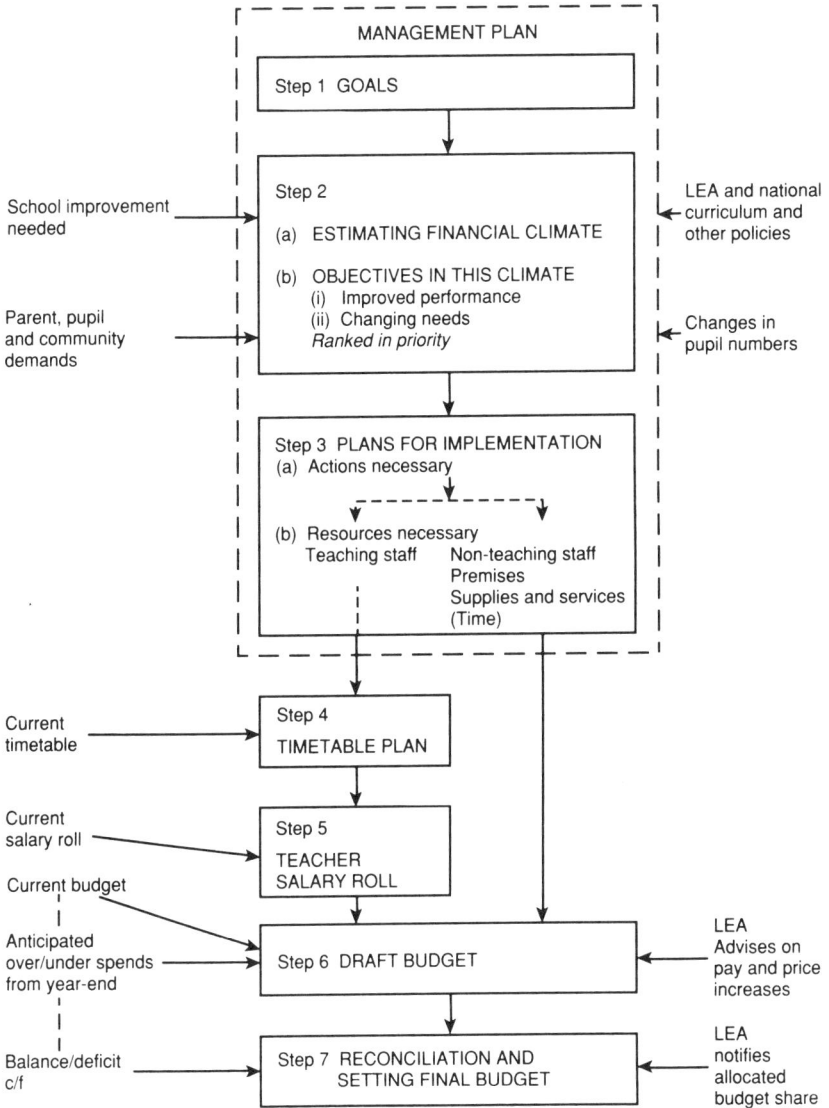

Figure 23   The 'limited plan' approach to budget making (Source: Knight, B.,
1989b)

Base budget

This has been strongly advocated by the UK Audit Commission in *Management within Primary Schools* (pp. 23–26), though the principle is equally applicable to secondary schools. It advocates a school plan as a starting point. However, it accepts that the major part of most schools' budgets will be irrevocably committed to on-going commitments or core activities, and so not available for alternative uses. But this budget core is seen as a strict minimum, not a comfortable optimum – if you like, the lowest minimum that would be tolerable in a desperate cuts situation. In the Audit Commission example below, 84 per cent is shown as base budget and 16 per cent as discretionary:

'The starting point of the budgetary process is the unavoidable expenditure facing the school. Once this first call on funds or **base budget** has been identified, the school can then explore options because resources in excess of the base budget are available for alignment with the school's aims. The guiding principle of the base budget is that it prejudges as few ways of meeting the particular needs of the pupils as possible.

... Vincent Square School is situated in a metropolitan district and has 220 pupils on roll; its total funding allocation is £232 300 . . . The largely unavoidable expenditure for the operation of Vincent Square School, excluding classroom staff, is:

	£
Repairs and maintenance	1 500
Energy	2 500
Rates	8 000
Water	1 000
Cleaning	6 500
Caretaking	9 000
Refuse collection	300
Equipment	200
Recruitment advertising	100
Adult free school meals	2 000
Support to governing body	300
Administrative supplies and equipment	2 000
TOTAL	33 400

These items include the running costs of the school premises because, although there will be some scope for efficiency savings, these costs are largely fixed.

The real flexibility in resourcing revolves around staffing decisions. The teacher staffing element of the base budget can be determined by reference to the organisation of the school into classes. A reasonable starting point would be the number of teachers (including the head) required to form groups of not more than 30 pupils, together with a part-time element sufficient to release the headteacher for $1^{1}/_{2}$ days a week for administration and for seeing parents. The base should also include other unavoidable staffing costs, such as midday supervision.

Applying this approach to Vincent Square implies a need for the 220 pupils to be formed into eight groups. If there were only seven groups, the maximum of 30 pupils would have to be breached in at least some of the groups but with eight groups all can be contained within the maximum. To enable the head to be released from teaching the number of teachers would be 8.3. . . . The estimated base staffing budget is:

	£
Headteacher (Group 2 point 10)	24 200
Deputy Headteacher (Group 2 point 2)	21 400
6.3 other teachers	105 100
	150 700
Add: premises etc. [above]	33 400
Midday supervision	5 500
Total base budget costs	189 600
Budget remaining	42 700

It is important to stress that neither Vincent Square not any other school can be expected to operate successfully on its base budget – it is simply a budgeting approach to identify the maximum sum of money available for deployment by the governing body to meet its school development plan.'

This approach has much to commend it. Like the earlier strategies it works from the given and so avoids time-consuming re-creation of the base budget. It does adopt a clean-slate attitude to the remainder of the budget, and so opens up more possibility of a thorough examination of alternatives linked to the school's plans and objectives; but by doing so it may of course create more internal concern and conflict.

Programme budgeting

Programme budgeting was introduced by President Johnson within the US government as PPBS – the Planning Programming Budgeting System. It was based on the idea that traditional line-item budgets were just an accounting system that did not clarify objectives, relate the budget to them, or match it against measurement of their achievement. The case was strong and widely accepted. However, it required much more data and time. So PPBS in its original form has now largely withered away in the USA. In US education it did not progress beyond a top-down technique within school districts.

The logic of programme budgeting is, however, strong. The line-item budget, disaggregating expenditure by categories like salaries and not by activities or programmes, is uncoupled from objectives, difficult to evaluate against performance, and driven by history as much as by identification of actual needs. The programme approach in education has been encouraged by recent trends – the move towards school self-management; the increased concern with effectiveness and efficiency; the borrowing of methods from the business sector; the demand for greater accountability; and the desire to increase team-working and collaboration within schools and with their communities.

Brian Spicer has set out the rationale for programme budgeting in Judith Chapman's book *School Based Decision Making and Management:*

> Our decision making about how resources are to be used must be less haphazard and more carefully attuned to priorities . . . our management and monitoring in use of resources must be elevated to the standards accepted as the norm for the corporate world. (p. 199)

Spicer stresses the need for 'strategic management', contrasting strategic planning ('doing the right things'), and operational management ('doing things right').

Programme budgeting has developed extensively in the Australian state of Victoria, largely following the original model set out by Brian Caldwell and Jim Spinks in *The Self Managing School,* and more recently in New Zealand. The original Caldwell/Spinks management model is shown in figure 24. This model separates policy-making, coloured black on the diagram, from policy implementation – i.e. strategy from operations. It bridges the gap between objectives and budget provision with two stages: formulating policies and deriving programmes and plans from them. It builds up the budget by aggregating the individual budget proposals for each programme and reconciling the total against funds available. An example of an individual programme budget is given in figure 26, p. 139. Each such budget has its own stated aims, guidelines etc.

(Caldwell and Spinks have modified the model in their recent book *Leading the Self Managing School* (1992), as in figure 25. The revised model separates long-term strategic management from annual operational management – thus solving the problem of timing with development plans discussed in Chapter 2. But the revised annual cycle, although highlighting the importance of the curriculum, reduces the emphasis on programmes and plans.)

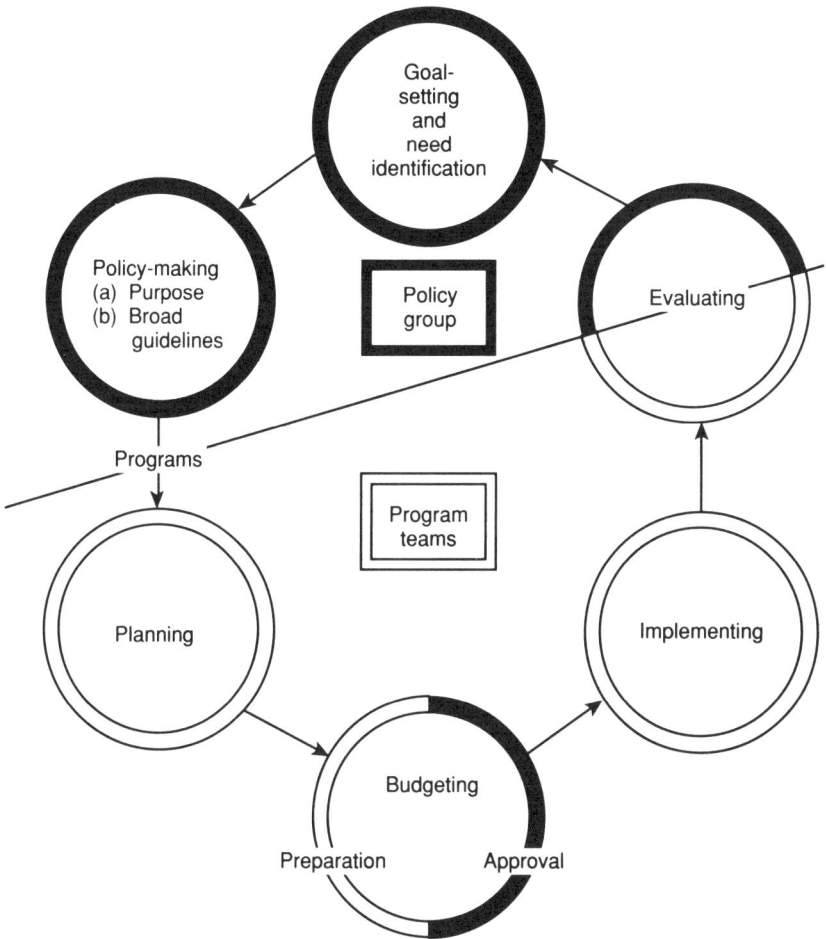

Figure 24   The Collaborative School Management Cycle (the original model)
(Source: Caldwell, B. and Spinks, J., 1988)

Programme budgeting seems to be taking root in Australia, although it
is too early to say whether this is permanent or whether it will die back like
PPBS. Its logic is powerful. But there are several reservations. First, it is
undoubtedly more time-consuming than the strategies discussed earlier.
The process is more elaborate, and collaboration is always more time-
consuming. Also, its bottom-up budget building ignores the Audit
Commission argument for a reserved base budget. Second, it has found it
hard to break out of conventional 'subject' compartments. It is difficult to
translate an objective such as 'Improve student cooperative working and

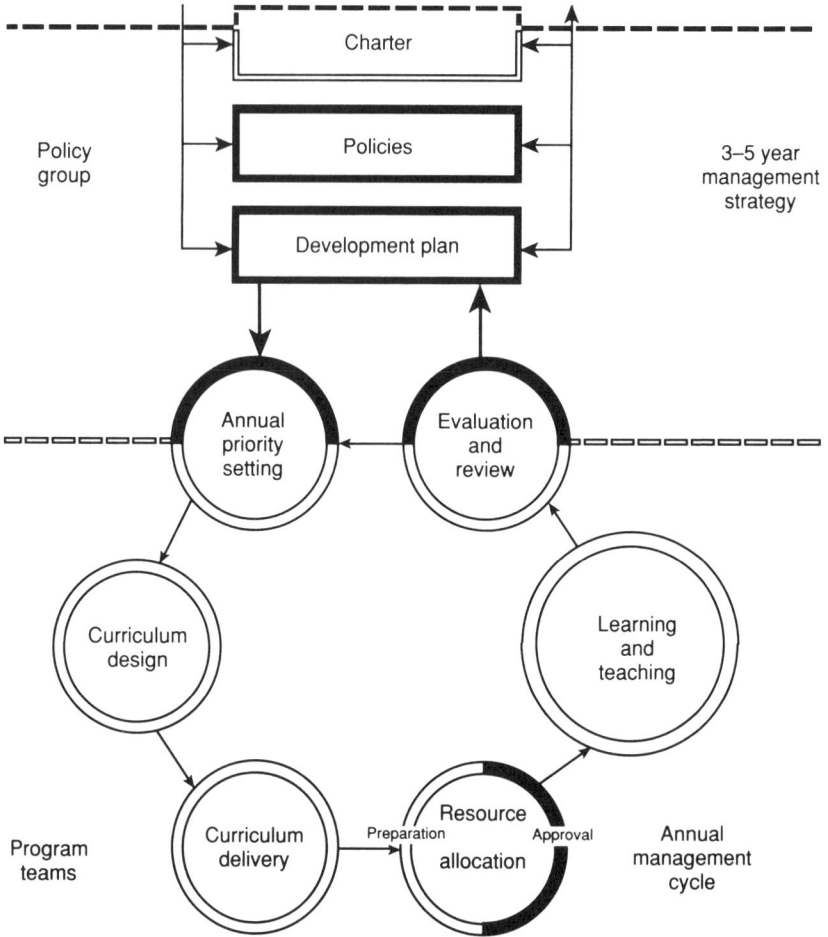

Figure 25 The Collaborative School Management Cycle (the refined model)
(Source: Caldwell, B. and Spinks, J., 1988)

problem-solving' into the budget. (In fairness this is equally true of other strategies.) Third, its collaborative character enhances the role of teachers in decision-making, and while this may enhance short-term efficiency and even effectiveness, it is not clear that it will encourage bolder long-term innovation.

Probably the real value of programme budgeting lies less in the technique than in the frame of mind. *Programme thinking* is what matters.

PROGRAMME: Special Education

Resources required

Planning elements	Teaching staff	Non-teaching staff	Materials & equipment	Books	Services
4.1 Teaching units provided by special education staff 37 units × $595/unit	22 015				
Related units of Planning, Marketing and Organization (PMO) 9 units × $595/unit	5 355				
4.2 Senior supervision of the programme by infant mistress 2 units × $738/unit	1 476				
4.3 Provision of teacher aide services to develop support materials 2 hrs × $7.22 × 40 weeks		577			
4.4 Support items for students' use			750		150
4.4 Books for students and staff to use, including a special focus for 1985				300	
	$28 846	577	750	300	150
	Programme total = $30 623				

Figure 26   Example of a budget for a specific programme (Source: Caldwell, B. and Spinks, J., 1988)

Zero budgeting

Zero budgeting was introduced by President Jimmy Carter into US government. It proved very greedy for information and died back quicker than PPBS. The author does not know of any school currently operating it. But as a concept – as opposed to a system – it is attractive. It involves wiping the slate clean and requiring each activity to justify its claims for any funds *at all*. It is particularly useful for questioning the status quo, reducing expenditures for which priorities have fallen, and making space for new needs.

Apart from being very time-consuming, it is also threatening: no one starts with any claim to anything! It is not realistic for annual operation, but it could be very useful for cleansing the stables periodically – say every five years, ideally linked with whole-school review. Alternatively, it could be used to scrutinise different areas of expenditure each year. A simple form of zero budgeting would use questions such as:

Should this function or activity be performed at all?
If so, on what scale? And at what quality level?
Should it be performed in this way?
Or are there better, or cheaper, alternatives?
How much should it cost?

The best strategy?

Tim Simkins and David Lancaster in *Budgeting and Resource Allocation in Educational Institutions* examined various approaches to budgetary construction. They suggested that each school needs to adopt a system that fits its own needs, and saw a wide range of possible criteria (pp. 105–108):

- Respond equitably to needs of different subject areas.
- Take account of priorities.
- Promote achievement of the school's objectives.
- Encourage innovation.
- Facilitate long-term planning.
- React rapidly to environmental change.
- Facilitate evaluation of 'sub-units' (departments etc.).
- Take account of patterns of power and influence.
- Take account of differences in ability to spend wisely.
- Avoid incurring substantial time or other costs.
- Be easily understood and widely accepted.

Budget format and presentation of information

Your budget format is not preordained. You can design it for your own needs, just as for any other planning document. Of course you may be required to keep accounts in a specified form by an LEA, school board or government department, but that is only required for that specified purpose. With modern spreadsheets there is no reason why financial information should not be shaken up, like a kaleidoscope, into different patterns. Indeed a main argument of this chapter is that this is essential for intelligent management: different information formats are needed for different purposes.

Line-item	Function
Employees	Instruction
Full time/PT teachers	Full time/PT teachers
Supply teachers	Supply teachers
Supply teachers (INSET)	Technical
Administrative/clerical	Books and equipment
Technical	Administration
Caretakers	Full-time teachers
Premises	Administrative, clerical
Electricity	Postage and telephone
Water	Premises
Cleaning materials	Caretakers
Refuse collection	Electricity
Maintenance	Water
Supplies and services	Insurance
Books and equipment	Teacher support services
Postage and telephone	INSET
Establishment	Supply teachers (INSET)
Advertising	Clerical support
Staff travel/subsistence	Student support and services
Insurance	Transportation
Miscellaneous	Catering

Figure 27 Alternative budget formats (abbreviated examples)

Budget layout

There are three main types in use.

Subjective or line-item (figure 27). This is the familiar layout by categories of expenditure; e.g. employees' salaries, premises, supplies and services, establishment expenses, miscellaneous, transport, catering. It is well-tried and effective for controlling and monitoring expenditure, because it collates similar expenditures together and allows comparison of like with like. But it is of limited use for strategic planning or relating expenditure to objectives, and it does not aid evaluation beyond the purely financial.

Function (figure 27). This classifies information by the function for which funds are spent; e.g., instruction, administration, premises, teacher support services, student support and services, transportation, catering. It is easier to see how money is being used and to question priorities, and so makes planning and evaluation somewhat easier. But it is less suitable for control – a category like non-teaching salaries may be spread over several functions. And it is still not closely related to objectives or activities.

Programme (figure 28). Here expenditures for each programme or activity are grouped, as discussed above under programme budgeting. In *The Self Managing School* Caldwell and Spinks list 41 programmes for Rosebery District High School (all-age) in Tasmania. Nineteen of them are subjects, but there are also programme areas like pastoral care, support services, special needs, administration, public relations, cleaning, grounds and some complementary areas such as extra-curricular activities, gifted children, drama festival, school magazine and council. An alternative to subject programmes could be broader groupings (e.g. creative and performing arts) or programmes for groups of students or by skill development (communication, numeracy, problem-solving etc.) – but these are difficult to create.

This programme format links expenditure more closely to objectives, though still largely on a subject, or function-centred, basis. It could recharge an element like premises to each programme unless this is retained as a function. But while it is the best of the three formats for strategic planning and evaluation, it is the weakest for control. Teaching or non-teaching salaries, for example, will be spread across many budget heads.

ROSEBERY DISTRICT HIGH SCHOOL, TASMANIA:
PROGRAMME BUDGET SUMMARY SHEET   Note: selected headings only

	Teaching staff	Non-teaching staff	Relief days	Materials & equipment	BooksServices & hire
101 Extra-curricular activities					
103 Administration	109 791	36 456	760	7 000	
105 Pastoral care	79 694			600	
111 Curriculum resource	23 252	3 910		7 073	
113 K–10 Music	27 798		152	2 040	30
141 7–10 English	61 405			600	2 200
142 3–10 Foreign languages	19 778			120	240
173 K–10 Special education	28 846	577		750	300
182 Public relations	738				
TOTALS	1 058 764	156 027	2 508	60 810	10 328

	Minor materials	Travel	Services	Contingency reserve	Other	Programme total
101 Extra-curricular activities						
103 Administration		380		200		580
105 Pastoral care	250		5 400	523		160 180
111 Curriculum resource		500				80 794
113 K–10 Music				100		34 335
141 7–10 English	100		200		290	30 610
142 3–10 Foreign languages			425	200		64 830
173 K–10 Special education						20 138
182 Public relations			150			30 623
	40			10		788
	5 739	7 340	10 625	3 680	1170	1 316 991

Figure 28   Example of a programme budget summary sheet (Source: Caldwell, B. and Spinks, J., 1988)

The best format? It seems clear that some kind of function or programme format is to be preferred for analysis and evaluation, but the traditional line-item format for control. There is no reason why schools should not use different formats for the different purposes. In fact both can be used together, and linked through a matrix, with programmes on one axis and a subjective format on the other. This then allows teacher salaries for various programmes, for example, to be aggregated into a total. The Caldwell and Spinks example in figure 28 is of this kind. A similar matrix is also the recommended budget framework for New Zealand Charter schools, with the following subjective entries: consumables, assets, general materials, printing and stationery, staff training, repairs and maintenance, salaries teaching, salaries ancillary, services, utilities, water (*Governing Schools: A Practical Handbook for School Trustees*, New Zealand Ministry of Education, 1990).

Aggregation or disaggregation?

Consider the following examples, A and B:

A	**B**	
Teacher salaries £176 000	Headteacher salary	£26 000
	Deputy headteacher allowance	4 000
	Incentive allowances	5 000
	Main scale salaries, administration	2 000
	Main scale salaries, teaching (full-time)	132 000
	Main scale salaries, teaching (part-time)	7 000
	TOTAL	£176 000

Which is more useful? Again, it depends on your purpose. If you want to analyse expenditure then B is greatly preferable. You are more likely to raise questions and look at 'what if' alternatives. Similarly for evaluation B is more likely to lead to answers about value for money, efficiency and effectiveness. But for control, A is better. It is easier to see the wood for the trees, and one salary figure is easier to check for monthly variation.

So again, two types of format are required. It may be that schools use the correct amount of aggregation for control, but do not supply themselves with sufficiently detailed disaggregation for analysis and evaluation. That may be one reason why those two processes are less well executed.

Finally, rounding off. Seldom are more than three characters needed for analysis and evaluation. Rounding off to the nearest thousand may suit large schools. For example, which would be best for the first item of B above?

Headteacher salary   £30 000 (rounded up)
                      or 26 000
                      or 26 400
                      or 26 380
                      or 26 383?

The figure £26 400 seems preferable. This kind of simplification – together with the actual physical layout and appearance of headings – can be of appreciable benefit at the analysis and evaluation stages. Any good spreadsheet should cope with this.

Raw totals ... or comparative figures?

It is very difficult to make sense of any single figure in a budget estimate or out-turn statement, just as it is difficult to make sense of your own domestic electricity bill unless you can compare it with previous similar bills and with neighbours' bills.

Example Mountaintop School: electricity 1993/94 = £15 000. Is this good? bad? high? low? It's impossible to say, unless you also know . . .
    Mountaintop School: electricity 1992/93 = £14 000. Is this 7.1 per cent increase reasonable? It is difficult to judge, unless you consider changes in student numbers . . .
    Mountaintop School: enrolment 1993/94 = 830
    Mountaintop School: enrolment 1992/93 = 800.
But it is still difficult to relate the two sets of data unless they can be combined as unit costs:
Mountaintop School: electricity per student unit costs
                       1993/94 £18.1
                       1992/93 £17.5
Now is this reasonable? Well, these unit costs show only a 3.4 per cent increase, probably no more than inflation. But it is still impossible to make much of a judgement unless you can compare this data with other schools. So the full set of data you need is:

	Mountaintop School		
	1993/94	1992/93	% change
Electricity	£15 000	£14 000	+7.1
Number of students	830	800	+3.7
Unit cost per student	£18.1	£17.5	+3.4
	Similar peer schools (average)		
Electricity	£16 000	£15 600	+2.6
Number of students	880	850	+3.5
Unit cost per student	£18.2	£18.4	−1.1

The situation is now more complex. Mountaintop spent less than its peer schools in 1993/94 on electricity, both in total and per student. But the percentage increase in its electricity costs from 1992/93 is greater – total and per student. So, like much cost data, this raises as many questions as it solves; but at least Mountaintop School now has a more sophisticated view of its energy costs.

As a general rule any budget *estimate* document should set out last year's figures against this year's, and should convert both to unit costs to allow easier comparison. A budget *out-turn* document for evaluation should ideally include a series of unit costs over three or four years or so, plus data from peer schools, to allow broader comparisons and detection of trends. But the final budget estimates, used for control and monitoring, do not need previous year's figures or unit cost data.

What are the best format arrangements?

The ideal situation would be:

Budget analysis	*Budget control and monitoring*	*Budget evaluation*
Programme*	Line-item	Programme*
Disaggregated	Aggregated	Disaggregated
New year and previous years	Current year only	Out-turn and previous years
Totals and unit costs	Totals	Series of unit costs, unit costs for peer schools

(*) aggregated into line-item totals by a matrix.

Budget construction

This is the phase which schools probably see as the most troublesome, but there is less to be said about it. The principle is simply to reconcile priorities and commitments with the funds likely to be available, probable student numbers and levels of salaries and prices. The problem is that these variables keep on varying, sometimes even into the new financial year. Unless income can be increased, expenditure has to be reduced either by removal of some areas of expenditure, or by reduction in the level of provision.

It is often said that the curriculum does, or should, determine the budget. This is generally incorrect. The curriculum in most schools is a sealed system, and reducing one area (say history) and expanding another (such as science) will make little percentage difference to the budget. The only exceptions are an expansion in a small group and resource-expensive area such as technology or in secondary schools an increase in options. The key decision is not on curriculum but on class organisation. When a small primary school reaches the point where it feels bound to create an additional class, it triggers a budget increase of 5–10 per cent. Even in a good-size secondary an extra class creates a 1 per cent increase.

One specific issue is contingency funds. It is hard to justify rolling forward indefinitely unspent funds – and especially if the rate of investment return is less than inflation. But in uncertain times schools look for security. Personally the author prefers dedicated capital replacement and building maintenance funds, accumulated year by year, which can also be used as fallback reserves if a dire contingency arises.

Internal (sub-unit) budgets

In larger secondary schools, large conglomerate departments will probably need to operate a similar but scaled-down budget system. A few schools do now treat departments or faculties like the autonomous departments of further education colleges.

Example Beckfoot Grammar School in Bradford (1000 students, ages 13–18) has created three areas, each housing a year-group (Y9, Y10 or Y11) and coinciding with department bases. Area leaders and their teams are responsible, with devolved budgets, for both pastoral and academic work in their area, and for the area premises.

This is the exception. But wherever budgets are devolved internally, even in the smallest school, the budget holders still need to go through the same initial process of strategic analysis.

* * *

This chapter has stressed the need for a thoughtful approach to the budget, particularly over budget analysis, choice of a budgetary strategy and selection of improved formats. There has not been space to explore the rich scope for 'political' activity that budgets create, discussed by Tim Simkins and David Lancaster in their Sheffield Polytechnic paper.

8 Budgetary control, evaluation and equity

Budgetary monitoring and control are often treated as being synonymous. Actually they are distinct: monitoring compares actual expenditure against estimated, whereas control safeguards funds and ensures they are spent as authorised.

Monitoring need not be confined to expenditure. It can also be used for income, capital or project expenditure and cash flows.

Monitoring raises questions about the roles and responsibilities discussed in Chapter 3. Who should do it? To whom should he or she report? Who has the authority to take corrective action, and within what limits? Governing bodies or headteachers do not want to be saturated with figures – but they must avoid the 'Why didn't you tell me . . .' syndrome. Budget information also needs to be reported regularly to internal budget holders.

Monitoring

Monitoring expenditure is mainly undertaken through regular budgetary tabulations, usually produced monthly as a computer printout. Their common form is:

Item	Total budget	Expected to date	Actual to date	Variance
Telephone	1200	600	500	–100
Postage	1200	600	700	100

The variance column may be initially confusing in that a minus figure shows an underspend, which is a 'plus' within the estimated budget. It is important to get a feel for monthly statements and an eye for important discrepancies. It is particularly important that trends – especially overspending! – are picked up early when corrective action is easier. But tabulations do not need exhaustive study each month, and time need not be wasted on minor items.

Your response to significant variances is likely to be in three stages:

1 Verification. Are the figures correct? There could be a miscoding or an error arising from data entry.

Are the figures representative of the actual situation? The figures represent actual payments that have been passed through the system. Are there invoices received but not yet paid or processed; or items ordered but not yet invoiced?

Commitment accounting is often used to overcome this problem, recording orders as commitments and deleting each commitment when paid. This does involve considerably more work and unless efficiently managed can create confusion. However, it is useful for reference when a heading seems to be underspent. Of course there may still be a major order about to be placed, which commitment accounting will not show.

2 Interpretation. What does the variance mean? There are four possibilities:

- An error, discussed above.
- An oscillation – a wobble in the flow of invoices which creates a temporary over- or underspend which is likely to be evened out in the next month or so.
- A 'one-off' – a definite variation on expenditure which should not recur.
- A trend – a tendency to over- or underspend for this item each month, so likely to lead to an accumulated deficit/surplus.

Table 8 gives examples for one item, postage, for each of these eventualities.

Table 8   Expenditure for postage, recorded for six months: four different patterns of variation

Month	Expected	Error Actual	Var	Oscillation Actual	Var	One-off Actual	Var	Trend Actual	Var
1	100	100	–	80	–20	100	–	120	20
2	200	200	–	220	20	200	–	240	40
3	300	300	–	320	20	500	200	360	60
4	400	1400	1000	400	–	600	200	480	80
5	500	500a	–	530	30	700	200	600	100
6	600	600	–	600	–	800b	200	720c	120

Notes: (a) Error now corrected
(b) The overspending in month 3 has been carried forward in following months
(c) At this rate overspending will be 240 at year-end.

3 Corrective action. If you consider the variance suggests a trend, the first question to ask is whether this is caused by a change in the *volume* of goods and services supplied, or in their *price*. If the former, you may be able to control use of this item so that its volume reverts to or near to the planned level. Obviously you cannot change a rise in price, but again you may be able to adjust the volume used to offset this.

Example There has been an increase in electricity expenditure. If consumption of units has risen, measures can be taken to reduce this. A rise in electricity prices could be cushioned by an appeal for economy.

If you cannot compensate fully for the new trend, or for any 'one-off' variation, you can use virement to transfer an allocation of funds from an underused to an overused budget head. However, this is only worth doing if the discrepancy is substantial. Too many adjustments to the original allocations make evaluation of the budget and projection for future years more difficult, unless they are very well documented.

Of course the most important variance is at the bottom right-hand corner – that for the 'bottom line' of total expenditure. But it is very risky to monitor the budget just from this figure. It is much safer to watch the major variances as they unfold, and ensure that your projection of final underspends exceeds that for overspends.

Refinements

Some refinements in monitoring are possible. With 'budget profiling' the 'expected' expenditure column can be projected not as one-twelfth of the annual figure but according to likely monthly expenditures, particularly where items are affected by seasonal or school-year variations. Some systems use variances to show projected surpluses or deficits likely to occur if they continue. However, unless this is very sophisticated it can be confusing.

A specialised feature is 'management by exception', whereby a computer is programmed to report under- or overspending outside defined parameters. This is particularly useful for monitoring internal budget holders' expenditures and flagging up those heading for problems.

■ Control

With the growth of school self-management there is more risk of abuse of school funds. David Goodman, an English District Auditor, captured this in an article in *School Governor*:

> **Under local management of schools, people will be no more or less honest than hitherto, but the risks will increase:**
>
> ● **Greater financial freedom increases opportunities for fraud.**
> ● **The drive for lean overheads will lead to reduced controls.**

- Decentralisation makes separation of duties more difficult to achieve.
- Local processing destroys the fear of detection by the centre.

It is not possible to prevent fraud completely; but it is possible, and important, to set up a *system* that is reasonably effective both to reduce temptation and to prevent unjust imputations against the innocent. The foundations for this will be laid for state schools by the standing orders and regulations of the delegating authority (LEA, school board or state government), but the detailed fabric will still need to be constructed by the school itself. The system needs to be a coherent and thought-out set of policies, regulations, practices and procedures. Some guiding principles can be established.

Separation of powers. Wherever possible different people should be responsible for different functions; e.g. cash receipts, banking, ordering, authorising payment, signing cheques, and keeping accounts and records. Under no circumstances should school funds pass through private accounts.

Responsibilities. These need to be clearly defined, particularly to provide supervision and separate powers.

Personnel. Personnel with access to school funds need careful selection and training. But apparent reliability and honesty are never a total defence against fraud.

Income. All cash should be paid into the school's account, not used for payments. Receipts should be issued for all moneys collected, with a recording and reconciliation system.

Banking, deposits, investments and loans. Policy should be clearly established.

Orders. These should be in written form (including confirmation of telephone orders) on specified numbered forms, signed by authorised personnel (usually internal budget holders). Triplicate books allow copies for supplier, budgetholder and finance clerk.

Contracts. These require rigorous definition of service standards and service specification, tender documentation and procedures for advertising, receiving, evaluating and awarding tenders and monitoring performance.

Payments. Payments should only be made on invoices backed by signed orders with delivery notes receipted for goods actually received, and authorised by one of two or three senior staff. Cheques require two signatories. Petty cash payments should be firmly controlled.

Records. Retention of orders, invoices, statements, receipts, vouchers and other records should be specified.

Inventories. Requirements should be specified, with provision for writing off (discussed earlier in Chapter 6).

Security. Provision for safes, holding of cash, security and supervision of premises should be reviewed, with insurance and possibly bonding arrangements.

Independent audit. Periodic reviewing by outsiders, or insiders not normally involved with finance, is important. The review should focus primarily on the control system and the efficiency of its operation, reinforced by spot checks.

Unofficial school funds. These are growing in importance with school self-management and need particular care. Governors and headteachers need to issue firm guidelines, incorporating many of the above features in a form acceptable to parents or teachers acting in a voluntary capacity. Fund raising events with large amounts of cash are particularly vulnerable so precautions are needed – two people should be present for receipt of moneys, for example.

To sum up, effective control needs a good system tempered by common sense. Oppressive, time-consuming or mistrustful regulations can be counter-productive. But governors and headteachers do need to be alert. It helps to ask occasionally – 'If someone in this school wanted to fiddle some money, where could they extract a substantial amount?'

Two useful checklists for financial control can be found in the CIPFA (Chartered Institute of Public Finance and Accountancy) *Audit Implications of Local Management of Schools* (1989), especially pp. 22–31, and the New Zealand Ministry of Education's *A Guide to Financial Management* (1990, pp. 32–38).

■ Evaluation of the budget

This last stage of the budgetary process seems the most difficult for most schools. There are three aspects:

1 Financial efficiency – comparing the out-turn budget with the start-of-year estimate.

2 Resource efficiency – looking at what the money was spent on.

3 Effectiveness – assessing whether the expenditure has achieved the outcomes hoped for.

The first two are reasonably straightforward but limited in value. The third is much more important but inextricably linked with total evaluation of the school. Also, the first two can be undertaken immediately the financial year is completed, but evaluation of outcomes needs a longer time frame, perhaps several years.

A solution is to see budgetary evaluation in two stages: *functional* evaluation of financial and resource efficiency, carried out annually; and *strategic* evaluation, occurring as part of the school's normal evaluation process, whenever it occurs.

■ Functional budget evaluation

This needs to be carried out as soon as possible after the year-end. It should be a reflective but practical process. It does not need a formal independent evaluation, but rather an informal mulling over of the data by those responsible for school finances, supplemented by some external comment (e.g. from an auditor, or senior staff or governor not deeply involved with the school's financial management), and by at least one internal budget holder. Probably one meeting would be sufficient. It is important that full out-turn figures are available, as well as comparative unit cost figures for previous years.

When looking at *financial efficiency*, questions need to be asked such as:

How satisfactory is the final out-turn total? (A large surplus may be as unsatisfactory as a deficit.)

How satisfactory is the balance of the main items in the budget; e.g. the ratio of, say, teaching to non-teaching or other main expenditures?

What about the budget format? Does this need improving? And is there sufficient comparative information for this evaluation?

How do the out-turn figures for each budget head compare with the estimates?

What are the main under- and overspends? Should any of them have been foreseen? Do any show trends likely to continue in the new financial year?

Are any longer-term trends apparent?

Were there any specific problems or difficulties in the budget process; e.g. inaccurate, late or inadequate information; poor communications; unclear responsibilities; difficulties with IT?

Are there any areas where additional savings or economies could be made, or financial efficiency improved?

What about the construction of the budget for the subsequent year, which probably occurred during the year in question? Were there any special problems here, or any aspects which should be improved?

For *resource efficiency*, a similar set of common sense questions seems appropriate:

> Could we have obtained this resource in any other way? Imagine that a particular resource had broken down or was not available – for example, no postal service, or no cleaning force. How else could you provide this service? This is often a silly question, but it can raise alternative sources of supply.
>
> Are we getting the best value from our teacher resources? Should we be improving this in any way; e.g. staff deployment, staff development, better support services, improved recruitment or retention?
>
> How well are we looking after, and improving, our physical assets; e.g. premises, capital equipment?
>
> Did we get good value for money from the supplies and services we bought? Could the purchasing, storage, maintenance, inventory and security arrangements be improved? Are the current contracts working satisfactorily?
>
> Are there any considerations relating to human or capital resources, or supplies and services, that we shall need to consider in the future; e.g. new needs, problems, technicalities etc.?
>
> Finally, a taxing question: if I owned this school, would I spend my money like this?!

Strategic budget evaluation

This should arise from the normal process of school evaluation but add a financial dimension to it. General school evaluation is likely to refer back to the stated objectives of the SDP and attempt to assess the extent to which these have been achieved, using performance indicators or success criteria where appropriate. Budgetary evaluation can begin with these evaluation conclusions – say of high, reasonable or low success (or failure) – and then link this to the allocation of resources for that particular feature. This may include non-financial budgets such as the timetable, allocation of rooms etc.

There are two essential requirements. The first is that evaluation does focus on outcomes; e.g. the actual improvement in students' English; the actual effect of increased group-work in terms of student learning and behaviour; the actual performance of teachers as a result of appraisal; the perceived change in parental attitudes, understanding and support. Of course this needs sensitive judgements, not crude quantifying.

The second essential is that there is an attempt to link these changes to the resources consumed – i.e. a cost-effectiveness review. As Chapter 10 makes clear, thorough cost-effectiveness studies are not easy, but some attempt to open up the issues in a school is important.

Here again we should be looking to common-sense, practical questions:

Did we allocate sufficient resources for attainment of this objective?

Does our achievement seem a good return on our investment? How does it compare with the performance of other similar schools?

Did we spend more or less in real terms on this objective than previously? If so, is there evidence of higher or lower achievement?

What would happen if we allocated more for this objective? Would any extra achievement be 'worth' the extra expenditure? What would happen if we allocated less?

What would happen if we spent nothing on this objective (the zero-budgeting concept)? Could the objective have been achieved by some alternative expenditure, or by none at all?

Probably some written report will be needed for this strategic evaluation – but it should be short and backed by an oral presentation (to staff? governing body?). There might also be an opportunity for a member of the school staff to make a special study of some aspect of functional or strategic budgetary evaluation, perhaps as part of a course of study or dissertation for a professional qualification.

Finally, there is another set of issues linked with budgetary evaluation … the fourth E to join Economy, Efficiency and Effectiveness, namely . . .

▓ Equity

Finance flowing through the budget of a state maintained school largely comes from state funds. Such expenditure will serve communal ends – the enhancement of national economic performance, the support of a democratic society, cultural and social advancement. But it will also serve the needs of individual students and their families, equipping students with the capability to compete effectively in the labour market, maximise earnings, extend their life choices and improve their personal welfare and quality of life. Now clearly if society is going to allocate its resources to benefit individuals, it is entitled to expect that its resources will be allocated fairly. It would be very unreasonable if public money was channelled unduly to one group rather than another. (In non-maintained schools parents will be equally anxious to ensure that their fees are allocated fairly for their child and not used to subsidise others – but the fee mechanism and the market context should ensure this.)

So is your school budget equitable for all students? Does each student receive what society, or parents, would see as a fair allocation of the resources and process of the school? Equity is a very slippery concept, and it is not realistic to expect a busy school to embark on deep philosophical debate or a complex research programme! Yet the questions do need addressing, since in some schools some groups of students benefit more from resource flows than others. So it is reasonable to expect that a school should carry out an 'equity audit' at intervals.

The checklist below will provide such an audit. It could be completed by a working party in a couple of hours, although it may need collection of additional data and a second meeting. It is a 'quick-and-dirty' approach, far from exhaustive, but a lot better than nothing. The framework owes much to that set out by Robert Berne and Leanna Stiefel in their excellent book on equity in school finance.

■ Checklist for an equity audit

Equity for whom?

Probably you will be concerned for the whole student body of your school. But you could narrow the focus to specific groups, defined by gender, ethnicity, social class or intellectual ability. Or you could extend it to stakeholders such as parents, the community, taxpayers or employers.

Comparison with whom?

Equity is a comparative concept, comparing one student or group of students with another. So with whom will you compare your selected group? Are you thinking of:

- inter-school comparisons, comparing allocations to the students of your school with their peers in similar schools elsewhere?

- intra-school comparisons, matching one student or group of students against another within your school?

- or both?

What is to be measured or assessed?

You can analyse allocations to students in many ways, so you need to select those which seem the most important and for which data can be provided.

Finance. Inter-school comparison of unit costs per student, between similar schools, is straightforward when the same financial framework is used. For example, comparing schools maintained by the same funding body should be easy, except for the proceeds of fund raising and income generation which may be an appreciable source of inequity and for which data may not be accessible.

Tracking allocation of funds to individual students or groups of students within your school is much more difficult. It involves quite complex costing of teaching time, building use and other resources: feasible for a research project but not realistic for most schools. Since the major cost will be teacher salaries, however, teacher time per student can be used as a crude proxy for finance (e.g. if a teacher provides 80 hours p.a. for a class of 20 students, each student is notionally allocated four teacher-hours p.a.).

Physical and human resources. Comparison between schools is possible if data are available for criteria such as:

> Student/teacher ratios
> Class size
> Number of ancillary staff per hundred students
> Area of classroom space/school buildings/playing fields per student
> Numbers of library books per student.

However, with devolution each school will make its own decisions on the mix of resources and so differences may reflect budget strategies as much as equity. For example, a school with a higher student-teacher ratio than its peer schools may have spent more on other resources.

Within the school, quantitative assessments for individual students or groups will be time-consuming, but qualitative judgements may be possible. For example, do certain groups see more of the 'best' or most experienced teachers? Or consume teacher-hours more expensively in small classes? Or occupy the best accommodation? Or consume more in goods and services? (Of course, there may be valid reasons for such differentiation.)

Also, do certain individuals or groups take more advantage of activities outside the timetable, such as extra coaching, music tuition, extra-curricular or residential activities? Of course it can be argued that these are open to all – but if they are taken up more by certain groups or individuals, is there an equity problem?

Time allocation. Comparison with other schools may be useful where there are significant differences in the school day, particularly in provision of learning time. But the most important comparisons are best made within a school. Usually children of the same year-group will have the same amount of daily seat-time. This seems equitable – but is it? Some students learn more slowly and need more time to make the same progress as others, so giving all students the same time inevitably handicaps some of them.

This issue was brilliantly staked out by John Carroll in his Model of School Learning, where he suggested that with fixed and equal time allocations differences in aptitude are simply translated into differences of achievement; whereas under flexible time allocations they are translated into the amount of time required to master the same task. (This powerful model of time allocation is discussed in the author's book *Management of School Time*, pp. 129–31.)

In recent years there has been much discussion, particularly in the USA, on the allocation of time to students within the classroom. Some of this allocation (e.g. the maximising of 'time on task') relates to the teacher's effectiveness. But it also relates to teachers' philosophy and values, at the extremes between teachers who are 'levellers', distributing their time equally, and those who are 'elitists', preferring to spend it on students who are likely to make the greatest gains.

Educational process. Is your school converting its budget into learning activities that are more appropriate for some individuals or groups than others? Does your school's history and philosophy lead to neglect or favouring of some groups – for example gifted children or children with other special needs – or certain curricular areas?

Outputs. When inputs or processes are translated into outputs, are there marked disparities between groups and individuals?

Example If a student with a low reading age makes no progress in a year, he may have had a fair share of resources but the outcome is not equitable compared with other students. Of course there may be special reasons – but it may be that the school is not allocating inputs in an imaginative enough way to secure improvement.

There is now a good deal of evidence about under-achievement of some ethnic minorities, students with English as their second language, girls in maths and science, boys in foreign languages, and children with social handicaps. Is there evidence for this in your school?

Outcomes. Does there appear to be problems of equity for groups of students in relation to ultimate outcomes such as continuation of education and training, employment, occupation and career advancement, avoidance of crime etc? Collecting data on these is more difficult.

What principles and values should be used in considering equity?

There are three different views of equity, based on different values and to some extent in conflict. Which will you adopt?

1 *Horizontal equity* (equal treatment of equals). This is a common-sense view ('fair shares for all') which has natural appeal. It lies behind some of the current thinking about vouchers and per-pupil formula funding. It is a useful yardstick for inter-school comparisons. But it has a serious weakness: children are clearly not equal, and even if one narrows the range to say children of a given grade or age, equal resourcing is only rough justice. But it is a starting point. Perhaps we can say that, other things being equal, students should receive an equal share of resources.

2 *Vertical equity* (appropriate unequal treatment of unequals). This recognises that different groups of students or schools have different needs and so require different levels of funding. In comparison between schools, special provision may be needed for features such as:

Small size (proportionately higher overheads)
Site-specific costs (e.g. split site; premises expensive in energy or maintenance)
Existing stock of premises and resources (some schools may start from a higher baseline)
Supplementary private funding and income generation
Quality of teaching staff (some schools may find it more difficult to recruit good quality staff)
Student material and school environment (some socially deprived areas may create a more adverse school environment).

For comparisons within the school, provision may be needed for child-centred differences:

Learning disabilities (e.g. English as a second language)
Pre-school and family impoverishment
Retardation (from absence or other disruption)
Physical and mental handicap
Student choice of, or nomination to, more costly courses.

3 *Equality of opportunity.* This is based on the idea that those who 'start the race behind' have no chance of equal success unless they are given special help to catch up. Positive discrimination is necessary for those who are less advantaged on grounds of wealth, race, sex, social class etc. Comparing schools you should be looking for differences in community or parental wealth and the extent to which this is translated into differences in funding or other advantages. Within your school you should be checking the extent to which children of wealthier or poorer parents or specific groups appear to be advantaged or disadvantaged. (Equality of opportunity really overlaps with vertical equity, but it highlights one important aspect.)

■ An equity action plan

If you have completed an audit, it is likely that some equity problems
will surface. How will you deal with these? You will need to consider
what specific resources are required, and how these can be built into the
budget. How can these resources be earmarked so that they are used as
intended? Also, are there any alternative strategies that might produce
better equity – market mechanisms, for example, such as 'loaded vouchers', 'internal vouchers', or 'performance contracting' (see Chapter 10)?
And how will you monitor outcomes to check that equity problems are
shrinking?

Finally, if this idea of an equity audit seems too time-consuming or
complicated, you could at least face up to some of the equity issues presented to New Zealand schools:

'Does your school have a gender equity policy? Have you made equitable
financial provision to implement this policy? Specific areas in which you
could budget for gender equity are:

staff training
purchase of extra PE equipment
equitable funding of sports teams
purchase of extra science/technology equipment
funding of women's studies programmes
purchase of non-sexist resource material
additional funding for careers advice for girls.

Have you made financial provision for implementing an equal educational
opportunity programme? Specific areas in which you could budget for this
are:

provision of resources for ESL
purchase of library materials in languages other than English
adequate funding for 'recovery' programmes and/or extension pro-
    grammes for gifted children.

Do students with disabilities have access to all sporting and recreational
facilities, and areas of the grounds? Do you need to make financial provision
to increase this access?'

(New Zealand Ministry of Education,   *Guide to Financial Management*,
1990)

---

9 Resource management

Resource management is an integral part of financial management, ensuring that your expenditure is well directed and achieves good value for money. Management of people, plant, goods and services, and time . . . each could justify a book in its own right, so this chapter can only pick out some of the issues.

Resource *management* implies the familiar cycle of analysing the current situation, clarifying objectives, making plans, allocating finance, implementing and evaluating. Of these the most important is analysis: the sharper your analysis of existing resource use, the greater your chance of improving it.

■ Human resources

The major part of every school's costs is salaries and related expenditures, and of these mainly teachers' salaries. Anyone involved in managing any school faces the same challenge: how to obtain the best return from this expensive human resource (if you like, value for money and cost-effectiveness). The challenge becomes much sharper when responsibility for teachers' salaries is delegated. However, every school has to operate within a framework of legislation, regulations and agreements, and these vary so much between systems that it is impossible to universalise. For this section we shall focus on the situation in England and Wales, although the principles should have application elsewhere. A good first step is . . .

■ A human resource audit

First, what can be said about the present school staff? This needs quantitative information on:

- mix of staff (teaching and categories of non-teachers, full- and part-time, their numbers and salary costs);

- profile (age, experience, gender, distribution of allowances);
- deployment (class contact, student/teacher ratio, administration time);
- trends (comparison with past and future).

You will also need qualitative assessments, possibly supported by outside opinion, of:

- competence and skills;
- attitudes and morale;
- the working and professional environment (a staff questionnaire might be revealing!).

Second, what sort of staff will the school need in the future? This requires a similar kind of assessment, however tentative. The gap between your audit of staff present and staff future will have implications for recruitment and retention, training and professional development and school policies and management. All aspects have implications for salaries.

Mix, profile and deployment of staff

Trends

In human resource management, as with the budget, the strongest determinant is often history. What was, is. Few schools review radically how they allocate their salaries budget, but there are signs of change. There is a trend towards a more differentiated use of people with staff being seen as core workers (permanent, full-time, highly skilled), periphery (part-time, often flexible, sometimes less skilled) and out-workers (consultants, contracted personnel or organisations). Similarly there is a tendency for the former black-and-white distinction between teaching and non-teaching staff to shade into a gradation: lead or senior teachers, teachers, probationary or beginning teachers, other professionals (e.g. librarians), para-professionals and instructors, technical and other ancillary support staff, adult volunteers, student volunteers.

Mix and profile

If you adopt a zero-budgeting approach to your staffing mix, taking nothing for granted, you may wish to consider some of the more radical strategies examined in Chapter 11. Certainly it would be logical to consider teaching and non-teaching salaries together, restricted only by those constraints imposed externally. Of course it is difficult to alter quickly the mix or profile of a school's staff, unless the school is growing or there is high turnover. But a long-term plan is still sensible. Even marginal changes may yield substantial savings or increased efficiency or flexibility.

Deployment

Staff deployment can be changed much more quickly. One major factor affecting the budget is your view on class size, and so the number of teachers needed. Others are class contact ratio, administrative time, and allocation of responsibilities with attendant allowances. The class contact ratio (i.e. the proportion of the number of lessons in a week or cycle that a teacher actually teaches) has a sharp effect on the budget, particularly in secondary schools. For example, a school with ten classes will need the following number of teachers:

10.0 working at 100 per cent class contact
11.1 working at 90 per cent class contact
11.8 working at 85 per cent class contact
12.5 working at 80 per cent class contact
13.3 working at 75 per cent class contact
14.3 working at 70 per cent class contact

The same allowance has to be made for administrative time. If a school allocates forty administrative periods in a forty-period week, with 80 per cent class contact, this requires an additional 1.25 teachers. To cost this you need to add to salaries the on-costs for superannuation, national insurance and a proportion of supply (relief) teaching, INSET, and recruitment expenses.

Non-contact time can be very worthwhile. It can improve curriculum and materials development, preparation, assessment, communication and not least, morale. But it is expensive. In primary schools there are similar costs attached to the administrative time of the headteacher. It is important to consider whether it is essential, or whether any tasks could be deleted or carried out by others more cheaply.

Allowances

Allocation of allowances for responsibilities has been determined by national regulations related to the size of the school, but the logic of LMS implies that eventually schools will largely or totally determine the number and size of allowances. There is a trend at the moment to flatter staffing structures, sometimes to save finance, sometimes to distribute allowances more evenly. Any school allocating allowances needs a clear set of objectives and criteria to achieve both value for money and fairness.

▪ Teacher salaries

A case for performance-related pay?

By far the largest single item in the budget, teacher salaries, is attracting close scrutiny, particularly now that LMS is in effect delegating decisions on salaries and conditions of service to the school level. Logically, now that schools are responsible for managing their own resources to achieve their objectives, there is a strong case for examining PRP (performance-related pay). For in theory at least, PRP relates expenditure to achieved performance. There is also a supporting argument of equity: it is not fair that a high-performing teacher should be paid the same as a low-performing one doing the same task.

The conventional response, and certainly the union response, is that teachers are not strongly motivated by performance-related awards, and that the whole range of teaching outcomes are not readily accessible to quantitative measurement. But in practice responsibility/incentive allowances have been used to reward merit – not for achieving targets certainly, but often for above-average teaching; and teachers are often keen to seek extra remuneration by taking on extra work or responsibilities.

There are a range of criteria by which teachers' salaries can be differentiated:

- qualifications and training (initial and in-service);
- experience;
- quantity of work – i.e. hours worked;
- role and responsibility;
- level and demands of work – i.e. difficulty of subject or students;
- quality of work – i.e. skills and competencies demonstrated;
- performance – i.e. achievement of defined targets against preset criteria.

Clearly the further down the list the more criteria are related to actual performance, but the more difficult they are to define and assess.

As PRP spreads in the private sector, and increasingly in the public sector including management and professional areas not too dissimilar to education, the defence of a 'special case' looks rather fragile. Frequently PRP has been welcomed by managers in the private sector:

- as a management tool;
- as a device to change the working culture and focus attention on performance;
- as a means of spending limited funds for salary increases more effectively.

It is widely seen as an essential feature of 'performance management'; i.e. management that is centred on improved performance.

Gordon Sapsed gives a clear account of the well-established IBM scheme in an excellent book on PRP edited by Harry Tomlinson (1992). This system relates an employee's pay to the job 'level' (there are only about eight levels in the whole company), years in the job at this level, and above all performance. 'Your individual job performance is the main factor that decides the amount of salary you will receive within the range of your job level' (p. 81). This enables the young high-flier to increase earnings rapidly if he or she obtains high performance ratings as in figure 29 (the rating scale is on the right-hand side).

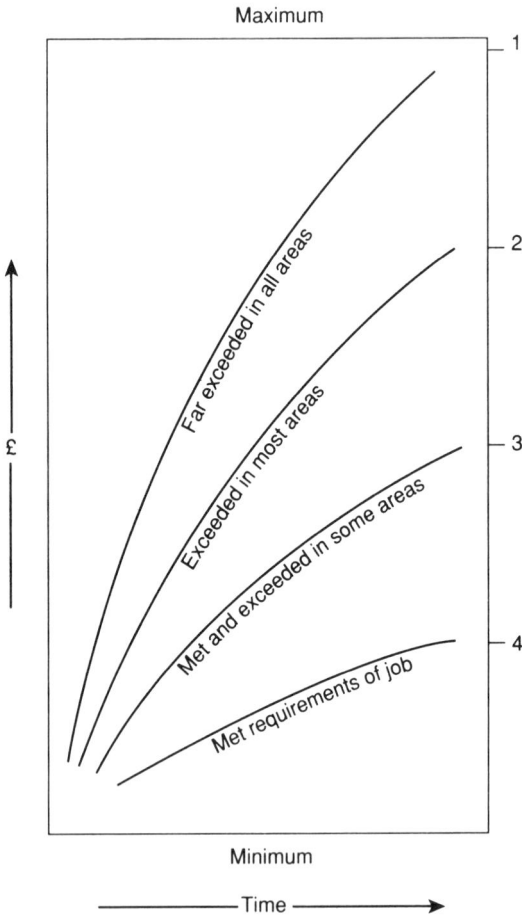

Figure 29   Performance-related pay in IBM: curves represent movement of employees' salary over time, giving proper pay for a particular category of performance (Source: Sapsed, G., 1992)

PRP inevitably has a close relationship with appraisal. It is appraisal that enables management and employee to establish targets and evaluate achievement, as well as identifying that personal development of the employee which will make further improvement possible. However, it does seem important that the two processes should be separate. Gordon Sapsed comments:

> IBM's merit pay system, while linked to the appraisal system, is not synchronised with it, and performance reviews are not regarded as personal pay negotiations . . . the performance management process is seen as separate from, although related to, the pay system. (p. 86)

So the logical case for PRP is strong. Certainly the British government needs no convincing (DFE, 1992):

> We have no doubt that moves towards properly designed performance-related pay arrangements would be right in principle: providing better rewards for the best teachers and clearly offering worthwhile incentives to motivate all teachers to improve their performance.

Ministers have pressed strongly for it over the past few years. And it can be argued that public and government support for an increase in teacher salaries is more likely if this is related to performance.

Will PRP work in schools?

Previous history is not encouraging. 'Merit pay' has been introduced extensively in the USA in several waves from the 1920s to the 1960s, but it has now largely died out. In the UK, even in the private sector, long-term benefits have been very uneven. Experience in the public sector is more recent and not yet very promising. There are very few examples in state schools. Even in the independent school sector, where the market economy might be expected to encourage PRP, there are virtually no examples of the systematic, structured sort now being advocated for state schools.

So will PRP work? There are certainly plenty of problems. Helen Murlis, an authority on pay systems and a contributor to Harry Tomlinson's book, makes a number of cautions (pp. 67–70):

- New PRP systems can seldom be implemented quickly.
- They need to match the culture and values of the organisation, and to be tested and developed in that context.
- 'Performance rewards are not easily justifiable or credible without properly conducted appraisals.'
- PRP cannot compensate for seriously inadequate basic salaries.
- 'Qualitative targets are as important as quantitative targets.'

She concludes:

> ... it needs to be stressed that this is an area where there is a considerable mismatch between the simple and appealing theory of paying more to people who perform better and the hard reality of delivery processes that really motivate and deliver improved performance.

So can PRP work in schools? Possibly – if it is built upon an existing foundation of well-accepted and effective appraisal; if it is well designed and introduced slowly; if it grows out of the present systems rather than replacing them; and if there are sufficient funds to finance proper PRP awards without depressing basic salaries.

There is a final point to be made. Reward systems in schools can be seen as of three kinds:

1 *Extrinsic:* salary, fringe benefits, promotion, status, some conditions of service.

2 *Environmental:* school climate ('what does it feel like here?'), ethos ('what is considered right here?') and culture ('how are things done here?'); working conditions and some conditions of service; equal opportunities; technical, clerical and moral support; collaboration, consultation, communication and openness; team working, positive feedback and recognition.

3 *Intrinsic:* satisfaction and enjoyment from the job; autonomy and responsibility; challenge and innovation; achievement of high standards, professionalism.

Now while teachers are certainly not immune to extrinsic rewards, there is solid research to suggest that they are strongly motivated by idealistic factors such as working with children, helping people and providing a valuable service. So while we should certainly not dismiss PRP – it may eventually produce a better reward system, and it is coming anyway whether we like it or not – it is certainly not the only or perhaps even the best means of improving human performance in schools. The trouble is that it is easy to design a PRP system (but very hard indeed to make it work) while it is difficult to improve the intangibles of environmental and intrinsic rewards. On the other hand, for the time spent the latter would probably give a better return on your budget investment in staff salaries. Independent schools seem to reward their teachers in this way.

Fringe benefits

Here too there seems to be a growing trend to extend removal and relocation expenses, travelling expenses and subsistence, company cars, leasing facilities, loans, private health insurance, 'golden hellos' (recruitment incentives), 'golden goodbyes' (increased salary in the final years to inflate the pension) and, in independent schools, reduced school fees and free or subsidised housing . . . as well as normal pension and related benefits.

The main issue seems to be value for money. Is this the best way of allocating budget resources? Fringe benefits are a form of categorical or earmarked funding in cash or kind. So you need to ask what is the purpose of each one, and is this achieved, or would the money be better spent as a cash grant? Company cars are a good case in point. Unless there is a tax advantage, it seems more sensible to pay cash and allow the employee to decide how to spend it.

Professional development and training

In theory this is a cost-effective way of gaining better performance from money spent on salaries. There seem to be two main issues. First, what is the percentage of money spent on INSET and associated teacher relief (including the cost of any 'free' INSET provided by the LEA/school board), appraisal and other professional development in the school, of the total teacher-related budget (i.e. salaries, fringe benefits and all on-costs, recruitment and administrative expenses)? Similarly, what is the percentage for non-teaching staff?

An exact calculation is not necessary, just an approximation. For most schools the figure will be very low – probably in the 1–2 per cent range for teachers, and less for non-teaching staff. So would it be worth spending more on INSET and professional development, financed from other budget heads or even from a slight staff reduction? But this raises the second issue: is INSET or appraisal actually effective in improving teacher performance?

The author's own view is that training and professional development for teachers in post is grossly underfunded in most schools and should be a substantially larger proportion of the budget. We should be looking at a much more highly trained and skilled teacher force. But any additional budget allocation will be wasted if such training and development is not properly managed, or if teachers are still deployed on lower-level tasks.

Non-teaching staff and volunteers

In every country, non-teaching staff are paid much less than qualified teachers, so schools should be looking to see whether non-teaching tasks can be taken off teachers, to leave them more time for their key tasks. This applies both to administrative and other chores for classroom teachers, and tasks for senior staff such as financial or premises management or examination administration. A recent study (1992) of secondary school teachers by Professor Campbell and Dr Neill of Warwick University found 'Teaching in the sense of giving instruction on subjects during lessons constituted less than one third of the teacher's working time.'

With proper training, non-teachers could take over a number of teachers' current tasks. For example, in the primary school classroom there are many high-level tasks (teaching reading, organising a project); but there are other middle-level skills (e.g. hearing children read, marking books) which a para-professional could do perfectly well, with the teacher's support. Children's physical welfare and caring for resources are already accepted as suitable for an aide. Many volunteers already undertake such middle- and lower-order tasks. In some secondary schools tasks such as examination administration and examination invigilation are already done by non-teachers.

Logically it makes good financial sense not to use highly skilled and expensive people for lower-order jobs. But there are problems! First, finance. If, for example, student registration and administrative chores are done by clerical staff, as they can be using modern technology, this may leave teachers time for more useful activities but it may not be possible to reshuffle their workloads so that the staffing saved pays for the extra clerical staff and technology. So although this system may be more efficient, it could actually cost more. There is more scope if the whole mix of teaching and other staff is altered.

Other problems are equally obvious – management, in organising the new arrangements, providing training, perhaps modifying premises; and not least, politics – in implementing unfamiliar change, negotiating with unions and staff, demarcating jobs etc. None of these need be insuperable, but they certainly make this type of change difficult. Nevertheless, there are great benefits to be gained. A number of good examples, with a discussion of the financial and practical issues, can be found in the report by Peter Mortimore and others for the DFE (see References). This suggests the use of the term 'associate staff' as more appropriate. For volunteers see p. 94.

Premises and grounds

After teacher costs, the next largest section of a school's budget is premises (maintenance, cleaning, energy, water, furniture and fittings, grounds, and premises-related salaries). It is worth checking that expenditure is well directed and value for money achieved.

■ Premises use

A thorough audit of premises usage is a good starting point. A good method is to walk all round the school, looking into each room, cupboard, nook and cranny, as well as the school grounds. While the use of many rooms will be self-evident, in almost every school there are rooms, storage, and circulation spaces that are underused, or even not used at all. Look particularly into the less public areas – lofts and basements, cloakrooms and odd corners. Also be alert for opportunities of change of use – exchanging rooms, stores etc. Ask the present users what improvements are needed, because sometimes a minor modification can greatly improve the working value of a space. A good survey like this will often turn up some changes that can improve the school's efficiency at no cost, and a list of desirable improvements that can be prioritised.

It is also worth considering community use of the school. A simple matrix, with rooms marked on one axis and times of the week on the other, with usage plotted in the appropriate cells, can show the extent and pattern of such use. Should it be increased (and if so, what action is needed for this to occur)? Or rationalised? Do the charges cover the real costs (energy, wages, administration, insurance, wear-and-tear etc.), and if they do, how do they relate to the market rate for similar accommodation? Generally schools should charge the economic or market rate – whichever is the higher – unless there is some reason otherwise. Either way it should be a conscious decision.

■ Premises maintenance and improvement

To ensure that expenditure is related to priorities and secures value for money, a process of planned management is needed. This ought to work through the usual cycle.

Aim. What is our overall goal(s)? Do we want to improve the appearance of the school? Or improve its comfort? Or its efficiency for teaching or learning? Or make it more accessible to the community? Or reduce expenditure short-term or long-term?

Objectives and priorities. What are our specific objectives – stated clearly so that achievement can be evaluated? For example, can we improve approaches and entrances so that the school is warmer and cleaner? Can we increase storage areas by 50 per cent? Priorities should be set:

Immediate (health and safety etc.).

Urgent this year (work deferred too long will cause problems).

High-priority – could be left a year or longer, but important for one of your objectives.

Medium-priority – similar, assisting one of your objectives.

Low-priority – desirable, but not closely related to current objectives.

Plan. This is a list of jobs to be done, in priority order, this year and in future years, with guide prices.

Budget. It is necessary to fit the plan for the coming year to the budget available. Part will need to be allocated for unplanned, day-to-day maintenance (possibly one-third, but the previous year's figures should guide). Ideally a programme of planned preventative maintenance should reduce this.

Implementation. There must be arrangements for who is to be responsible; tenders and contracts; checking work.

Evaluation. How did the year's programme go? Were the objectives achieved? How close was expenditure to the budget allocated?

Improvements, adaptations and refurbishment may be financed from the maintenance budget but are probably best fed from a separate budget head. This makes year-to-year maintenance comparisons easier. To avoid just reacting to the latest request, you need to go through a similar cycle: goals, objectives, plan etc. But for major projects accurate costing is important, along the lines suggested on page 181.

Other premises matters affect school finance. With both cleaning and grounds maintenance there are a set of interrelated issues: the standard expected; use of technology; and the actual delivery, whether through employees, consortia or teams, or hired contractors. Each can affect both expenditure and value for money.

Vandalism and theft is a very emotive cost. Here you need a detached view, best gained by a kind of balance sheet (very rough figures only):

- What was the financial cost of vandalism and theft to your school last year, in repairs, redecoration and losses not covered by insurance (and possibly in extra cost of insurance, and other items)?
- How much more would you need to spend to reduce it, and would this be cost-effective?

In many cases additional expenditure may not be justified. In others – and particularly considering the non-financial costs of vandalism – some investment in security measures may well repay. (Of course there are non-financial precautions possible, not least increased community use of the site.)

■ Energy management

Unless your school is very energy efficient, you should be able to save 10 per cent of your school's energy costs without too much trouble – enough for a substantial increase in books and equipment in most schools. This should not mean any reduction in the level of service, and it's all good for the environment.

To make savings you really need to begin with an energy audit, establishing how much you spend and what you spend it on (including the tariffs), with a study to see where savings could be made. You will then need a school energy policy with objectives, ideally linking to the curriculum, and an energy savings group; and a programme, with both investment for improved efficiency and day-to-day measures. There are no complicated principles at work here – just the need for a systematic 'management' approach. Water costs can be tackled in the same way.

Excellent brief Good Practice Guides and Energy Consumption Guides are produced by the Building Research Energy Conservation Support Unit (see Addresses).

■ Supplies and services

These should be the easiest resources to manage, since they are familiar in everyday life. But there are a few principles to be noted.

First, responsibilities. Who is authorised to order supplies or services? What are the internal school regulations to ensure proper control of purchases and payment? Generally authority should be delegated as close to the classroom teacher as possible, avoiding petty restrictions but ensuring that there are proper controls (see p. 149).

Second, purchasing policy. Staff responsible for purchasing need to think:

>   What exactly is it that we need? Of what quality?
>   What about the 'hidden factors' – safety, durability, maintenance, security and delivery?
>   When is it needed? The more time, the better prospect of a wise purchase.
>   What is available? And at what price?
>   Are there cheaper alternatives?
>   How well does this match our needs and budget?
>   Do we need further advice or research?

There are also the obvious points that the larger the purchase the more the care needed; and that with multiple purchases wherever possible one item should be purchased and tested first. All this seems common sense, but it is still easy to make unwise purchases.

Third, is there any prospect of bulk purchasing or discounts? Many English schools purchase extensively through regional purchasing consortia and can obtain extremely favourable prices. But there is also scope for local clusters of schools to use bulk purchasing power to negotiate contracts, for example in painting and decorating or local supplies.

Example In the Taranaki district of New Zealand, all the primary and secondary schools and the Further Education Colleges have each taken a $500 share to set up a collective purchasing agency. A purchasing officer seeks discounts and lower prices for the complete range of goods and services on their behalf. The organisation appears to be very successful and any profits are shared equally.

Fourth, do services need to be put out to tender for contract? If so, you need to define clearly the level and quality of service you require, convert this into a description of the work to be done, draw up a contract document, advertise, evaluate tenders and award the contract ... and monitor the contractor's performance – tricky business. (There is an excellent booklet available, *Buying for Quality*, produced by the School Management Task Force for the DFE.)

Finally, there are the issues discussed in Chapter 6 such as depreciation, inventories and stock control. None of this is *theoretically* difficult, but there does appear to be considerable variation in efficiency between schools.

■ Time

Of all the resources available to schools this is the least considered and the worst managed. Of course it does not help that you cannot see, hear or touch it – though perhaps you can feel it? Yet, all the money in your school's budget has to be converted into 'resource hours' before the resources it brings can actually be used, as in figure 30.

So while in one sense your use of school time does not cost you anything – it is just there, a limited and expendable but infinitely flowing resource – in another sense more intelligent use of it can bring much more efficient and effective use of your money.

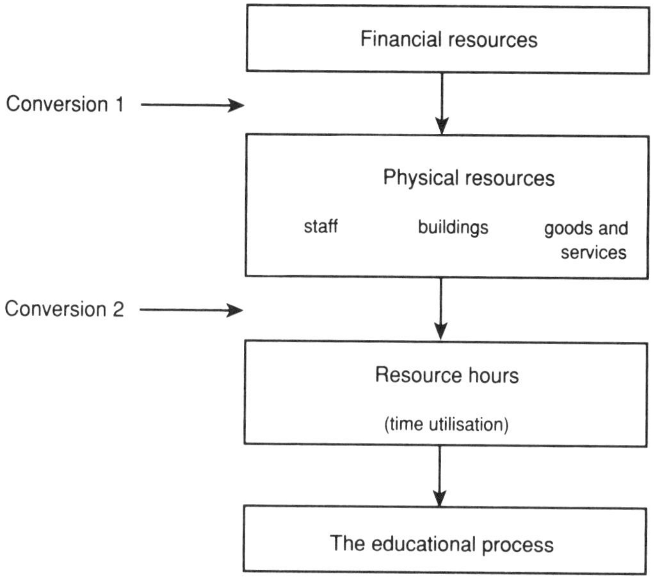

Figure 30   Conversion of financial resources for use in the educational process
(Source: Knight, B., 1992)

Example Suppose two identical schools have an even number of daily
lessons, and school A divides them equally, morning and afternoon, while
school B provides more periods in the morning. There is very strong anecdotal evidence that the latter arrangement leads to more successful learning.
So both schools have the same budget and spend it on the same *amount* of
time – but school B has chosen a more effective *structure* and so gains
greater educational returns for the same expenditure.

School time has four main features, each affecting costs and outcomes:

Time structure. There are *macro*-structures, such as the school week, the
framework of the school day, and the school year (state schools are
unlikely to be able to *manage* the last of these). There are *micro*-structures,
such as lesson and session lengths and frequency, course structures (e.g.
modular), and timetable arrangements for out-of-school activities and
special events. And there are individual time patterns, less formal but
determining how students, teachers and other adults in the school spend
their time and so how learning takes place.

Time quantity. This is the actual amount of learning time in the school day and year. Administrators tend to feel that more is better. In England and Wales currently there is a trend for a slight extension of the day, consolidating for secondary schools at 25 lesson-hours per week. There is little research evidence to support the idea that more time in the school week creates better learning – although more time does create space for an extended curriculum. There is also a strong trend in developed countries for extended time for informal education: out-of-school and leisure activities, coaching, television, home computers and distance learning. But most of this is not directly linked to school learning, although perhaps it could be.

Time quality. This describes the way in which time is structured and used in schools to affect the quality of learning. It is discussed under 'Classroom time' below.

Time flexibility. In most schools time is far from flexible, as the regularity of the bell and the timetable matrix testify. Yet every learner is different, and so needs different time arrangements from other learners. And the time needed for many learning tasks cannot be predicted in advance. Most organisations consider flexibility a virtue *per se,* and schools should cherish it more.

■ Utilisation of plant

Schools are very poor users of plant. In most schools buildings are used for less than 25 per cent of the time they are available (from 8 a.m. to 10 p.m. every day, assuming 350 days per year). Even from 8 a.m. to 6 p.m. they are used less than 45 per cent of available time per year. (In both cases there may be use in lunch hours and for extra-curricular and community activities, and in holidays, but often this is marginal.)

This would horrify any industrialist! Sound financial management should seek much fuller use of this plant – and even more so in the future as schools become more capital intensive. However, there are difficulties. To make full use of school plant requires radical approaches to the school day and school year, and any change to school time arrangements can be difficult and unpopular. Secondly, although more intensive use achieves a better return on capital, it does cost more in energy, maintenance, administration, salaries and possibly transport and teaching salaries. The addition is a very small percentage of the budget (unless there are additional teacher costs) but it still has to be found.

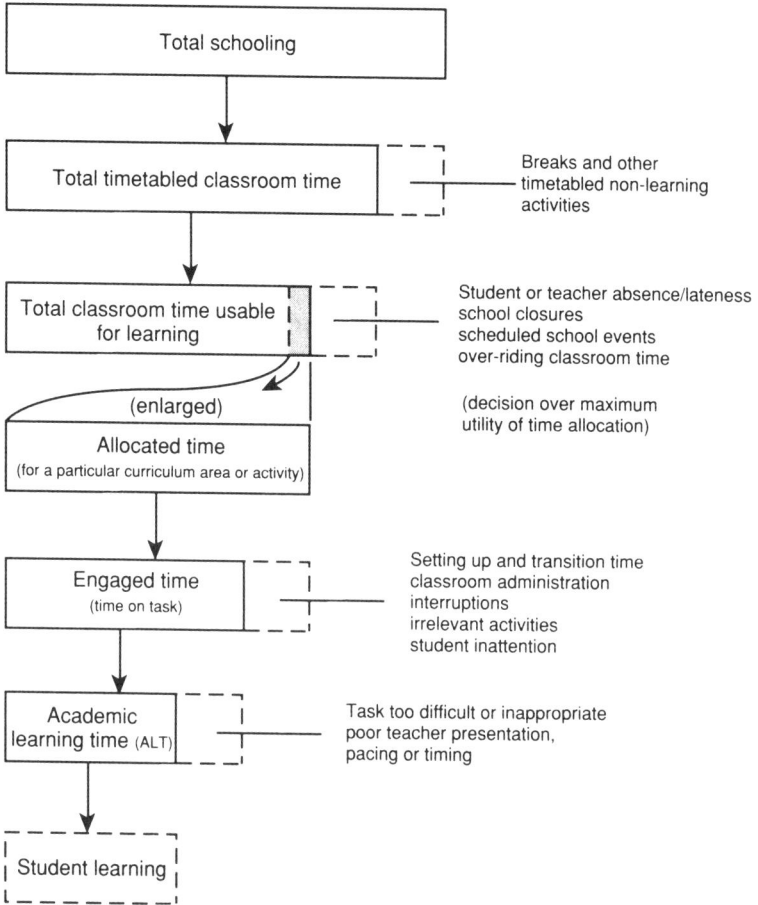

Figure 31 Allocation of time for learning (Source: Knight, B., 1989b; adapted from Husen and Postlethwaite, 1985)

■ Classroom time

Almost all school finance is ultimately expended in, or supporting, the classroom. Yet research evidence suggests very strongly that its translation into effective learning varies enormously from classroom to classroom and from school to school, as figure 31 suggests.

So budget expenditure cannot be divorced from day-to-day classroom and school management.

The US Mid-continent Regional Educational Laboratory (McREL) has devised a tool for assessing efficient use of school time for students learning, summarised in figure 32. Improvements in academic efficiency and so in cost effectiveness, can arise if we take appropriate action to improve attendance, reduce non-instructional activities and increase student effectiveness. (For a fuller description, see Knight, 1989b, p. 145.)

◼ More efficient school day structures

The present conventional school day, ubiquitous worldwide, occupying all morning and often much of the afternoon, with a fixed structure where all students and staff are normally on site at the same time and follow the same routine, has financial merit. It is compact and so reduces recurrent costs (although as suggested above it makes poor use of the

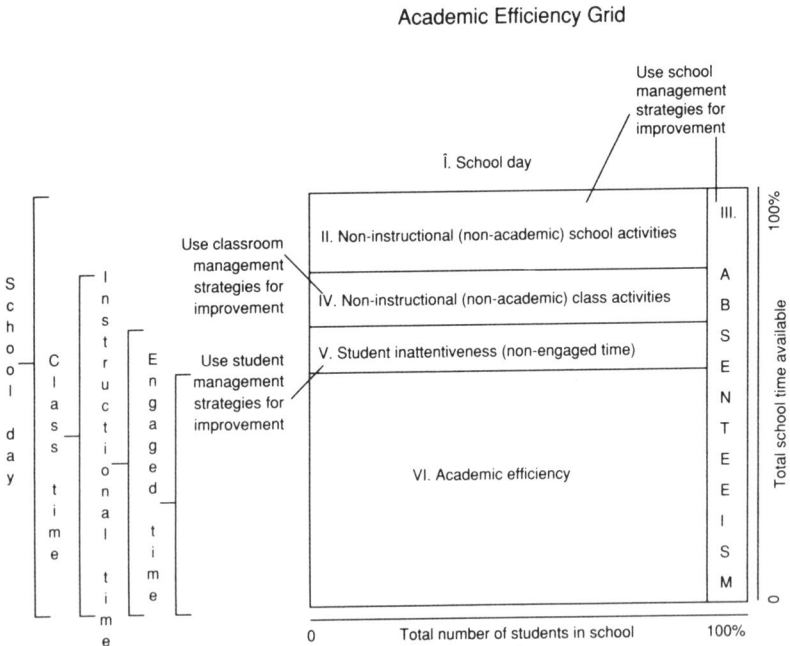

Academic Efficiency Grid

Figure 32 Tool to analyse efficiency of school time use (Source: McREL, 1988; quoted in Knight, B., 1989b) Reproduced with permission of Mid-Continent Regional Educational Laboratory.

capital investment). Its timetable and firm social control facilitate a class-orientated system of learning, at its best an efficient and cheap system.

But . . . it also has severe disadvantages. It makes it more difficult for schools to combine in delivering the curriculum – increasingly important as the curriculum becomes more complex. Its inflexibility is hostile to individual and individualised learning and the use of new technology, and it often restricts interaction with the community in prime time. So we should look seriously at improved versions, as suggested on page 226.

There is only space here to scratch at the surface of the possibilities available to improve our use of school time, which have been discussed more fully in the author's *Managing School Time* and *Designing the School Day*.

10 Costs, cost-effectiveness and productivity

If you wish to manage your school's finances effectively, you need to pass beyond planning and control of expenditures into cost analysis and management. Unfortunately this is less pressing than budget management, and conceptually more difficult. Costs are fuzzy creatures. Also there is no tradition of cost management in schools. Perhaps for these reasons many schools ignore it.

▄▄ Concepts of costs

A simplified explanation was given in Chapter 1 page 8 and you may wish to reread that. A more challenging and difficult conceptual analysis is set out in Chapter 2 of Hywl Thomas's book *Education Costs and Performance*. He summarises some of the main views held by economists about costs. In particular he distinguishes between an objective view of costs as determined by the market value of a transaction, and a subjective view where cost is based on the chooser's personal evaluation of the transaction – the 'commodity view' and 'utility view' of costs respectively.

Example A rich and a poor school both buy the same photocopier. The market value of the machine is the same for both; but for the poor school the sacrifice of other opportunities is much greater. We could perhaps say that the photocopier is more costly for that school, but no more expensive.

If you are interested in differentiating between different types of cost, you may find a standard textbook on cost accounting useful; for example Horngren's *Cost Accounting – A Managerial Emphasis*.

▰ Unit costs

It was suggested in Chapter 7 that unit costs are valuable and often essential for cost comparison, across years or between schools. These will usually be costs of inputs, normally under budget heads like teacher salaries, electricity etc. It is, however, very easy to produce unit costs for the educational process, and with more difficulty for outcomes. These have other qualities. They are useful for cutting schools costs down to a manageable scale. Few of us have much idea what £500 000 looks like – we are not used to it in our everyday life, any more than we are to, say, an electricity bill of several thousand pounds. And they raise questions in the mind …'Is this the best way of spending …?' 'What if ….?' 'What other ways …?'

▰ Process unit costs

Process costs can be easily established based upon usage of time. Table 9 sets these out for schools in England and Wales in 1988/89.

Table 9   Average school-time unit costs (£) in England and Wales 1988/89

	Primary	Secondary
Cost of educating one pupil		
For one minute	0.018	0.028
For one 35-minute period	0.63	0.98
For one hour	1.08	1.67
For a school day	5.76	9.19
For a school week	28.82	45.97
For a school year	1 095.30	1 747.00
For 4 35-minute periods per week for a year (typical course)		148.00
For 4 periods per week for 5 years (typical 5-year course, e.g. French)		741.00
Cost of educating one class of average size (taken as 24.25 primary, 20.43 secondary)		
For one minute	0.44	0.57
For one 35-minute period	15.29	19.92
For one hour	26.21	34.15
For 4 periods (e.g. week's science)	61.16	79.69
For one period per week for a year	581.00	757.00
For 4 periods per week for 1 year (a typical course)	2 324.00	3 028.00
For 4 periods per week for 5 years (e.g. a 5-year science course)	11 620.00	15 142.00
For one school day (e.g. a primary class)	140.00	188.00
For one school week	699.00	939.00
For a school year	26 561.00	35 691.00

Table 9 (continued)

	Primary	Secondary
Cost of one school		
(Primary 200 pupils, secondary 800 pupils)		
For one hour	216.00	1 337.00
For one day	1 153.00	7 356.00
For one school week	5 764.00	36 778.00
For one school year	219 060.00	1 397 600.00

These costs exclude debt charges and school meals but include central LEA administration, transport and aid to pupils.

Source: CIPFA Education Statistics 1988–89, net expenditure per pupil pp. 57 and 62, published in Knight, B. (1989b, p. 16)

Table 9 represents an average across all the schools of England and Wales, but you can easily produce a similar table for your own school. Just calculate the global per-student cost (global budget total divided by number of students on roll) and then divide this by the number of school days in the year, lesson hours in the day, etc. With a calculator it takes just a few minutes.

Refinements are possible. Student unit costs for a small class can be calculated by taking the cost of an average class and dividing by the number of students in the small class. This will not be completely accurate, as a small class incurs less premises-related and support costs. But since teaching costs are the main determinant it will be close enough, and will flag up the increased unit costs created by small classes. Similarly unit costs can be established for students of different ages.

What do these process unit costs mean? Well, they are only average costs, and so should be handled with caution. Also they are theoretical or notional, so they are useful for giving insight and understanding but are not a day-to-day management tool.

It is possible and very useful to calculate marginal unit costs; i.e. the extra or reduced costs that will be created by each additional or subtracted student. These need to be calculated in a different way, by looking at the budget and for each head asking: 'What extra expense will be created by one additional student?' (Or saving for each student less.) For many items the answer will be little or nothing. Even for teacher staffing it is most likely to be nil. But if you keep asking the question for the second such student, and third, and so on, eventually an additional teacher or other resources will be required. This process calculates reasonably accurately the lumpy nature of rising or falling roll expenditure in practice, as suggested in figure 20. It enables schools to project accurately the net effect of roll changes, and dispel the simplistic view that more pupils must represent a financial gain and less pupils a loss. The opposite may be the case.

▰ Outcome unit costs

Despite their many uses, input or process unit costs have one great drawback: they do not relate costs to outcomes.

The importance of assessing school outputs can be seen very easily. If two pupils of equal ability study French for five years, each at a cost of £800, and one gains a grade A pass at GCSE and the other a convincing 'ungraded', then the input costs are the same, but the output costs per unit of acquired skill in French are rather different. A grade A pass is more 'valuable', and so any department that produces more of these from the same resources must be producing them more cheaply. To give an absurd example, if a hundred students took GCSE after a five-year course and a hundred passed, the average cost would be £800 per pass; if only one passed and the rest retained nothing from the course whatsoever, the cost of that pass would be £80 000.

In secondary schools it is quite easy to produce such unit costs for examination passes. Passes at different grades can if necessary be given a weighting – 7 points for a grade A, 1 point for grade G etc. The input/process costs can then be divided by the total points to establish the cost of one point, and so of each grade of pass. Any quantitative measure (e.g. numbers of students learning to swim at different levels) can be calculated in the same way.

Such costing only costs the final outcome, so it does not necessarily cost the 'value added' by the school. All students do not start equal – they bring different levels of prior learning. However, it may be possible to cost this. In England and Wales, schools will eventually be able to measure the gains of their students between the assessments at the end of each Key Stage, and to cost these in a similar way to that suggested above. A-level passes are already being costed in this way with the ALIS system.

Outcome unit costs are good for raising questions, sometimes provocatively. The outcome costs of low-performing schools can be horrendously high. They can be particularly useful in community education, flagging up the cost – and value – of adult classes or use of leisure centres. But hard-pressed headteachers and principals may say that they are some trouble to work out, and are still not particularly *useful*.

The trouble here is that schools are just not used to costing their processes or outcomes. Ask a headteacher for school team results, or examination or test scores or similar, and there is a flood of statistics. Ask about the school budget and even about items like energy costs and you will nowadays get knowledgeable answers. But ask what it costs to teach a student to spell or read to a given level, or to master percentages or calculus – and meet a baffled silence. Yet surely these are proper questions, and only if we can answer them, however approximately, can we being to look at some of the alternative strategies that are becoming available.

■ Costing

In industry and commerce highly developed costing routines are in common use, including 'job costing' (costing of the output) and 'process costing' (costing the production process). There is considerable use made of standard costs – predetermined target costs per unit against which actual costs can be matched. There is a much freer use of cost centres and cost apportionment, and much better understanding of fixed and variable costs, unit costs and costing procedures. It is very doubtful that schools will develop in that way: the 'production cycle' is so slow, and the nature of the process so different, that copying this commercial practice would not seem very helpful. Nevertheless schools need to become more confident and skilled at costing, as they become more responsible for their own finance and more involved in entrepreneurial activities, and as technological changes make greater impact.

■ Costing a major project

There are a few common-sense rules.

1 Clarify the objective of the project at the outset.

2 Try to identify *all* costs and *all* benefits including any income or cost-reduction. Look for implied commitments like maintenance, insurance, security and for hidden costs. It may make the bottom line look frightening at first, but it is more reassuring if all costs have been foreseen. It is also very reassuring to any potential donors.

3 Include non-financial costs, like costs of time, premises use, wear and tear, environmental considerations and even perhaps intangibles like morale. It may be possible to put a financial equivalent against some of these, but if not some statement of costs involved needs to be registered.

4 Distinguish between start-up and steady-state costs. You may need to cost a major project for year 1, year 2, year 3 and year *N* (steady-state).

5 If there are alternatives for an item, isolate the costs relevant to each so that they can be compared easily.

6 Make clear the price base – probably prices as in the first year of operation.

7 Try to include firm estimates, but if not make the best guess you can. *BOP* estimates are very useful for this:
  O = the most optimistic but still realistic estimate you can make (i.e. the cheapest cost you could reasonably imagine for this item);
  P = the most pessimistic but still realistic estimate you can make;
  B = the best estimate between O and P. If there is no reason to estimate closer to one than the other, split the difference.

8 Use sensitivity analysis. Which of the items in your total estimate would be most likely to alter the bottom-line figure; i.e. which are the large items most vulnerable to change? Now rework your estimates for these.

9 Before you finish, ask:
  Are there any alternative ways of doing this we have not considered? Or any costs or benefits we have omitted?

10 Always finish with the bottom-line figure. Is it sensible? Practicable? Achievable? etc. Projects have a nasty habit of finishing less modestly than they began. Is it likely to achieve our objective? And what are the opportunity costs? What else could we buy with this money? Is this the best use for it?

Figure 33 sets out a simple example to illustrate some of these rules, for a small refuse disposal project. It shows clearly the merits of a more systematic approach to costing. This does identify some of those costs that might have been overlooked – the path and shelter for example, or the caretaker's time. The last would have been better expressed as a cash equivalent, say £500 per year. This would have more than doubled the notional annual costs (but while this may be a cost, it is not an additional expenditure – would the school notice this diversion of two hours per week?).

Inclusion of the non-financial costs within the costing statement makes it untidy, but does make it easier to form an overall judgement. These could be listed separately as a later section, and for a substantial project this might be necessary.

The separation into start-up and steady-state costs is important, even for a small project, but the start-up costs involve a problem of presentation. Should they be seen as a one-off expenditure – because they probably need to be financed in one year, unless there is some loan or leasing arrangement? Or can they be regarded as notionally spread across, say, five years? The latter allows the total annual cost to be estimated and shows that Option B is cheapest – £350 p.a. compared with £400 – although it still costs more initially.

A sensitivity analysis quickly shows that the figures for the local builder are the most likely to change the final assessment – particularly that for the chimney, since it is the largest item, and also crucial for costing one of the

	FINANCIAL			NON-FINANCIAL	
Items	Details	Option A (£)	Option B (£)	Details	Units
Start-up costs					
Option A: ready-made incinerator	From suppliers	550			
Option B: purpose-built brick chimney	Local builder		800?		
Both options:					
Path to incinerator	Local builder	400?	400?		
Shelter for rubbish	Local builder	300?	300?		
Total start-up costs		1250?	1500?		
[Total, amortised over 5 years, per annum		250	300]		
Annual steady-state costs					
Caretaker				Time displaced from other duties	2 hours per week
Depreciation					
option A, 5-year replacement		110			
Option B, unlikely in 10 years			–		
Firelighters, 50 packets p.a.		50	50		
Environment				Fires, etc.	Fumes? Soot?
Total, annual steady-state		160	50		
[Total, notional annual cost		410	350]		
Benefits					
Financial	Reduced refuse disposal charges	300	300		
Environment				Less rubbish stored on site	100 sacks saved; Smells reduced
Total benefit		300	300		
		300	300		

Figure 33 Example of costing a simple project, with the objective to reduce expenditure on refuse disposal (prices current)

options. So for a final decision firm estimates will be needed.

Less obvious are the final considerations. On these figures neither incinerator would meet the original objective of reducing expenditure. But do the environmental advantages which have now been identified amount to a revised objective, worth paying for? Then there are other issues behind the costing: would either incinerator work satisfactorily? Are there hidden snags – or advantages?

Finally, is this the best use of our money? Is an incinerator too marginal to our main job of educating children? What else could we buy with this investment? Here we move away from the commodity view of costs to the utility view. For a large school this expenditure may be very sensible, for a small one much less so.

This example may seem trivial, but the author has seen many cases where schools have undertaken a more substantial project with much less searching examination.

▓▓ Costing organisational change

Apart from new projects, schools need to be aware of the cost implications when their curriculum or other aspects of organisation alter. An excellent example has occurred in England and Wales recently with the introduction of the National Curriculum. Two studies for the National Union of Teachers (1991 and 1992) by Coopers & Lybrand Deloitte showed that central government, LEAs and the schools themselves have substantially underestimated the cost implications.

In the case of primary schools, the study found that the extra costs for additional teaching staffing (mainly for curriculum planning and assessment), incentive allowances, new books and equipment, additional materials, and some modifications to premises, amounted to £129 per student in the first year of the new curriculum, falling gradually to £109 over five years – say an additional or replacement demand on the delegated budgets of an average primary school of some 12–14 per cent.

For secondary schools the situation is similar (see the author's account in *Managing Schools Today*, October 1992). A 'reasonable model of resource allocation' to introduce the National Curriculum effectively was costed at £280 per student in year 1, tapering to a steady-state of £108, extra costs of 20 to 8 per cent respectively. This extra burden was created by additional staffing for smaller class subjects like technology; assessment, meetings, curriculum and materials development; incentive allowances for new responsibilities; in-service training; increased technician and resource assistant support; new textbooks and resource materials; library improvements, stationery and materials; a substantial expansion in information technology; equipment, particularly science and technology; and modifications to premises.

These studies have been quoted because it appears that few schools have made a systematic cost audit of the requirements of the National Curriculum. Of course it can be argued that no school could see the complete picture; that the phased introduction of the new curriculum and some lag in response to it masked its full implications; that schools had been conditioned by years of stringency to effecting change on a shoestring; that schools were still too preoccupied with other changes, notably their recent acceptance of responsibility for their own budgets.

Yet the overriding impression remains that schools have been caught out. Major change has crept, or swept, on them, and they have not responded by quantifying their requirements even though many of them listed 'introduction of the National Curriculum' as an objective in their development plans. Somehow no warning light flashed: *Major change coming up – thorough costing needed*. The same story can be told in other countries.

■ Cost-effectiveness

Henry Levin in *Cost-effectiveness – A Primer* suggests:

Cost-effectiveness analysis … can lead to a more efficient use of educational resources; it can reduce the cost of reaching particular objectives; and it can expand what can be accomplished for any particular budget or other resource constraint.

Under the heading of cost-analysis he distinguishes:

1 Cost-effectiveness analysis, allowing comparison of different methods of achieving the *same* goal, such as improving test scores or reducing truancy or dropouts, by linking data on their costs and effectiveness.

2 Cost/benefit analysis, allowing comparison of the value of *alternative* goals or programmes, such as allocating resources to more able or less able students, by relating data on costs to the benefits of the alternatives expressed in monetary terms. This monetary expression of benefits allows comparison of different programmes, but it also involves the problem of setting financial values on non-financial benefits.

3 Cost utility analysis, allowing the comparison of alternative goals or programmes according to their costs and also their assessment for value by appropriate observers. An example would be evaluation of different reading schemes by competent assessors and weighting of their grading according to the costs involved. This has the advantage – and the disadvantage – of requiring less stringent data.

Of these three approaches, probably cost-effectiveness has the greatest value in schools. However, its use is far from straightforward. Identification of the questions to·be answered needs great care. The concepts of cost and effectiveness, while easily expressed in simple terms, are complex in practice. For example, deciding which costs should be allocated to a particular method or programme is not easy. Equally, deciding which outcomes should be assessed for effectiveness, and in what form, requires careful judgement, and often exposes conflicts of values.

An extensive recent cost-effectiveness study is described in Hywel Thomas's book *Education Costs and Performance: A Cost Effectiveness Analysis*. The study examined the cost-effectiveness of three sixth form colleges, six schools, two further education colleges and one tertiary college in educating three cohorts of students for A-level examinations. Many of Thomas's findings relate to policy issues outside the individual school or college: for example, he concluded that in his study the sixth form colleges were substantially more cost-effective than most of the school sixth forms for A-level attainment, whether in actual grades, value-added by adjusting grades for student performance at 16+, or pass rates. FE colleges fluctuated between the two groups on different criteria, but fared badly on dropout from courses.

Other findings from this study are related to financial management within schools. Thomas found a positive relationship between class-hours provided for A-level groups and ultimate outcomes, but no relationship for size of group: 'The number of candidates in a group has no significant effect on outcomes . . . While [group] size has no significant impact on effectiveness it has the most powerful effect on unit costs.' So would larger groups compensated with more contact time be better value for money? Of less importance, Thomas found that if an A-level group was taken by two teachers rather than one, or three rather than two, or a woman rather than a man, grades improved by just over 0.1 of a grade. In other words, one student in eight or nine improved a grade in their subject. Similarly, 'good' degree qualifications were associated with improvement of about half a grade per student, but older or longer serving teachers with slightly lower grades.

The author's own view is that cost-effectiveness analysis is a powerful concept that should be in every school manager's mental toolkit. But it is not feasible for most headteachers to make their own cost-effectiveness analysis – it is far too complex and time-consuming, as a glance as Thomas's book will show. However, they can use the results of an external study. Even here great care is needed in making sure that the findings can reasonably be applied in a new setting.

Particular care is needed with the interpretation of data. A striking example lies in the well-known study by Henry Levin (1985) of the cost-effectiveness of four educational interventions for increasing student achievement in mathematics and reading in elementary schools: computer-aided instruction of the 'drill-and-practice' kind (CAI); cross age tutoring in daily 20-minute sessions of younger by (a) older students with adult supervision, and (b) adult tutors; increased instructional time (one hour per day, half each for maths and reading); and reduction of class size (35 to 30 students; 30 to 25; 25 to 20; and 35 to 20). Research evidence across a number of studies on the effect of these interventions was carefully analysed to produce their estimated effectiveness, expressed in expected 'months of student gain' per year of instruction. The costs of each intervention were then estimated and linked to the achievement table to produce an estimate of 'months of additional student achievement gain per year of instruction for each $100 cost per student'. This data is set out in Table 10.

Table 10   Cost-effectiveness of four educational interventions

	1 2 Effectiveness in months of additional student gain per year of		3 Cost per student per subject ($)	4 5 Cost-effectiveness in months of additional student gain per year of instruction for each $100 cost per student	
	Maths	Reading		Maths	Reading
CAI	1.2	2.3	119	1.0	1.9
Peer tutoring	9.7	4.8	212	4.6	2.2
Adult tutoring	6.7	3.8	827	0.8	0.5
Increased instructional time	0.3	0.7	61	0.5	1.2
Reducing class size					
35 to 30	0.6	0.3	45	1.4	0.7
30 to 25	0.7	0.4	63	1.2	0.6
25 to 20	0.9	0.5	94	1.0	0.5
35 to 20	2.2	1.1	201	1.1	0.6
CAI (cost efficient form, see text)	1.2	2.3	75	1.6	3.1

Adapted from Levin, H. (1985, pp. 82–84)

Levin's conclusion was that:

…it appears that the specific CAI interventions evaluated in this study was more cost-effective than adult tutoring, reducing class size or increasing instructional time. However, it was considerably less cost-effective than peer-tutoring in mathematics and slightly less cost-effective in reading.

This CAI, however, was assumed to be delivered within a conventional school day. If we assume it could be delivered in a more cost-efficient form, with schools open longer to double access to computers (a perfectly feasible arrangement, explored further in Chapter 11), then the cost per student per subject would fall to about $75. The figures for CAI can then be revised as in the bottom line of table 10, making the 'cost-efficient' CAI over 60 per cent more effective than its predecessor, and now the most effective intervention for reading (although still not for mathematics).

So, assumptions underlying cost-effectiveness analysis need scrutiny!

▉ Productivity

▉ The nature of school productivity

Teachers often talk about improving standards or results, but never productivity. It is a term that schools are not comfortable with – it seems too mechanistic. Yet productivity is a central issue in other industries and indeed the economy as a whole.

Productivity is the improved relationship of outputs to inputs, achieved by the better use of labour, management, technology, information and capital in the production process.

INPUTS ← decreases — PRODUCTIVITY — increases → OUTPUTS
in use of resources

Inputs can be measured in physical units (the number of teachers, books etc.), or in financial units, or in units of working time (person-days, person-hours etc.).

For schools, measurement of outputs is notoriously difficult and a whole range of measures can be used. Those that relate to the long-term goals of schooling are often only available long after students have left school – improved earnings, skills and employment, status and health, effectiveness as citizens and as consumers, creativity etc. Measures that can be related more immediately to the school process – examination results and test scores, continuation of education, attendance and delinquency – are really proxies for the other measures. There is little agreement about how they should be used, and how account can be given to qualitative as well as quantitative outcomes.

Educationists have long puzzled over the nature of the school 'production process' and its productivity. An early pioneer study was made in England and Wales by Maureen Woodhall and Mark Blaug (1968). Their major finding was that:

> **... unless the quality of those who leave school has increased in some way that no-one has been able to measure, it takes more resources today to produce a standard secondary school leaver than in 1950.**

They found that although outputs had risen, inputs had risen faster, and estimated this decline in productivity at a rate of 1–2 per cent a year, at a time when productivity in manufacturing and service industries was rising by a similar amount.

Eric Hanushek has published a similar study of productivity in US schools in the period 1960–80, with a lucid overview of the underlying issues (*Journal of Economic Literature*, September 1986). He shows that there was little improvement in terms of high school graduation and college entry after 1965, while school test scores fell sharply in the period 1960–80, although student/teacher ratios fell while spending per student rose by 3.8 per cent in real terms annually. He concludes: 'The constantly rising costs and "quality" of the inputs of schools appears to be unmatched by improvement in the performance of students.' In other words, there was decreased productivity (unless a reduction in student quality can be proved).

In the UK there has been a rise in recent years in the number of examination passes and the percentage of students continuing in education. There is also evidence of improvement of the curriculum in its range and quality. But there is little evidence of increased text scores – rather a litany of complaints from employers and parents – and certainly no evidence of any single process like spelling or an aspect of mathematics being learned more effectively, more cheaply or more quickly.

Why is it so difficult to improve school productivity? Tim Simkins (1987) describes the difficulties encountered by economists as they have moved from macro 'production function' studies, relating outputs to inputs, to a second generation of micro-level studies focused on resource flows within the classroom, and then more recently to the nature and process of schools as economic organisations. A convincing comprehensive theory still eludes them. William Boyd and William Hartman argue (1988) that there are a range of problems. The goals of schools are ambiguous and not universally agreed and the outcomes difficult to measure. There is not yet a generally accepted model of how the school 'production process' works, and how it can be improved. Schools are loosely coupled organisations, so that it is difficult to connect a drive for increased productivity from the headteacher (or Minister of Education!) to any response in the classroom.

Schools are also complex organisations, with 'production' occurring inside two black boxes, the classroom and the learner's mind. Intangibles like school climate and ethos are increasingly seen as important. Finally, there are 'political' problems. Hartman studied budget decision-making in four US high schools and commented:

> ... the possibility of linking distribution of resources to improving student achievement was *never* considered explicitly ... the

primary objective of the allocation process ... was equality among teachers in workload and in meeting the teachers' self-declared needs for instructional supplies and equipment.

There is also a Catch 22 to school productivity: if it comes from improved outcomes alone there will be no reduction in cost; but if it springs from a reduction in teaching costs, there will be fewer teachers and so less variety and flexibility, teacher-to-student contact and social control. (These are all difficult to measure and so likely to be overlooked in any scrutiny of productivity.)

■ Improving school productivity

How can school productivity be improved? There seem to be three kinds of strategies available.

Diffusion strategies

There are a number, all of which seek to improve school performance by 'diffusion' of new attitudes and skills throughout the school. All share a focus on outcomes, spreading of good practice and improvement of existing processes. They do not use specific interventions in student learning, or seek to alter the level or mix of inputs (though they eventually may do this to some extent).

Making schools more effective. There are a range of current approaches – the effective schools movement (e.g. the International Congress for School Effectiveness and Improvement, and particularly the work of Professor Michael Fullan in Ontario); the self-managing collaborative school (well advocated by Brian Caldwell and Jim Spinks); 'performance management'; 'quality management'; and indeed the general emphasis on development plans and improved school management.

It seems reasonable to assume that this kind of approach is likely to lead to better management and therefore better outcomes in the long term. And it may cost little initially – although it can lead to changes in budget allocations and resource management. It does also require a great deal of time and commitment; it is not easy to introduce in schools hostile to it, or blind to the need for it; and from a hard-headed financial viewpoint, it may be difficult to see an immediate association with improved outcomes or productivity. This is a long-term investment.

Enhanced professionalism. Here improved training and professional development is seen as the key to improved teaching and learning. So advances in the quality and quantity of INSET, mentoring and coaching, effective appraisal, school-based initial training and improved school climate are crucial. There are immediate but marginal financial implications – perhaps 1–2 per cent of the budget. The downside is similar to that above – time and commitment; resistance from the culture; and slow maturing results.

'Working smarter'. Peter Drucker began a recent article in the *Harvard Business Review* (November 1991): 'The single greatest challenge facing managers in the developed countries of the world is to raise the productivity of knowledge and service workers.' He argues that the more effective use of skilled labour – 'working smarter' – is the solution, and he suggests five stages:

1 Defining *essential* tasks (and shedding unnecessary or less essential ones).

2 Concentrating work on these tasks.

3 Defining performance, in quality and quantity: 'What works? And how is it done?'

4 Close partnership of managers and job holders – with the latter's knowledge of their own jobs the starting point.

5 A continuous learning – and teaching – process to improve techniques.

This kind of approach has much in common with 'performance management' and 'total quality management'.

Market forces. Unlike the previous strategies, this is not controlled by the schools. In a sense it springs from politicians' despair at improving schools from within. It is state governments that decide whether state schools are to operate in a planned system or in a market. For the latter, they set parents free to choose schools and schools free to meet parents' preferences. Grant maintained and LMS schools are already in that position in the UK, as are Charter schools in New Zealand. There are trends in that direction in several Australian states, and in parts of the USA (e.g. the Californian Charter schools, starting in 1994).

The implicit aim of the 'market forces' strategy is improved performance, but it is not yet clear that this will be achieved. It is quite possible that some schools may improve and others deteriorate. Current research shows some schools changing their educational process to meet market competition (e.g. increasing homework or emphasising discipline) but others concentrating on cosmetic processes like improving the school's appearance or public image.

For schools in a competitive market there are implications for financial management. Such schools are likely to be more entrepreneurial, with more emphasis on fund raising and income generation; more interested in developing distinctive features by investing in specific areas; more concerned with improved presentation, by expenditure on the appearance of the school's buildings, printing and stationery, PR and advertising.

High-tech alternatives (see Chapter 11)

Despite the false dawns of programmed learning, language laboratories and computer assisted learning, there are still hopes of a technological breakthrough. The logic for this occurring at some time is strong, but the implications for school organisation are profound. And it will be costly.

Low-tech alternatives (see Chapter 11)

Some of the low-cost alternatives like peer tutoring and extensive use of volunteers have great promise – in theory. In practice they have hardly been tried. This loops back to the 'political' resistance to productivity changes. Stirring up the natives with non-traditional alternatives may not be a very rational choice for a headteacher or principal.

* * *

What is the future for productivity in schools? The author's own guess is that we shall see only slow gains from improved school effectiveness, 'working smarter', better professional development and market forces – though we should not despise them. Peters and Waterman continually stressed the importance of 'small wins' for their successful companies. For major gains we probably need some alternative technologies, but the problem is – which? (And how?) These radical alternatives are examined more fully in the final chapter.

Looking back, this chapter may seem of limited immediate use to a busy school manager. But unless you can come to grips with some of the issues raised here in the context of your own school, you will remain a tactician rather than strategist. Some appreciation of costs, cost-effectiveness and productivity must underlie any substantial advance in relating financial management to school improvement.

11 Alternative and future strategies

Different approaches

One generation's sense is the next generation's nonsense. We can look back to earlier school financial management and wonder at our forebears' eccentricities. Why ever did they do things like that? So what will future generations find absurd in our arrangements?

There seem to be two factors in this mismatch between present and future perceptions. First, the future is different, and so the systems to serve it need to be different. Second, our present arrangements are constrained by a paradigm of assumptions and attitudes which the later generation may shed. So to see how strategies for financial management may – or should – alter, this chapter begins by first attempting to forecast the future for schools, and then critiquing our current paradigm of schooling.

The future for schools, and their finance

Schools in the Information Age

The Information Age – that mass of technological, industrial, economic and social change which is now upon us, comparable in importance to the Industrial Revolution – is already affecting the process and goals of education and is likely to do so increasingly. Knowledge or traditional skills are not enough. What is now important is the ability to access information, use and communicate it, supported by the ability to learn and retrain lifelong, work in teams and solve problems, and by qualities such as initiative and resourcefulness. The year-by-year change may be small but the cumulative effect will be revolutionary.

The technological impact of the Information Age on schools is likely to be different. In *Managing School Time* (1989), the present author suggested:

... f the information society is driven by the development of new electronic technology for the transfer, storage and retrieval of information and for communication, and if education is largely (but not solely) concerned with information and communication, then it is difficult to believe that education will not eventually be transformed, just like other information and communication industries.

... the main thrust of the new technology will be to individualise education, tailoring it to the needs of each student. So it will no longer be necessary for education to be age-related or status-related (school age or adult, full-time or part-time). It will not need to be school-based – students can learn at home, at other centres or through a wider network. And education will not need to be time ration related; students can take as little or as much time as they need.

... In the foreseeable future the new educational technology will not affect all aspects of school. The main impact will be in 'classroom' areas... it will be used much less extensively in areas of practical or affective activity such as practical science, technology, the arts and physical education... Even in the classroom areas it will only be used for part of the time. The inappropriateness or lack of technology and its software for particular areas and activities, the limitations of finance and the reservations of teachers will delay its full use ...

It is important to keep a realistic view. No area will be immune – values for example could be taught by interactive video – but no area will be completely taken over. Probably the actual time spent by students in using the new technology will only be a small proportion of the week. But – and this is the key point – a school cannot be part changed and part unchanged.

Now you may say that despite all the hype so far the new technology has only had a marginal impact on teaching and learning. That is true, but it misunderstands the nature of such change. We are currently in that exploratory stage where technology is being tried in various ways. This smouldering, often irregular advance may well continue for some years... until the critical mass develops of tried technology at the right price with proven systems and user confidence – and with the ability to deliver the same outcomes at least as cheaply as the conventional classroom. At that point fundamental system change will occur. Figure 34 represents this process.

In figure 34 the line AE represents our expectations of change – a straight line because we find it difficult to think exponentially. AD

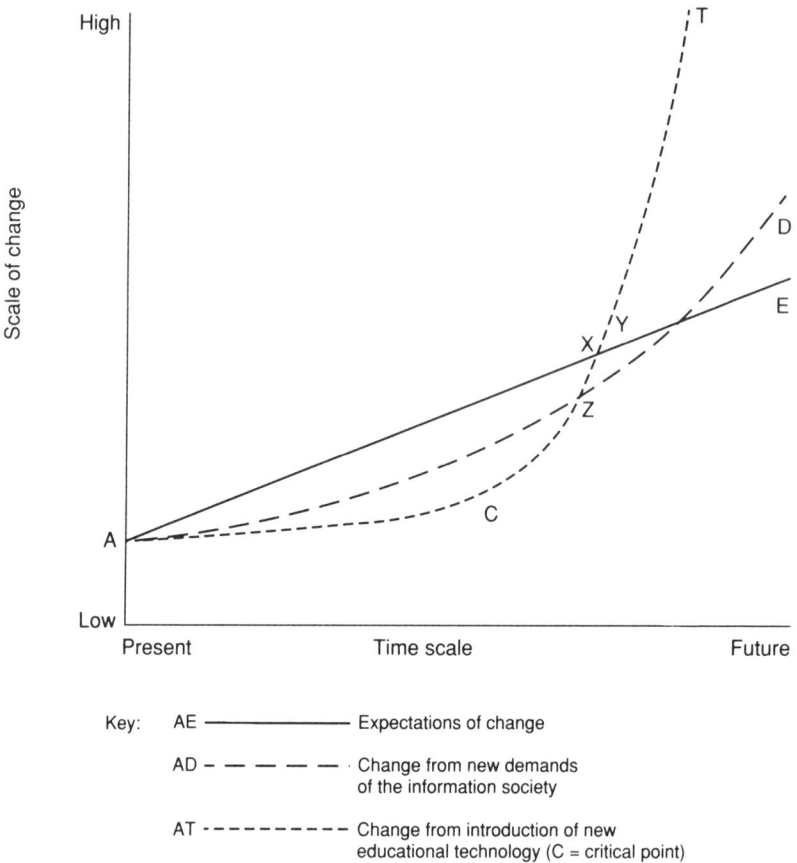

Figure 34 A model of future system changes in schools (Source: Knight, B., 1989b)

represents the exponential changes in the education process demanded by society. AT represents the impact of new educational technology – much less than expected at first, but accelerating rapidly at the point of critical mass, C.

Future financial prospects

The financial implications of such changes are substantial. There will be large capital outlays for the new technology itself, adaptations of buildings, furniture, storage and security. Recurrent costs will include software and consumables, INSET, technician support, maintenance, depreciation and insurance. John Abbott, the experienced Director of Education 2000, a project with heavy IT implementation, estimates the cost at £100 per pupil per annum, say an increase of 6–12 per cent p.a. in unit costs. This is a substantial increase, lifting school expenditure to a new, capital intensive plateau. It is unlikely that in most schools it could be financed by savings in other areas – it would be equivalent for example to a 9–15 per cent reduction in teacher budget. Moreover the curriculum and student development needed in the Information Age will require more person-to-person contact and so smaller classes, with more time – and so are unlikely to be cheaper.

More mundane changes are also predictable to some extent. Demography will vary from country to country, but generally the severe fall in student numbers is now levelling in developed countries, while in developing countries increasing numbers of school age children drives the system to the point of decline. In developed countries an increase in funding is required for extended participation – pre-school, post-compulsory and adult/third age – and community education; and probably for increased consumer demand for 'quality' in education, corresponding to advances in quality in other areas of consumption. Moreover, if productivity in schools lags behind that in industry and commerce, education will require more expenditure to maintain salary levels.

All the above factors require increases in funding in real terms for schools, some of these substantial, with the only possible savings from demography, or increased productivity, or increased fund raising or fees. But is increased funding for education, despite rhetoric about its importance, likely to appear? The position will vary from country to country, but in general the competing demands of an ageing population, increased social welfare, and other government services which are also affected by similar cost-push factors, seem likely to resist this (unless there is substantial growth in the GNP).

So, productivity is likely to become a central issue. Governments will look to improved productivity both to reduce pressures on their budgets and to improve the outcomes of the educational system. But productivity comes in various forms:

- 'Higher-cost' productivity – i.e. increased outcomes in relation to inputs, but requiring a higher level of inputs.
- 'Zero-cost' productivity – i.e. increased outcomes for the same level of inputs.
- 'Lower-cost/fixed outcomes' productivity – i.e. the same outcomes for less inputs.
- 'Lower-cost/improved outcomes' productivity – i.e. increased outcomes for less inputs.

Governments will prefer, but perhaps not obtain, the last of these. They will be less interested in productivity gains that require greater outlay.

▨ An unhelpful paradigm?

A paradigm is that set of values and beliefs which people construct around a particular reality and which then governs their behaviour. The present paradigm of schooling developed as a response to the needs of the Industrial Revolution and the nation state, and became firmly established in the later part of the nineteenth century. It now prevails worldwide. The paradigm assumes that education should generally be:

- provided largely by the state, free and compulsory within defined ages;
- universal, open equally to the children of all its citizens (but with special assistance for the disadvantaged);
- uniform, with centrally specified curriculum and assessment and with some uniformity of administration;
- provided within those institutions we call schools;
- delivered by teachers using traditional technology (printed paper, talk and chalk) with students grouped in classes;
- delivered within a fixed time-frame ('all in/all out' school day and year).

It is in the nature of a paradigm that it does not change until problems and anomalies become so acute that a new paradigm provides a better fit with new conditions. It may, however, incorporate some adjustments, provided they do not affect the core beliefs. So, for example, the current trend worldwide for greater parental participation in school management adjusts the paradigm but does not alter it. Site-based management is similar. The current UK movement towards quasi-independent grant maintained schools and the weakening of an LEA administered system appears to threaten parts of the paradigm, but even here central financing and control remains.

The problem with paradigms is that, although they appear to explain reality and provide constancy in a changing world, they lock our thinking into a particular pattern and discourage our considering alternatives, some of which may be more rational solutions to our current problems.

An example will illustrate this. Please sketch the rectangle 'A' on a piece of paper, and then divide it into four portions.

```
┌──────────────┐
│              │
│              │         A
│              │
└──────────────┘
```

Now look at the alternatives in figure 35 overleaf. Was your division similar to B, C or D? Or less regular, like E, F and G? Or more eccentric, like H, I and J? This is not a paradigm, of course, but it is a small illustration of how a set way of looking at things channels our thinking.

Our present paradigm is likely to become vulnerable to technological and other Information Age changes. But until it shifts, it hinders alternative thinking about the system of financial management we have created to serve it. It hinders particularly any radical approach to productivity. For why should educational productivity improve in the future if it has not done so in the past?

The remainder of this chapter looks at alternative strategies that singly or together might help to solve the productivity conundrum. Space is limited, however, and so it is not possible to explore all their full implications or the equity or value issues which lurk beneath them.

■ High-tech (and high-cost) strategies

Probably most of the technology we need already exists: the microcomputer, modem and telephone, compact disc and video, networks, cable TV and satellite communication. It is rapidly becoming more reliable, miniaturised and cheap. Teachers and headteachers are becoming more confident in its use. But linking of devices has a long way to go, as has the quality of software and resource materials. And it is not really clear yet how such technology can be best used, and whether (or how) it can improve outcomes. There is certainly very little expertise about how school organisation can be adapted to allow its full use (and given the degree of capital investment this is an important issue).

However, we can analyse the possible effects of new technology and their relationship with productivity. They can be categorised:

1 Improved quality of education through the actual experience presented. Examples could be advantages of video over textbook pictures or computer modelling over static graphs.

2 Improved quality of education from the process of using new technology; e.g. interrogating a database rather than combing reference books, word-processing and redrafting an assignment rather than writing a single draft.

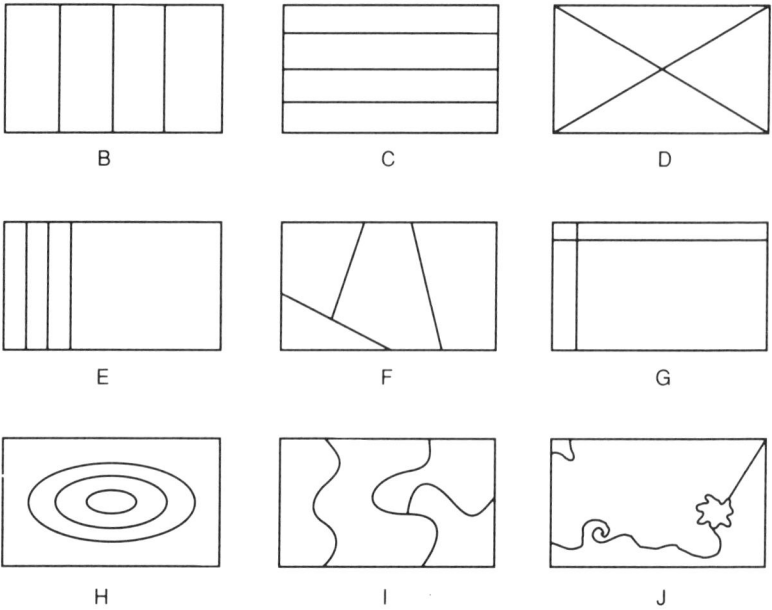

Figure 35   Alternative approaches to a problem

3 Improved level of achievement by students spending additional time using technology, outside of normal class hours.

4 Learning an element of the curriculum more efficiently; i.e. with greater understanding and recall for the same investment of time, or the same achievement in less time (largely the same thing).

From the viewpoint of financial management it is important to note that the first three can only provide 'higher-cost' productivity. Only (4) offers the possibility of 'zero-cost' or 'lower-cost' productivity, and this only if the time saved can lead to financial savings (e.g. if more effective learning allows the amount of the week for which students are taught by high-salary staff to be reduced).

Peter Drucker warns (p. 71) in the article quoted earlier:

Thirty years ago we were sure the efficiency of the computer would lead to massive reductions in clerical and office staff ... Yet office and clerical forces have grown at a much faster rate since the introduction of information technology than ever before. But there has been virtually no increase in the productivity of service work.

He makes a similar point about hospitals. The implication is therefore that, while any use of new technology may (but not necessarily will) improve productivity, the only use likely to avoid extra expenditure is a speeding up of learning. So however attractive other aspects may be, we should concentrate initially on developing technological systems to speed up basic learning of key knowledge, concepts and skills (for example the drudgery of spelling, grammar, elementary mathematics, learning of a foreign language). This is comparable to the trend in industry and commerce for less complicated and more repetitive mechanical processes to be automated first.

A high-tech strategy has other implications for financial management. It requires careful projection of estimated costs, both start-up and recurrent, as discussed in Chapter 10; careful purchasing (but there is never a best time to buy new technology); proper allowance for maintenance, security and depreciation. It also implies a different mix of elements within the budget, as discussed below.

Low-tech (and low-cost) strategies

A wide range of alternative low-tech strategies are available to schools, many of them needing little or no additional funding. They are focused on individual students and either complement class learning or improve student motivation. Because most are low-cost they deserve close attention: they could offer good value for money, improved outcomes and increased productivity. But . . . all of them involve change in working practice and most threaten the paradigm of the traditional school.

Individualised or flexible learning (outside the normal class framework)

This umbrella heading covers a range of possibilities: personal self-directed study; study periods in or outside the timetable; structured individual study programmes (e.g. the Dalton plan, as at Bryanston School, Dorset); Supported Self Study and Flexible Learning, with tutoring an essential element (e.g. schemes promoted by the NCET (National Council for Educational Technology and the Training Agency); programmed learning; distance learning by correspondence. (Homework is discussed separately below.)

All of these focus on the needs of individual students, and evaluation of some of the Supported Self Study schemes have been very positive. However, many of the schemes require costly tutoring, and there is usually a need for a person to coordinate, plus non-teaching support and a range of additional resources. Materials can be costly unless there are large economies of scale in production. Even correspondence schemes are quite high-cost, while unstructured individualised study, although low-cost, offers the least gains. So extended individualised learning may be very valuable for the skills it teaches and so broaden the range of outcomes, but where it requires a heavy staffing component or heavy investment in development it may not achieve high productivity gains.

Homework

Homework is already extensively used, but under-managed. Many schools do not examine its use critically enough for quality, quantity, type of assignment, potential for relating study to the home and community environment, relationship with classroom work, and involvement of parents. So it probably has considerable scope for development. From the school's viewpoint it is very cheap.

Use of the home as a learning resource

Although primary schools in particular often go to great lengths to develop home–school partnerships, most schools do not tap homes fully *as a learning resource.* Yet the sum of the learning resources in parents' homes far exceeds that in the school itself – the books, computers, televisions and videos, newspapers and magazines, holidays and visits and the human skills and expertise.

Probably a real attempt to maximise use of these huge learning resources, coordinated with school learning and linked with school–parent liaison, would be very cost-effective. It would certainly be a low-cost strategy, perhaps only involving a part-time coordinator and some expenses. As far as the author knows, it has not really been tried. (Oddly, though, schools frequently exploit learning resources *outside* the home, i.e. in the community.)

Home–school learning liaison

There are many well-attested schemes to show the value of home–school liaison. Most of these are intended to increase parental support and understanding or improve pastoral care, but some have been targeted on learning improvement. J. Tizard reported in a 1982 research article on a London borough scheme whereby two classes of children were heard to read about three times per week by their parents, who were supported with briefing meetings and home visits. These children made highly significant reading gains, in comparison with two control classes and two other classes who received additional reading support from a teacher. Parents were pleased to be involved, even if non-literate or not fluent in English. Teachers reported improved keen-ness and behaviour.

Such a scheme is not very expensive – mainly the additional cost of a part-time aide. Tizard comments:

> The findings of the present study suggest that staffing resources at present allocated . . . for remedial work in primary schools might be better employed, at least in part, in organising contact and collabo-ration between class teachers and parents . . . *on specific practical teaching matters* (my italics), and that this might prevent many chil-dren from falling behind in their reading in the first place.

Pre-school enrichment

There is now strong evidence emerging from the USA that schemes pro-viding positive support to deprived families, such as Headstart, improve long-term outcomes such as continuation in school, school attainments, avoidance of criminality, employment and progression to higher education.

Community education

Many schools are now into community involvement and interaction: linking the curriculum with community activities and needs; serving the community; gaining community support, financial and human; pro-viding adult classes and activities, and training or support for specific groups; enrolling adults in school classes and vice versa; letting school facilities . . . the list is endless.

Community education certainly makes more use of the school's capi-tal assets; it may improve the school's resourcing, financially or other-wise; it will usually make schooling richer and warmer. It can be self-supporting financially, though usually it is not. But it is unlikely to lead to measurable gains in outcomes from school students.

Adult volunteers and peer tutoring

These were discussed earlier in Chapter 5. Both are low-cost. They require a coordinator, possibly part-time, and some materials/support costs. Levin has shown (p. 188) that peer tutoring can be very cost-effec-tive, and the same is almost certainly true of volunteers. But both can appear as competition against conventional teaching, and both require extended or flexible school day arrangements for effective use. Take-up in schools has been slow.

Counselling

Several studies have suggested that funds spent on counselling students who are under-achieving can be more effective in improving performance than the same amount of teaching time. Unfortunately this is still an expensive, labour-intensive process. So while it may improve productivity, it is not likely to reduce expenditure and may actually increase it.

Coaching

Anecdotal evidence suggests that one-to-one or small-group academic coaching can have a similar effect of raising student confidence and morale. However, coaching is little used in most state schools outside normal classes, other than a little squeezed into odd moments. Schools in the USA often have a session at the end of the day where teachers are available to help students with problems. Schools could possibly provide coaching as a service for a fee – as some independent schools do, and like many private coaching agencies. Remission could be provided for low-income families.

Coaching provided on that basis would not improve productivity more than private coaching does; but from the school's viewpoint it would be cost-effective, producing increased achievement for no extra cost *to the school*.

Rewards and incentives

Schools are not heavily into incentives. They often make extensive use of symbolic rewards, although some schools could develop a more positive rewards policy. Why not incentives? Parents use them often, but are they acceptable in schools (e.g. cash or other attractive rewards for under-achieving students who improve)? As an example, Norham Community School in North Shields has provided free cinema tickets or excursions donated by local firms to reward students with 100 per cent attendance.

A medical alternative: the biology of learning

Sports medicine has had a profound effect on the performance of athletes, and space medicine on that of astronauts. It will be surprising if ultimately medicine is not used for similar advances in learning. This will require a cross-fertilising of knowledge about the operation and chemistry of the brain, neurology, hormones, allergies, diet and vitamins, additives and pollution etc., as well as genetics, paediatrics and psychology. There is no accepted term for it. Education medicine is hardly the right phrase. Perhaps we can think of the 'biology of learning'.

Such an advance – projected, since there is little attempt yet to coordinate work in this area – could offer dramatic gains in productivity. It could be relatively low-cost, and could be funded by parents, or schools (as with free school milk to improve physical performance) or by states (as with immunisation programmes). But of course there will be a range of attendant problems.

* * *

Low-tech strategies such as these ought to be attractive to school financial managers. They are mostly low-cost; most offer improved performance, to a varying degree; they are considerably under-used, even untried, and so probably have more potential than better known strategies. But . . . they are less familiar, more threatening to teachers and more difficult to develop. They do not always fit into existing budget classifications, or existing school organisation.

■ Facilitating alternative strategies

■ Organisational change

There are already signs of change in schools as organisations, with a growth of part-time and temporary staff and use of consultants and contracted firms. The boundary of schools has loosened, with more interaction with their communities and consortia of other schools and colleges.

We can extrapolate this trend further. Charles Handy argues in *The Age of Unreason* for the creation of a responsive learning organisation which alone can cope with chronic unpredictable change. He describes a 'shamrock organisation' (Chapter 4), with three leaves to the stem: a small professional core (directing the organisation); outworkers (specialists to whom a large part of the organisation's work is contracted); and a flexible labour force of part-time and temporary workers, particularly important for service industries which cannot stockpile products.

Handy suggests (p. 169) that as a shamrock organisation a school should make its core activities the devising of an appropriate education programme for each child and arranging for its delivery – the core of the curriculum by itself, but the remainder contracted out to independent specialist agencies ('mini-schools'). Here we can envisage buying in or contracting out for foreign languages, technical education, special needs, physical or arts education etc.

Example Ombudsman Educational Services of Libertyville, Illinois has provided special programmes for school boards since 1975. Currently it has twelve projects in Illinois, Arizona and Minnesota with over 2000 students. It is contracted to provide a compressed individual programme for 'at risk' students in off campus premises, using individualised learning plans, extensive competency-based computer instruction, personal tutoring and positive reinforcement. Good achievement gains and low drop-out are reported, and fees are lower than current school board unit costs. Similarly Dialogos International Inc. of Raleigh, North Carolina, provides languages teaching for school boards.

Handy also urges the virtue of 'federalism', with organisations delegating powers to the centre for an agreed purpose. The recent growth of school clusters and consortia is already pointing in this direction. Other possibilities could include 'intrepreneurship' (insiders taking responsibility for particular developments and being rewarded for them) and franchising (e.g. of outside coaching).

Developments like these may or may not improve productivity. They certainly make it easier to introduce some of the alternative strategies discussed earlier. They have substantial implications for school financial management, costing and budget construction. In particular they make decisions on 'mix' more important – not just between teachers, other staff, premises, goods and services, but between the core, the flexible workforce and outworkers.

■ School day design

Most of the other alternatives explored above – use of new technology, individualised or flexible learning, improved homework, use of the home as a resource, community interaction, adult volunteers, peer tutoring, counselling and coaching, student credits and incentives, better understanding of the biology of learning – are focused on students as individuals. Yet the traditional school day is organised for students in groups (i.e. in classes). So the traditional day is not a favourable environment for such alternatives to flourish.

The present author has argued strongly in *Designing the School Day* (pp. 46–50, 151–55) for a two-part or 'tight–loose' day, the first part an extended traditional morning, the second a flexible and extended afternoon and evening to allow activities focused on individual students to flourish, in school and beyond it, as in figure 36. This would also encourage home tuition. Other models are also possible.

An alternative school day strategy is not an optional extra. It is a necessary condition for widespread (rather than minimal) adoption of alternative strategies. It also supports the new approaches to school organisation discussed above. It has some direct financial implications, discussed

Model for primary schools

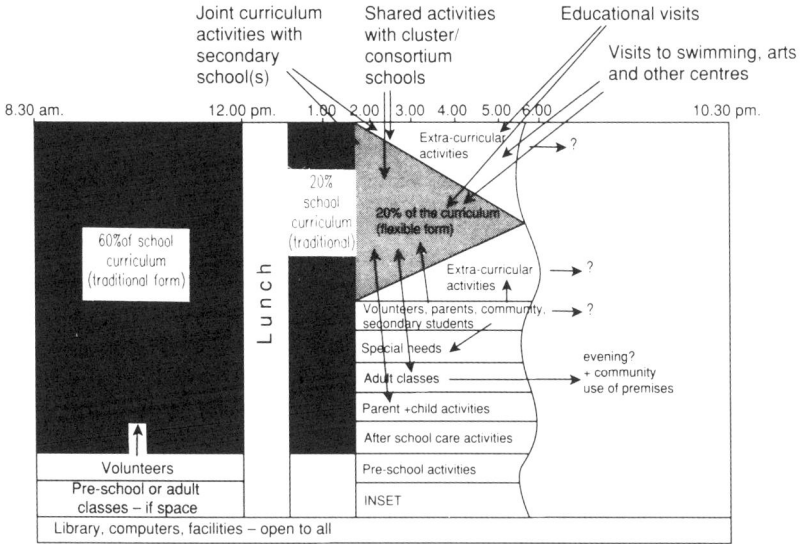

Model for secondary schools

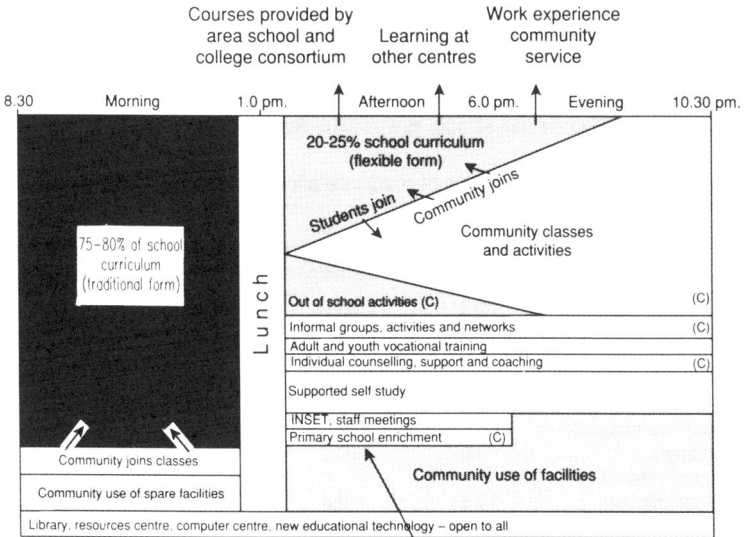

Key: (C) = particulary suitable for community volunteers

Figure 36 An alternative model of the school day (Source: Knight, B., 1992)

briefly on page 174, but its main relevance to financial management lies in the opening of new possibilities for advances in productivity.

■ Alternative financial strategies

New approaches are possible, particularly in relation to some of the alternatives discussed earlier.

New models of allocation

Concern is often expressed at the high proportion of school budgets spent on teachers' salaries and associated costs. This often springs from the realisation that a substantial increase in classroom learning resources or non-teaching support staff is only equivalent to a small decrease in teacher salary expenditure. It is underpinned theoretically by the economists' law of diminishing marginal returns (for a clear exposition see Monk, 1990, pp. 356–58). However, little change in the mix of resources has actually occurred.

The alternative approaches discussed earlier in this chapter are, however, likely to prompt new models of resource allocation, as table 11 suggests. Column 1 shows allocation of resources for a conventional school (based on that set out in table 4 on p. 106), while columns 2, 3 and 4 show alternative allocations. Column 2 (high-tech strategies) shows an increase in INSET and non-teaching salaries to support the new technology, with minor premises adaptations. The cost of the new technology itself is reflected in the sharp rise in classroom supplies.

Table 11 Alternative patterns of resource allocation in schools (budget %)

	1 Current allocation	2 High-tech strategies	3 Low-tech strategies	4 Organisational changes
Teacher salaries	72.0	63.0	67.0	30.0 Core 20.0 Flexible 20.0 Outworkers
INSET	1.0	2.0	2.0	1.0
Non-teacher support salaries	8.0	11.0	11.0	10.0
Premises-related expenditures	10.6	10.8	11.0	10.6
Classroom supplies	3.7	8.0	4.3	3.7
Other supplies and services	——4.7	——5.2	——4.7	——4.7
TOTAL, other than teaching	28.0	37.0	33.0	30.0

Note that these figures are illustrative only – see text

Column 3 (low-tech strategies) shows double the investment in INSET and more use of para-professional non-teaching staff. Increases in premises expenditure reflects extended all-day use, and in classroom supplies the growth of individualised learning.

Column 4 (organisational changes) shows the division of teacher salaries to reflect changes in school organisation, and an increase in para-professional non-teaching staff.

Please note that the figures are only illustrative to show the sort of changes that might occur. They are actually quite timid – changes in some schools may be much more fundamental in 20 years' time. If the total budget remained unaltered, the table implies a reduction in teacher staffing salaries to fund the changes (but even here this remains by far the largest element). The original level of teacher salaries could be retained for a budget increase of:

Column 2: 9%   Column 3: 5%   Column 4: 2%

Directing resources to individual students

If we are really going to tap the marvellous learning capacity of each human being, we need to enable resources to flow to individual students to meet their specific needs, not just to categories of expenditure or pro-grammes. There are two steps to be taken.

1 Costing individual students' activities. At present, state schools have lit-tle or no idea of their 'production costs' for individual students. Just ask the cost per student-hour for physics, or reading, or a foreign language, or swimming . . . and meet an embarrassed or indignant silence. Yet this kind of *process* costing is commonplace in many industries, and the pre-requisite for productivity gains.

More important, we need to look at *performance* costing: the cost of reaching a given level of performance, or of adding specific value; e.g. in physics, reading, a foreign language, swimming etc. Process costing is useful for illuminating financial management. It gives insights. But per-formance costing allows comparisons with the alternative strategies available. Some of these will only take root when they are shown to be more cost-effective.

Such process and performance costing per student will be an essential management tool in the future, for both analysis and planning and for evaluation. It is not of course needed for the budget statement used for authorisation and monitoring.

2 Funding individual students' activities. The next step is to use this costing information to give each student access to resources to meet his or her needs. This could be achieved in various ways, but probably the simplest would be an internal voucher or credit system. Suppose, for example, that 80 per cent of the curriculum is provided in the normal way, but for the remainder each student is given credits (perhaps so many 'units'). He or she could then spend these units on courses or activities to meet particular learning needs, in consultation with parents and a tutor.

With modern IT systems it should be straightforward to log up the credits used by each student (possibly with more available for purchase?). One student's allocation might look like this:

Budget allocation for J. Smith, 24 units (1 unit £10)

Item	Quantity	Cost per student hour (£)	Total cost(£)	Units
[Class teaching	800 hours	1.20	960	N/a]
Use of IT	150 hours	0.50	75	7.5
Supported Self Study	40 hours	1.00	40	4.0
Peer tutoring	50 hours	0.40	20	2.0
Small-group coaching	10 hours	2.50	25	2.5
Community or optional school classes	40 hours	1.25	50	5.0
Progress counselling	2 hours	15.00	30	3.0
TOTAL			1200	24.0
[cf. Conventional timetable	1000 hours	1.20	1200]	

The system would be not unlike a community education centre that costs and offers a range of courses and activities, except that here payment is by credit and not by cash. It would require an effective support system to assess the needs of each student, provide advice, organise enrolment and assess progress.

■ Conclusion?

This text has argued that a more thoughtful and analytical approach to school management is needed. It is not just a matter of doing things right, but of doing the right things. The following have been suggested:

- Establishing long-term planning, and linking this effectively to the budget and to student outcomes (Chapter 2).
- Defining roles and responsibilities clearly and setting up efficient systems (Chapter 3).

- Allocating funds within the school efficiently and with greater consideration of the alternative mechanisms available (Chapter 4).

- Systematic fund raising and income generation (Chapter 5).

- Anticipating and offsetting the effect of cuts, inflation, and operating below capacity (Chapter 6).

- Policies for depreciation and capital replacement, stock and risk management (Chapter 6).

- Deeper analysis of budget alternatives, and a more thoughtful approach to budget construction and format (Chapter 7).

- Effective systems of budget monitoring and financial control, and both functional and strategic budget evaluation (Chapter 8).

- An equity audit and action plan (Chapter 8).

- Improved management of human resources, premises, supplies and services, and school time (Chapter 9).

- Greater use of unit costs as a management tool (Chapter 10).

- Systematic costing of projects and changes (Chapter 10).

- Focusing on cost-effectiveness and productivity (Chapter 10).

- Exploring alternative strategies to improve productivity (Chapter 11).

Any school adopting even some of these should be both more efficient and more effective. However, the importance of improved financial management runs much deeper. In the next 20 years or so we shall see more profound changes in schooling than at any time in the history of education – changes prompted by developments in technology and the biology of learning, but supported by new approaches to learning and improved management of schools. This will shake our idea of how students should be educated and what they can achieve, and our conception of what a school should be. It will demand vision, lateral thinking, and leadership. It will be vital that such changes are facilitated by imaginative financial management. If this book assists that process, our time will have been well spent.

And finally, what about your school students? What benefit will they gain?

Bibliography, references and addresses

■ Select bibliography

This is a very personal selection, containing titles that the author has found useful, and/or which he feels would help readers who wish to start burrowing more deeply. Titles relating to specific aspects will be found under References.

Financial management: practical and theoretical aspects

For the UK, a useful book is Fidler, B. and Bowles, G. (eds), *Effective Local Management of Schools*, Longman (1989). It is uneven but contains some helpful chapters with a blend of theory and practice, as well as an extensive bibliography. There is an accompanying workbook which contains some useful exercises.

Hart, J., *Successful Financial Planning and Management in Schools*, Longman (1993), is a useful manual on operational practicalities. Downes, P. (ed), *Financial Management in Schools,* Blackwell (1988), contains a good deal of sound practitioner's advice, now somewhat outdated in detail for the LMS context in England and Wales, but still useful for schools first receiving financial delegation.

Levačić, R. (ed), *Financial Management in Education,* Open University (1989), is an OU reader with 20 extracts, some practical and some theoretical. So it is a good introduction to the subject but with the limitations of any anthology.

A comprehensive and authoritative handbook written for US school administrators is Wood, R. Craig (ed), *Principles of School Business Management,* Association of School Business Officials International, Reston, Va (1986). A number of the contributions have relevance outside the USA.

There is a growing number of useful practical articles appearing in periodicals, particularly *Managing Schools Today* (Questions Publishing, 6 Hockley Hill, Birmingham B18 5AA) and *The Times Educational Supplement*, with research articles in *Educational Management and*

Administration (Journal of the British Educational Management and Administration Society). Theoretical articles occur in *Economics of Education Review* and *Journal of Educational Finance.*

The annual yearbooks of the American Education Finance Association are a good source; for example:

Guthrie J. (ed), *School Finance Policies and Practices*, Ballinger, Cambridge, Mass (1980).

Odden, A. and Webb, L. (eds), *School Finance and School Improvement: Linkages for the 80's,* Ballinger, Cambridge, Mass (1983).

Monk, D. and Underwood, J., *Macro Level School Finance: Issues and Implications for Policy*, Ballinger, Cambridge, Mass (1988).

Cost and management accountancy

The standard texts on cost and management accountancy (but *not* financial accounting or public finance) have much to offer, and cover a much wider field than just accounting. They are written for commercial organisations, but much of the material on costs, budgeting, financial control etc. is useful. You need to apply it to the school context – and be prepared to skip. Almost any text on cost and management accounting would be useful.

Horngren, C., *Cost Accounting: A Management Emphasis* (4th edn), Prentice Hall, Englewood Cliffs, NJ (1977), is particularly useful. The latest 7th edn (1991) by Horngren and Foster seems less comprehensive, although accompanied by Dearden, J., *Management Accounting* (same publisher, 1988).

Other good examples are:

Durie, C., *Management and Cost Accounting* (3rd edn), Chapman Hall (1992).

Emmanuel, C., Otley, D. and Merchant, K., *Accounting for Management Control,* Chapman Hill (1991).

Financial management development outside the UK

A useful short summary of recent devolution developments can be found in Chapter 2 of Hill, D., Oakley Smith, B. and Spinks, J., *Local Management of Schools,* Paul Chapman (1990). Caldwell, B. and Spinks, J., *Leading the Self Managing School,* Falmer Press (1992), contains a short overview in Chapter 1 of trends in school management in English-speaking countries in the 1990s.

Canada. A very concise account of the Edmonton experience is provided in Smilanich, R., *Devolution in Edmonton Public Schools: Ten Years Later* (1988), a mimeographed paper from the author, Centre for Education, One Kingsway, Edmonton, Alberta T5H 4G9. Additional information on

Edmonton and other school districts of Western Canada can be found in Brown, D., *Decentralisation and School-Based Management*, Falmer Press (1990).

Australia. There does not seem to be an overview publication. Spicer, B., 'Programme budgeting – a way forward in school management', in Chapman, J. (ed), *School Based Decision Making and Management*, Falmer Press (1990), describes financial management in the state of Victoria.

New Zealand. The key document is *Tomorrow's Schools* (1988) New Zealand Ministry of Education, Wellington, updated with *Today's Schools* (1990). Good practical implementation material occurs in *Governing Schools: A Practical Handbook for School Trustees*, and various guides for schools; see References below.

USA. Because of the differences between states and school boards, no overview books exist. There have been a number of articles in the periodical *Phi Beta Kappa*.

Developing countries. A useful book is Bray, M. with Lillis, K., *Community Financing of Education: Issues and Policy Implications in Less Developed Countries*, Pergamon Press (1988).

Coombs, P. and Hallak, J., *Managing Educational Costs*, Oxford University Press, New York (1972), draws widely on Unesco experience to draw out general principles.

The microeconomics of education

For non-economists, books on the economics of education can prove difficult as soon as they descend into technical theory. But they do give insight into how schools operate which cannot be gained elsewhere. The best introduction seems to be Simkins, T., 'Economics and the management of schools', in Thomas, H. and Simkins, T. (ed), *Economics and the Management of Education: Emerging Themes*, Falmer Press (1987). This lays out the evolving approaches, with useful references. Good all-round coverage is provided in Monk, D., *Educational Finance: An Economic Approach*, McGraw Hill, New York (1990), again with an extensive bibliography.

A new recent interdisciplinary approach to the economics of organisations should bring new insights, but it is extremely theoretical. It is well set out in Barney, J. and Ouchi, W. (eds), *Organisational Economics*, Jossey-Bass, San Francisco (1986). Perhaps more useful is the economics of other service areas such as health care. A recent work is McGuire, A., Henderson, J. and Mooney, G., *The Economics of Health Care*, Routledge & Kegan Paul (1988). But . . . it is a technical economics work, not easy for non-economists.

Two books deal specifically with non-profit organisations and so are relevant to most schools. Anthony, R. and Herzlinger, R., *Management Control in Non-Profit Organisations,* Richard Irwin, Ill (1975, revised 1980), is a very solid, comprehensive review of the problems of financial and general management in such organisations. Drucker, P., *Managing the Non-Profit Organisation,* Butterworth-Heinemann (1990), has many practical ideas on the management of schools, hospitals, museums etc.

The macroeconomics of education

This is a very important area for governments but is not very relevant to the individual school. A good introduction are the appropriate sections in Husen, T. and Postlethwaite, T., *The International Encyclopedia of Education,* Pergamon (1985). Standard works are:

Psacharopoulos, G., *Economics of Education* (3rd edn), Pergamon (1978).

Benson, C., *Economics of Public Education* (3rd edn), Houghton Mifflin, New York (1978).

Musgrave, R. and Musgrave, P., *Public Finance Theory and Practice,* McGraw Hill, New York (1984).

▌ References

Acorn Fundraising (1991), *The Fund-Raising Manual for Schools,* Laurel House, Bishops Hull Road, Bishops Hull, Taunton, Somerset TA1 5EP.

Audit Commission (1988), *The Local Management of Schools: A Note to LEAs,* Bristol: Audit Commission.

Audit Commission (1991), *Management Within Primary Schools,* London: HMSO.

Berkshire LEA (1989), *Guidelines for School Development Plans 1990–91,* Berkshire LEA document.

Berne, R. and Stiefel, L. (1984), *The Measurement of Equity in School finance,* Baltimore: John Hopkins University Press.

Boulton, A. (1986), 'A developed formula for the distribution of capitation allowances', in *Educational Management and Administration,* 14(1), pp. 31–38.

Boyd, W. and Hartman, W. (1988), 'The politics of educational productivity', in Monk, D. and Underwood, J., *Microlevel School Finance – Issues and Implications for Policy,* Cambridge, Mass: Ballinger.

Bray, M., with Lillis, K. (1988), *Community Financing of Education,* Oxford: Pergamon Press.

Caldwell, B. and Spinks, J. (1988), *The Self Managing School,* Lewes: Falmer Press.

Caldwell, B. and Spinks, J. (1992), *Leading the Self Managing School*, Lewes: Falmer Press.

Campbell, R. and Neill, S. (1992), *The Use and Management of Secondary Teachers Time After the Education Reform Act 1988*, Warwick: University of Warwick Policy Analysis Unit.

CIPFA (1989), *Audit Implications of LMS*, London: CIPFA.

CIPFA (1990), *Education Statistics: 1990–91 Estimates*, London: CIPFA.

Clifford, A. (1991), 'Volunteering for duty', in *Managing Schools Today*, 1(3), pp. 14–15.

Coombs, P. and Hallak, J. (1972), *Managing Educational Costs*, New York: Oxford University Press.

Coopers & Lybrand (1988), *Local Management of Schools – A Report to the Department of Education and Science*, London: HMSO.

Craig, I. (ed) (1987), *Primary School Management in Action*, Harlow: Longman.

Davies, G. and Ellison, L. (1991), *Marketing the Secondary School*, Harlow: Longman.

Department of Education and Science (1988), *Education Reform Act: Local Management of Schools*, Circular 7/88.

Department for Education (formerly DES) (1992), *School Teachers' Review Body: First Report 1992*, London: HMSO.

Devlin, T. and Knight, B. (1990), *Public Relations and Marketing for Schools: A Do-It-Yourself Manual*, Harlow: Longman.

Downes, P. (ed) (1988), *Local Financial Management in Schools*, Oxford: Blackwell.

Drucker, P. (1989), 'Why service organisations do not perform', in Riches, C. and Morgan, R. (1989), *Human Resource Management in Education*, Milton Keynes, Open University Press.

Drucker, P. (1990), *Managing the Non-Profit Organisation*, Oxford: Butterworth-Heinemann.

Drucker, P. (1991), 'The new productivity challenge', in *Harvard Business Review*, November/December 1991.

Fidler, B. and Bowles, G. (1989), *Effective Local Management of Schools*, Harlow: Longman.

Fielden, J. (1980), 'Educational costing for troubled times', in *Proceedings of the Eighth Annual Conference of the British Educational Administration Society*, Sheffield City Polytechnic (now Sheffield Hallam University).

Goodchild, S. and Holly, P. (1990), *Management for Change: The Garth Hill Experience*, Lewes: Falmer Press.

Goodman, D. (1990), 'Sharks and sharp practice', in *School Governor*, November.

Halstead, K. (1983), *Inflation Measures for Schools and Colleges*, Washington DC: US Department of Education.

Handy, C. (1991), *The Age of Unreason*, London: Business Books.

Hanushek, E. (1986), 'The economics of schooling: production and efficiency in public schools', in *Journal of Economic Literature*, XXIV, September 1986, pp. 1141–77.

Hargreaves, D. (1989), *Planning for School Development: Advice to Governors, Headteachers and Teachers*, London: DES.

Harrold, R. (1988), *Curriculum and Financial Performance in Non-Government Schools*, Hawthorn, Victoria: Australian Council for Educational Research Limited. [Address: Radford House, Frederick Street, Hawthorn, Victoria 3122, Australia.]

Henley Distance Learning (1992), *Management in Education*, Henley-on-Thames: Henley Distance Learning Ltd.

Hentschke, G. (1985), 'Emerging roles of school district administrators: implications for planning, budgeting and management', in Augenblick, J. (ed), *Public Schools: Issues in Budgeting and Financial Management*, New Brunswick, USA: Transaction Books.

HM Treasury (1992), 'GDP deflators', in *Autumn Statement 1992*, Cmnd.2096, London: HMSO.

Hoenack, S. (1988), 'Incentives, outcome based instruction and school efficiency', in Monk, D. and Underwood, J., Microlevel *School Finance – Issues and Implications for Policy*, Cambridge, Mass: Ballinger.

Husen, T. and Postlethwaite T (1988), *The International Encyclopedia of Education*, Oxford: Pergamon

Kelly, A. (1992), 'Turning the budget on its head', in *Managing Schools Today*, 1(7), pp. 24–27.

Knight, B. (1983), *Managing School Finance*, Oxford: Heinemann.

Knight, B. (1987), 'Managing the honeypots', in Thomas, H. and Simkins, T., *Economics and the Management of Education: Emerging Themes*, Lewes: Falmer Press.

Knight, B. (1989a), *Local Management of Schools – Training Materials* (2nd edn), Harlow: Longman.

Knight, B. (1989b), *Managing School Time*, Harlow: Longman.

Knight, B. (1991), *Designing the School Day*, Harlow: Longman.

Knight, B. (1992), 'What price the National Curriculum', in *Managing Schools Today*, 1(2), pp. 18–21.

Lancaster, D. (1989), 'Aspects of management information systems', in Fidler, B. and Bowles, G., *Effective Local Management of Schools*, Harlow: Longman.

Levačić, R. (ed) (1989), *Financial Management in Education*, Milton Keynes: Open University Press.

Levačić, R. (1989), 'Rules and formulae for allocating and spending delegated budgets: a consideration of general principles', in *Educational Management and Administration*, 17(2), pp. 79–90.

Levin, H. (1983), *Cost-Effectiveness – A Primer*, Beverley Hills: Sage Publications.

Levin, H. (1985), 'Costs and cost-effectiveness of computer-assisted instruction', in Augenblick, J. (ed), *Public Schools: Issues in Budgeting and Financial Management*, New Brunswick, USA: Transaction Books.

March, J. and Olsen, J. (eds) (1976), *Ambiguity and Choice in Organisations*, Bergen: Universitetforlaget.

Mid-continent Regional Educational Laboratory (1988), *Achieving Excellence: A Site-based Management System for Efficiency, Effectiveness, Excellence*, McREL, 12500 E. Illiff Avenue, Suite 201, Aurora, Colorado, 80014, USA.

Monk, D. (1990), *Educational Finance: An Economic Approach*, New York: McGraw-Hill.

Mortimore, P., Mortimore, J., with Thomas, H., Cairns, R. and Taggart, B. (1992), *The Innovative Uses of Non-Teaching Staff in Primary and Secondary Schools Project: Final Report*, London: University of London Institute of Education.

Murlis, H. (1992), 'Performance related pay in the context of performance management', in Tomlinson, H. (ed), *Performance Related Pay in Education*, London: Routledge.

National Union of Teachers (1991), *Costs of the National Curriculum in Primary Schools*, London: National Union of Teachers.

National Union of Teachers (1992), *Costs of the National Curriculum in Secondary Schools*, London: National Union of Teachers.

New Zealand Ministry of Education (1990), *Governing Schools: A Practical Handbook for School Trustees*, Wellington.

New Zealand Ministry of Education (1990), *A Guide to Financial Management*, Wellington: Learning Media, Ministry of Education (ISBN 0 478 05544 7).

Ouston, J., McMeeking, S. and Higgins, P. (1992), 'Schools and honeypot management: the impact of project funding mechanisms on the implementation of educational innovation', in *Educational Management and Administration*, 20 (3).

Peters, T. and Waterman, R. (1982), *In Search of Excellence*, New York: Harper Collins.

Publishers Association (1989), *The Book Check Action File*, London [19 Bedford Square, London WC1B 3HT]. Versions for primary schools (ISBN 0 85386 174 9) and secondary schools (ISBN 0 85386 167 9).

Sapsed, G. (1992), 'Performance-related pay in IBM', in Tomlinson, H. (ed), *Performance Related Pay in Education*, London: Routledge.

School Management Task Force (1992), *Buying for Quality*, London: Department for Education (ISBN 0 85522 416 9).

Simkins, T. (1986), 'Patronage, markets and collegiality: reflections on the allocation of finance in secondary schools', in *Educational Management and Administration*, 14(1), pp. 17–30.

Simkins, T. (1987), 'Economics and the management of schools', in

Thomas, H. and Simkins, T., *Economics and the Management of Education: Emerging Themes*, Lewes: Falmer Press.

Simkins, T. (1989), 'Budgeting as a political and organisational process in educational institutions', in Levačić, R. (ed), *Financial Management in Education*, Milton Keynes: Open University Press.

Simkins, T. and Lancaster, D. (1987), *Budgeting and Resource Allocations in Educational Institutions*, Sheffield: Sheffield City Polytechnic (now Sheffield Hallam University). Paper in Educational Management 35.

Smilanich, R. (1988), *Devolution in Edmonton Public Schools: Ten Years Later*, mimeographed paper from the author, Centre for Education, One Kingsway, Edmonton, Alberta, TFH 4G9, Canada.

Spicer, B. (1990), 'Programme budgeting: a way forward in school management', in Chapman, J. (ed), *School Based Decision Making and Management*, Lewes: Falmer Press.

Spinks, J. (1991), 'Difficult Decisions', in *Managing Schools Today*, 1(1), pp. 55–57.

Thomas, H. (1990), *Education Costs and Performance: A Cost Effective Analysis*, London: Cassell.

Tizard, J., Schofield, N. and Hewison, J. (1982), 'Collaboration between teachers and parents in assisting childrens' reading', in *British Journal of Educational Psychology*, 52 (1).

Tomlinson, H. (ed) (1992), *Performance Related Pay in Education*, London: Routledge.

Turner, A. (1990), 'Making your first million', in *School Governor*, April 1990, pp. 25–27.

Wallace, M. (1991), 'Flexible planning: a key to the management of multiple innovations', in *Educational Management and Administration*, 19(3), pp. 180–92.

Western Australia Ministry of Education (1987), *Better Schools*, Perth: WA Ministry of Education.

Wood, R. Craig (ed) (1986), *Principles of School Business Management*, Reston, Va: Association of School Business Officials International.

Woodhall, M. and Blaug, M. (1968), 'Productivity trends in British secondary education 1950–1963', in *Sociology of Education*, winter 1968, 41 (1).

Some useful addresses

America 2000 Project, New American Schools Development Corporation, 1000 Wilson Boulevard, Suite 2710, Arlington, Va 22209.
American Association of School Administrators, 1801 North Moore Street, Arlington, Va 22209.

Association of School Business Officials International, 1760 Reston Avenue, Suite 411, Reston, Va 22090.

Audit Commission, 1 Vincent Square, London SW1P 2PN (tel: 071 828 1212).

BESO (British Executive Services Overseas), 164 Vauxhall Bridge Road, London SW1V 2RB.

Building Research Energy Conservation Support Unit, Building Research Establishment, Garston, Watford WD2 7JR (tel: 0923 664258).

Central Statistical Office, Government Buildings, Cardiff Road, Newport, Gwent NP9 1XG (tel: 0633 812828).

Centre for the Study of Comprehensive Schools, Queen's Building, University of Leicester, Barrack Road, Northampton NN2 6AF (tel: 0604 24969).

Charities Aid Foundation, 48 Pembury Road, Tonbridge, Kent TN9 2JO.

CIPFA (Chartered Institute of Public and Finance Accountancy), 3 Robert Street, London WC2N 6BH.

Community Education Development Centre, Lyng Hall, Blackberry Lane, Coventry CV2 3JS.

DFE (Department for Education), Sanctuary Buildings, Great Smith St, Westminster SW1P 3BT (tel: 071 925 5401).

Directory of Social Change, Radius Works, Back Lane, London NW3 1HL (tel: 071 284 4364).

Education 2000, The Garden City Corporation Offices, Broadway, Letchworth Garden City, Herts. SG6 3AB.

HM Treasury, Parliament Street, London SW1P 3AG (for GDP deflator, telephone 071 270 5689).

Pacific Institute, 20–24 Uxbridge Road, London W8 7AT (tel: 071 727 9837).

Phoenix School Management Software, Morgan Barnett Associates, Lisker House, Lisker Avenue, W. Yorkshire LS21 1DG.

Publishers Association, 19 Bedford Square, London WC1B 3HJ.

REACH (Retired Executive's Action Clearing House), 89 Southwark Street, London SE1 0HD.

Index